THE MAGIC LAND

INVITATION TO TRAVEL SERIES

UNDER THE DIRECTION OF LOWELL BRENTANO

RALPH HANCOCK, ASSISTANT EDITOR

The
Magic Land: Mexico

By Ralph Hancock

COWARD-McCANN, INC.
NEW YORK

To

MY MOTHER

Contents

ACKNOWLEDGMENTS

There is one department of our government that is particularly helpful to those interested in the factual data pertaining to other countries. Businessmen, foreign traders, tourists, students, and writers especially have found the Bureau of Foreign and Domestic Commerce an excellent service organization. The author has drawn on the resources of this bureau many times in the past and wishes to acknowledge his gratitude for the liberal use of its material in this volume. The Pan American Union and the American Automobile Association were equally helpful, and are highly recommended sources for those desiring additional material and information on Mexico and the other American countries. Travelers will find that the Asociación Mexicana de Turismo (Mexican Tourist Association) and the Pemex Travel Club are courteous service bureaus where free maps and literature may be had for the asking. To all of these our thanks. For the addresses of these and other good sources of information on Mexico see page 292.

INTRODUCTION

Those who have never been to Mexico may say, "What, another book on Mexico?" But anyone who has so much as put a foot across the border will understand how impossible it would be to describe this country in one book or a hundred books.

The Spanish "tourists" who landed on the unexplored coast near Veracruz in 1521 called it a fabulous country. New Spain, they named it. Then, realizing finally that this new land was five times as big as Spain with a civilization three times as old, they acknowledged the only name by which it could be called—Mexico, the name by which it had been known for countless centuries.

Subsequent visitors have added their own adjectives, no two of them alike. Artists will tell you enthusiastically about the blue lakes and the snow-capped volcanoes, the gaudy costumes of the natives and the colorful markets. Writers wax poetic describing the picturesque beauties of Acapulco and Guanajuato and Taxco, or grow philosophically serious discussing the *ejido* and the *Sinarquistas* and the Revolution (which, by the way and by nationalistic Mexicans, is now labeled Evolution). Businessmen talk of potentials; the untapped mineral wealth in the mountains, the dormant electric power in the rivers, or the forests so thickly timbered with cedar and *oyamel* that the native charcoal burners rarely see the sun.

Mexico has a culture that was centuries old before Columbus was born, and she experienced a hundred years of Spanish colonial history before the *Mayflower* made history for us. She is as new as tomorrow's front page. She is our neighbor who lives next door, a neighbor we have scarcely met, although the meandering brown stream of the Rio Grande is all that divides her physically from us.

There is Mexico City with its background of snow-capped volcanoes, the gay and charming capital of the republic, one of the most beautiful cities in the world—and one of the most sophisticated. Then there are the villages, quaint, medieval, and primitive. The range of Mexican culture runs the gamut between these extremes. And the people who make this culture? They are as different, inherently, as the geography or the climate. From one state to another they vary in customs, in dialect, frequently in language. The products they produce are even more varied, ranging from henequen fiber to cattle, petroleum to silver and gold, bananas and coffee to corn and cotton. In fact, Mexico's geography, culture, people, climate, and products are more varied than those of any area of similar size in the world. If one word could describe this land, that word would be *magic!*

It is not our hope that we have produced herewith just another guide to Mexico. But if this invitation to travel encourages you to seek your own interpretation of our neighbor's problems and stimulates you to a fuller enjoyment of her culture and her colorful inhabitants, then it has served the only purpose for which it was written. To that end, yes, any number of books on Mexico!

THE MAGIC LAND

CHAPTER I

MEXICAN BACKGROUNDS

U SUALLY those facts and figures that pertain to the geographic, economic, and historic backgrounds of a country are dull no matter how one struggles to dress them in clothes of sparkling metaphors and scintillating adjectives. The background description of Mexico, however, poses no such problems. A bare listing of salient facts and figures about Mexico contains so many unusual contrasts, such extraordinary features and romantic aspects, that any additional coloring would be lily-gilding of the most blatant sort.

GEOGRAPHIC

AREA AND BOUNDARIES

Mexico, the third largest Latin-American republic (Brazil and Argentina are larger), is 758,258 square miles in area, or roughly one quarter the size of the continental United States. Its long northern boundary borders the states of California, Arizona, New Mexico, and Texas, going generally southeastward in an undulating line of 1,549 miles. The long arm, like a cactus in shape and climate, extending 760 miles into the Pacific Ocean from the California border is the peninsula of Baja California. It parallels Mexico's west coast to form the narrow Gulf of California. Counting the coast line of the peninsula, the country has a long Pacific coast line of 4,437 miles.

Mexico's narrowest point is the 140-mile-wide Isthmus of Tehuantepec in the south. At various times within the memory of man it has been the site of a proposed ocean-to-ocean highway, a canal, and, lately, an eight-track railway carrying huge flatcars running sideways and hauling aboard them the ocean steamers wanting a quicker

1

short cut than the Panama Canal. The best idea so far is Miguel Covarrubia's book *The Isthmus of Tehuantepec*, written and illustrated by him. Its detailed portrayal of a little-known but highly fascinating region is the first step toward a lucrative tourist business —more lucrative, at least per peso invested, than any scheme heretofore dreamed up.

Eastward from the Isthmus of Tehuantepec the Yucatán peninsula juts into the Gulf of Mexico pointing to the northeast toward Cuba and Florida. Someday there will be an auto ferry service from some point on the peninsula to a near point on Cuba. There is already such service between Havana and Florida. And then when Mexico completes its Veracruz-Yucatán highway, American tourists will be able to drive a circle tour, U.S.–Mexico–Cuba–U.S., unequaled anywhere in the world for scenic variety and tourist interest.

Southward, the border with Guatemala on the Pacific side and with British Honduras on the Caribbean side forms a jagged line 553 miles long. The line runs over the shoulder of Tacná, highest mountain in Central America, and across the low, flat, jungle-covered land of Tabasco and Quintana Roo, still largely unexplored and unknown.

Mexico's east coast from the Yucatán peninsula to the Rio Grande is washed by the Gulf of Mexico. Including the coast of the Yucatán peninsula, this east coast line is 1,774 miles long. This, with the western coast, gives Mexico a coast line of 6,211 miles, as compared with 4,833 for the United States.

TOPOGRAPHY

Wild and precipitous mountain ranges and peaks are a salient topographical feature of Mexico. A continuation of the South American cordillera begins in the Isthmus of Tehuantepec and extends through southern Mexico, dividing above Mexico City to form two coastal ranges, the Sierra Madre Oriental and the Sierra Madre Occidental. Between these ranges and transversed by others lies the vast central plateau, a rugged tableland constituting almost three quarters of Mexico's area. It is known as La Mesa Central de Anahuac. Roughly 1,500 miles long and with a maximum width of 530 miles, the floor of this plateau ranges in altitude from 4,000 feet in the north to 8,000 near Mexico City. It is widest in the latitude of

Mexico City. The surface is cut up into numerous *barrancas* (ravines), some of great depth. Two natural passes afford outlets to the eastward; one at Jalapa, now traversed by the Interoceanic Railway, and through which Cortés built a road during the Conquest; and one at Saltillo, utilized by the National Railways. Through this latter pass the American soldiers climbed to the plateau during the Mexican War. Paved highways now use these passes also, and in addition several other man-made passes, to connect the Mesa Central with the east coast, and run through Guadalajara and Taxco to the Pacific.

Thus the topography of the main body of Mexico is characterized by innumerable valleys lying between chains of mountains and by a narrow coastal fringe that is widest along the Gulf of Mexico just south of the United States border.

The third highest mountain in North America, the Pico de Orizaba (18,686 feet), is midway between Mexico City and the gulf port of Veracruz; the famous Popocatépetl (17,883 feet) and Ixtaccíhuatl (17,738 feet) are clearly visible some forty miles east of the capital. The view is especially good toward the end of the rainy season when the air is clear and the peaks are getting their first snowfalls. Many other lofty peaks, most of them extinct volcanoes, rise in the southern portion of the country. One active volcano, Parícutin, near Uruapan in the state of Michoacán, began erupting after an earthquake in February 1943. The surrounding territory for many miles has been partially devastated by volcanic ash. It is today the outstanding thrill and awe-inspiring tourist attraction in Mexico.

Mexico has no important navigable rivers and very few lakes. Some small islands off the coasts are under its sovereignty.

Two peninsulas, each constituting slightly more than 7 per cent of the country's total area, complete its physiognomy. The Yucatán peninsula, flat and only slightly above sea level, is inaccessible by land from the rest of Mexico. The peninsula of Baja California is an extension of the continental coast range; the only land approach is through the United States from southern California.

Mexico's mountainous nature is a factor of primary importance in its economy, since it creates tremendous problems of transportation and communication and has a powerful bearing upon agriculture. Many sections of the republic are virtually inaccessible, with resultant lack of economic and cultural development.

GEOGRAPHIC HANDICAPS

Figures on the total area, however, give little indication of Mexico's land resources. In fact, if its territory had been more habitable and agriculturally productive in proportion to its size, its population would have been many times larger than it is today. Farming and the exploitation of raw materials are very difficult, even impossible in some areas. More than half the total area of the country consists of rugged land—mountains, cliffs, and gorges.

Mountains and jungles cut off the southeastern states of Yucatán, Campeche, Tabasco, and Chiapas from the main body of Mexico. Neither highways nor railways connect the two sections, and their isolation is broken only by steamer, telephone, telegraph, and air transport. This is the most dramatic instance of the geographic handicaps to Mexican development. A large proportion of the Mexican people live outside the reach of modern rail or highway transportation. In some places airplanes now reach territory not heretofore served by anything more modern than burro trails.

ARABLE LAND

If the total arable land of Mexico were divided equally among the approximately 22,000,000 inhabitants, each would receive less than two acres. The 1940 census showed that only about 7 per cent of the national territory was usable for farming. It also showed that slightly more than half this area was always lying fallow, so that in any given year only 3 to 5 per cent of the total land was used for food production. Even with the greatest conceivable investment in irrigation and drainage, probably no more than 12 per cent of the total area will ever be arable. (This might be compared with 44 per cent for Italy, 43 per cent for Germany, 40 per cent for France, and 31 per cent for Spain.) In addition, only 9 per cent of the total arable land gets natural rainfall, about 12 per cent is irrigated, and 70 per cent is semiarid.

CLIMATE

Although the Tropic of Cancer almost bisects Mexico, the climate in the greater part of the country is more closely related to altitude and rainfall than to the subtropical latitude. Generally speaking, there are two distinct seasons: the dry season, October through May, and the rainy season, June through September.

Three climatic zones may be distinguished.

The tropical zone, with altitudes ranging from sea level to 3,000 feet, consists of the coastal plains, the Yucatán peninsula, and certain areas in southern Mexico. The mean temperature is from 77 degrees to 80 degrees Fahrenheit, with a minimum of 60 degrees and a maximum of 119 degrees. Rainfall within this zone, south of the Tropic of Cancer, is heavy (up to a hundred inches), but ranges to desert conditions in the northeastern section bordering the United States.

The subtropical and temperate zone—elevation from 3,000 to 6,000 feet—is in general warm and temperate, with adequate rainfall and a mean annual temperature in the neighborhood of 75 degrees.

The cool zone, or that above 6,000 feet, which includes the central plateau and Mexico City, is temperate to cool and cold, the annual mean temperature being about 63 degrees. Rainfall is generally sparse.

The most densely populated section of Mexico, the central plateau, is pleasantly cool the year round. Although it is just south of the Tropic of Cancer, the 5,000-to-8,000-foot altitude gives it a climate much cooler than the tropical latitude would suggest. Thus Mexico City and most of the other cities commonly visited by tourists have an ideal vacation climate—warm summer days, only slightly cooler winter days, and cool nights always. There is a wide variation between day and night temperatures, and this should be taken into account when one reads any figures on Mexico's temperatures. While the January twenty-four-hour average is 54 degrees, for instance, some January days get as warm as 75 degrees.

To the north the plateau slopes gradually to a lower altitude, becoming warmer and more arid. It is bounded on the east and west by mountain ranges that slope down to the narrow coastal plains. The climate in the coast cities, such as Acapulco and Mazatlán on the Pacific and Veracruz and Tampico on the Gulf of Mexico, though hot and humid, is made comfortable by sea breezes.

On the south the plateau is broken into by the rough mountains and valleys that make up southern Mexico. In this area there are regions high enough to receive occasional frosts and valleys low enough to have a hot tropical climate. Oaxaca, at an altitude of 5,128 feet, has a climate much like that of Cuernavaca; the low Isthmus of Tehuantepec has temperatures comparing with those of Acapulco.

This broken mountain region falls away on the east to the low-lying and flat Yucatán peninsula. This is *tierra caliente,* or hot land. Here the climate is warm and humid throughout much of the year, with a variation of only seven to twelve degrees in average temperatures between winter and summer.

Summer (June to October) is the rainy season all over Mexico. The rains come, not in the form of all-day drizzles, but in brief afternoon showers, which leave the evenings and mornings bright and clear.

Most United States citizens who are used to heavy humidity climates winter and summer are agreeably surprised to find that 90 degrees in Mexico City is delightfully comfortable; that 70 to 80 degrees is almost chilly. For personal decisions based on Mexico's climatic conditions, see "Clothes," page 24.

HISTORIC

In contrast with the nomadic and primitive tribes that inhabited the northern regions of America before Europeans set foot on this soil, Cortés and his hardy followers found in Mexico a mighty empire and a civilization that in many respects fairly compared with and even excelled that of Spain. Tenochtitlán, over whose ruins stands today the modern City of Mexico, was a thriving metropolis of several hundred thousand inhabitants—a city built in large part over artificial islands, connected by extensive causeways strung across the waters of Texcoco Lake, which filled the entire expanse of the Valley of Mexico.

ANCIENT MEXICO

It is generally accepted that the earliest inhabitants of Mexico, much as of the rest of this hemisphere, migrated by way of Bering Strait from Asia, anywhere from ten to twenty thousand years ago; but the latter history of the hundred and some odd Indian tribes that peopled Mexico when Cortés landed on these shores is to this day an unsolved mystery. It is estimated that the Toltecs, who were called "Builders" because of the stately temples and colossal pyramids they left to posterity, settled in the central plateau of Mexico in the early days of the eighth century; while the Aztecs, who superseded them some five centuries later, drifted down from some distant northern region, probably all the way from Alaska. Alaska was the original locale of Asiatic migration to America, the subsequent slow progress of which spread southward and eastward as far as Hudson Bay and Patagonia.

The unraveling of Mexico's pre-Conquest history rests with the archaeologists and ethnologists, but Bernal Diáz del Castillo, a lieutenant of Cortés whose chronicle provides the sole comprehensive record of the Conquest, was willing to concede that Moctezuma's court outshone Spain's in magnificence; that the Aztec language was more expressive and sonorous than either Spanish or Latin; that the sonnets and lyrics of the Texcocan poet-prince Netzahualcóyotl were marked by singular beauty; that the art works in precious metal and stone wrought by native craftsmen were more beautiful than anything produced in Spain; and that Tenochtitlán's architecture was more imposing than that of Toledo.

And while the Aztecs and Toltecs were building their great cities in the central plateau of Mexico, the equally inscrutable Mayas evolved a civilization in Yucatán that was in many respects superior to that of their European contemporaries. Chichén Itzá, Uxmal, and Tulum belong among the magnificent treasures of man's past and are a source of wonder to men of science and art from all over the world. Few of us realize to what extent our own modern civilization is indebted to these ancient American dwellers.

By evolving maize from wild plants, the civilization of aboriginal Mexico introduced agriculture in America. Rubber, henequen, quinine, common and sweet potatoes, pumpkins, cocoa, peanuts, peppers, tobacco, ipecac, cascara, vanilla, chicle, indigo, copal, and cochineal form but a partial list of aboriginal Mexico's contribution to our own present-day welfare.

THE CONQUEST

In 1519 Hernán Cortés, an intrepid Spanish adventurer, landed on Mexican soil on the site now occupied by the city of Veracruz, heading a motley force of only four hundred men, recruited in the Spanish crown colony of Cuba. Cortés achieved one of the most amazing conquests in all history. He burned his ships, thus destroying all chance of retreat, and started on the long and weary march to the Aztec capital on the high Mexican plateau. The success of his project was due as much to shrewd diplomacy as to brilliant generalship. He was also aided by the belief prevalent among the Indians that he was the reincarnation of their "Fair God," Quetzalcoatl, and by the traditional animosity of the Totonacs, Tlaxcalans, and other native tribes toward the mighty Aztecs. The Indians, moreover, were terrorized by the thunder-making cannon and muskets and—since horses until then were unknown on this continent—by the mounted soldiers, believing them to be centaur-like monsters. Cortés induced some of the dissentient tribes to join him and captured Tenochtitlán after almost two years of fighting, during which the Aztec emperor, Moctezuma II, was slain. Following the Conquest, the Venice-like Tenochtitlán was ruthlessly demolished; the great temples were razed to the ground, the canals drained, the causeways destroyed, and over the ruins of this ancient Aztec capital a new city was built, patterned after the cities of Spain.

COLONIAL ERA

For three hundred years thereafter, Mexico, known as New Spain, was a colony of the Spanish crown. During that time Spain became the world's mightiest empire, owing in large part to the vast riches in silver and gold extracted from Mexican mines. On the other hand, it implanted on this soil its language, religion, culture, and customs. The first university on this continent was established by the Spanish clergy in Mexico, as well as the first printing press. Meanwhile, by the gradual assimilation of bloods, Mexico's population acquired a new racial complex.

INDEPENDENCE

In 1821, after a series of frustrated revolts inspired by the great patriot Father Hidalgo, Mexico wrested its independence from Spain. Although the country's liberal leaders aspired toward creating a republic, their hopes were thwarted by Agustín de Iturbide, a former officer of the Spanish army, who by an adroit coup seized power and was made emperor. Iturbide's reign endured but a year, and in 1823 Mexico became a republic.

Embracing an enormous area, handicapped by ponderous natural barriers, and devoid of adequate communication, the new republic was assailed by many grave problems and trials. Its heterogeneous population lacked a sense of civic consciousness and national unity. It was not prepared for the institution of democracy; its republican form of government was a premature undertaking. Thus, denied internal stability, in 1846 it was drawn into a war with the United States, resulting from the annexation of Texas. A peace treaty was signed a year later, by which Mexico ceded to the United States the territory comprising California, New Mexico, and Arizona.

In 1858, with the rise to the presidency of Benito Juárez, a Zapotec Indian of humble origin whose personality in many respects bore a resemblance to that of Abraham Lincoln, Mexico attained its first definite progress toward a valid republican rule. It was Benito Juárez who, in curtailing the temporal power of the Church, which up to that time actually owned more than two thirds of all national wealth, destroyed the final vestiges of Spanish colonial rule. The promulgation of these liberal laws, however, resulted in foreign intervention. The defeated clericals, aided by foreign mineowners and bondholders, decided to crush Mexico's liberalism by importing a European king backed by European troops, and with this aim their representatives negotiated at the courts of Spain and France.

These enemies of Mexico's liberalism finally induced Napoleon III, the French emperor, to send an army to Mexico and to install in Chapultepec Castle the Archduke Maximilian of Austria as emperor. Benito Juárez, however, was not disposed to abandon his cause. His guerrilla bands, scattered over different parts of the country, incessantly harassed the French invaders, who finally, upon the insistence of the United States government, withdrew from the Mexican territory, abandoning Maximilian to his fate. After a final desperate stand at Querétaro, Maximilian was captured and shot, whereupon Benito Juárez resumed the presidency.

In 1876 General Porfirio Díaz became president and ultimately a mail-fisted dictator. Betraying the liberal tenets of Juárez, he ruled Mexico for over thirty years. And although Díaz encountered a formula for ending civil strife, and for the first time since its inception the Mexican republic could devote itself to economic development, it was in the methods by which he stimulated such development that Díaz committed his most disastrous blunders. In his eagerness to attract foreign investment, he actually gave away Mexico's national resources to foreign interests. He allowed the Indians to be

despoiled of such lands as they still possessed. Mexico under the
Díaz dictatorship was a feudal domain possessed by an opulent few
and peopled by millions of paupers. Peace achieved at such a price
could hardly endure. When senile decay brought about the dictator's fall, the accumulated resentment of the masses burst into a
nation-wide upheaval.

RECONSTRUCTION

Francisco Madero, who led this popular though desultory movement of liberation, became president. He was inspired by ideals of
democracy and popular suffrage, but lacked a definite program that
might have enabled his administration to achieve economic allevia-
tion of the exploited Indian masses; thus he was soon confronted
by a counterrevolutionary movement that resulted in his downfall
and untimely death.

During the following decade the country, seeking a crystallization
of its national hopes and ideals, was torn by almost continuous civil
strife. With the enactment by Carranza of a new federal constitution
in 1917, the popular liberal movement finally evolved a concrete
political as well as economic platform, giving origin to a new era of
revolutionary reconstruction. Mexico's true revolution came into
being with this new bill of rights.

The Revolution—a peaceful and orderly process of social and economic transformation—has been in the course of its gradual mate-
rialization for quite a long time, reaching its most flourishing stages
during the last few years.

ECONOMIC

The several factors that make up the economic background of
Mexico disclose considerable information of value to the visitor
earnestly seeking a true cross-section picture of the country. Here
too, in a subject drier than history or geography, are those unusual
contrasts and extraordinary features that need no coloring to make
them interesting.

POPULATION

Mexico's estimated population in 1947, based upon the 1940 census, was over 22,000,000. Only the United States and Brazil in the

Western Hemisphere outrank Mexico in number of inhabitants, while none exceed it in variety of races.

The average density of population in Mexico is twenty-nine per square mile, but large areas are virtually deserted. An estimated half or more of the people live within a radius of two hundred miles of Mexico City. The Federal District, within which the capital lies, had a calculated population of 2,225,000 in 1947. The other large cities, with recent population estimates, are: Guadalajara, 255,000; Monterrey, 220,000; Puebla, 150,000; Mérida, 106,000; and Tampico, 94,000. Mexico is basically a rural country with few large cities but with numerous small towns and villages.

Almost two thirds of the Mexican people are of mixed race, with Indian blood predominant. The estimated one quarter to one third of the population that consists of pure-blooded Indians is steadily shrinking. The number of Indians and the persistence of their cultural traits and practices are nevertheless very important factors in Mexican life, culturally, politically, and economically. Unmixed Europeans, a small percentage of whom are relatively recent immigrants, account for approximately one tenth of the inhabitants; the great majority of them are of Spanish descent. There is a large American colony in Mexico City, and numerous Americans dwell in other parts of the republic. Most of the Americans living in Mexico are technical employees of industries and construction companies, salesmen and agents representing American firms, artists and writers, tourists escaping northern winters and tourists escaping northern summers, and Americans escaping state income taxes. But if your income is derived from a source within the United States, don't attempt to escape the federal income taxes!

The sharpest cleavages in the Mexican social structure are along economic lines—a great mass of people living at a subsistence level, a small middle class (growing with the industrial growth of the cities), and a minute group of wealthy people.

Agriculture is the basic occupation in Mexico. Agricultural workers and their families constitute two thirds of the population.

PRODUCTION

Mexican agriculture is diversified because of climate, topography, soil, and other physical circumstances. However, only about 3 to 5 per cent of the land is under cultivation. Irrigation now plays an important role in Mexican agriculture, and substantial sums are being and will be spent upon new irrigation projects.

Normally Mexico produces most of the foodstuffs needed for domestic consumption, except wheat. Other products sometimes short in the local markets are corn, sugar, lard, and rice. The principal agricultural products, in order of value, are corn, cotton, sugar cane, wheat, henequen, bananas, sesame, tomatoes, and coffee. Other crops and forest products are various grains and forages, beans, tropical and other fruits, tobacco, common vegetables, chicle, rubber, naval stores, and lumber. Livestock of all kinds are raised in Mexico, the most important being beef cattle.

Although agricultural activities are prevalent throughout Mexico, some degree of specialization by regions exists. The central states and northern highland region produce corn, wheat, and other small grains; the Laguna district (largely by irrigation), Mexicali, and Matamoros produce cotton; states bordering on the United States, cattle; southern Sonora, Sinaloa, and Tamaulipas are the source of much of our winter vegetables; higher elevations of Veracruz and Chiapas states produce coffee; in the semitropical and tropical portions of this region are produced citrus fruits, pineapples, bananas, chicle, sugar cane, and copra; and in the Yucatán, henequen.

The principal manufacturing industries, in order of their importance, are cotton textiles, wheat mills, breweries, soap, vegetable oils, tobacco, iron and steel, and rayon textiles. More than 35 per cent of Mexico's industrial production is estimated to be centered in the Federal District in factories of various types. Other important manufacturing centers are: Monterrey—iron and steel, glass, beer, textiles, furniture, matches, chemicals, enamelware, incandescent lamps, paper products; Puebla—textiles, railway equipment, cement tiles, ceramics; Aguascalientes—railway equipment; León—shoes, clothing, textiles; Guadalajara—iron and steel, textiles, shoes, soap, bricks, tile, pottery, glassware; San Luís Potosí—fiber products, leather, soap, flour, beer.

Other cities and towns are the sites of locally important and specialized industries; native handicraft industries flourish throughout the country.

Mexico is one of the richest mineral countries in the world. It outranks all other countries in silver production, is rich in gold, and produces a large variety of industrial minerals, including lead, zinc, copper, iron, tin, mercury, antimony, manganese, tungsten, molybdenum, cadmium, arsenic, coal, and mica. Deposits occur in practically every state of the republic, the richest zone extending along the Sierra Madre Range from the United States border in the northwest to the lower Gulf coast. Important smelters are located in the states of Sonora, Coahuila, Nuevo León, San Luís Potosí, and Zacatecas.

Mexico's oil fields, the output of which ranks seventh in world production, are located along the Gulf coast; the Tuxpan region in the state of Veracruz yields over 60 per cent of the national production. Refineries are situated near the fields and also in Mexico City. Petroleum is usually exported from the port of Tampico. The petroleum industry, which was expropriated by the government in 1938, is controlled and operated by a federal agency, Petroleos Mexicanos. Its products are sold in Mexico under the brand name "Pemex."

TRANSPORTATION

Transportation is one of Mexico's greatest problems, primarily because of the mountainous topography and the long distances that make the construction and maintenance of roads and railways difficult and costly. The republic has not been able to afford adequate facilities for land communication between all parts of the country, although important highways are under construction or contemplated. Airplane services have helped to overcome some of the transportation difficulties.

COMMUNICATIONS

Telegraph and Cable. The domestic telegraph business is a monopoly of the federal government, under the administration of the Ministry of Communications and Public Works. International radio-telegraph messages originating in Mexico are sent over the beams of the federally owned "Radiomex" system, which connects with other international systems at points to which it has direct circuits, including New York, London, Buenos Aires, and Lisbon. There are arrangements also with the Tropical Radio Telegraph Company, the MacKay Radio and Telegraph Company, and RCA Communications, Inc. A subsidiary of the Western Union Telegraph Company under franchise from the federal government handles a large volume of international telegraph and cable messages in Mexico, using cables connecting at Tampico with New York and at Salina Cruz with South America.

Telephone. There are two major independent telephone systems in Mexico, owned by subsidiaries of United States and Swedish companies. The systems are interconnected everywhere in the republic except in the Federal District. In addition to a small installation fee, the charge for telephones in Mexico is a flat monthly rate, with no limit on the number of calls, except out-of-town and international calls. The total number of telephones in Mexico in 1947 was about 205,000.

Radio. Broadcasting in Mexico is conducted along competitive lines as in the United States. Radio chains and independent stations, relying upon commercial advertising for their revenue and requiring only a federal license, operate in all the principal cities of the republic. Some international connections have been formed. Programs are generally divided into fifteen-minute and half-hour intervals, but there does not appear to be the same rigid adherence to time schedules as in some other countries. Short radio spots are a popular form of advertising.

CURRENCY AND EXCHANGE

The currency unit of Mexico is the peso. Under a special stabilization agreement between the Mexican and United States Treasuries, the peso is pegged at 4.85 to the dollar, one peso being equal to $0.206185.

CHAPTER II

BEFORE MEXICO

THE recent tremendous increase in travel to Mexico is not entirely the result of efforts like this. Rather it is more the result of Mexico's own awakening to the potential money value of the numerous tourist interests within her borders. The awakening took definite shape during the administration of Manuel Ávila Camacho (president, 1940–46) when the AMT (Asociación Mexicana de Turismo, Mexican Tourist Association) was set up as a government-sponsored tourist information and promotion service. Large quantities of attractive travel literature were printed by this organization and distributed free throughout the United States. It attempted some standardization of hotel and resort services and some regulation of prices; it licensed qualified guides and worked to simplify the entry requirements for United States and Canadian citizens.

All this interest to assure the welfare and pleasure of tourists has paid off. It even became an important factor in the solution of Mexico's postwar economic problem. President Miguel Alemán, who succeeded Camacho, inherited an economic headache unparalleled in Mexican history. Mexico came out of World War II with a comfortable dollar balance, a backlog of buying power that could and did command the best market for the first postwar manufactures. But the buying spree was short-lived. Spiraling living costs, a Florida-type real-estate boom, excessive building and construction, and an expanding industrial program with at the same time a drastic reduction in exports, largely through the curtailment of United States wartime buying, had so reduced the backlog by January 1947 that Mexico was frantically looking around for new ways to bolster her economic condition. Several restrictions were placed on foreign purchases to stop the flight of dollars remaining on hand, but very few measures could boost the curtailed exports to replenish the short supply of dollars.

It was in this crucial period that Foreign Minister Jaime Torres Bodet suggested that an increase in Mexico's tourist trade would bring in the much needed dollars. Directives were issued to all Mexican consular offices in the United States that effected substantial streamlining of tourist procedures. At least one staff member in each consulate was assigned to work full time with tourists and travel agencies and be responsible for the issuance of tourist cards. His office hours were set at nine to five, an extension of several hours over previous service. Forms for the tourist to fill out were made more brief, and every consulate was amply stocked with attractive travel literature made available by the AMT. All of this has been a good investment, for Mexico's international financial position at the beginning of 1948 was beginning to show signs of stability. But before you begin your contribution to Mexico's economic stability, here are a few things you should know.

ENTRANCE REQUIREMENTS

Although not now required, these documents may prove helpful to the traveler entering Mexico or returning to the United States: a certificate of smallpox vaccination, a certificate of good conduct from one's local police department, a letter of introduction from a chamber of commerce or similar civic organization (particularly for those planning to do business in Mexico; see page 290), and letter of credit or other banking reference.

Under regulations adopted several years ago, passports are not required by United States or Canadian citizens entering Mexico as tourists.

TOURISTS

Although tourists may visit the border towns for periods not to exceed twenty-four hours without a permit, tourist cards (*tarjetas de turista*) must be obtained for visits to the interior of Mexico. Tourist cards are required for all persons fifteen years of age and over. These cards are good for a period of six months and may be renewed for an additional five months upon request at the Departamento de Migración (Immigration Department) of the Secretaria de Gobernación (Ministry of Interior), Bucareli 99, Mexico, D.F., Mexico, or at branch offices of this department in other parts of Mexico.

Tourists entering Mexico on a tourist card are forbidden by law to engage in any kind of business or to change their status in any manner while there. The law is very clear on this point and severe penalties are imposed for legal infractions.

Tourist cards are obtainable from the nearest Mexican consulate in the United States—see your local telephone directory if you live in New York, New Orleans, or San Francisco—or from the Mexican Tourist Bureau, Rockefeller Center, New York City, or at the immigration offices on the Mexican side of the international border. They may be obtained either in person or by mail for $2.10. Tour parties are generally accommodated with a list that is applied for by the person conducting the tour. Some travel agents provide this service in addition to arranging transportation and hotel accommodations.

NATURALIZED CITIZENS

The Mexican authorities make no distinction between naturalized citizens and persons born in the United States. However, naturalized citizens should carry their naturalization papers to ensure their entry into Mexico as American citizens and as evidence of their right to re-enter the United States.

ALIENS

An alien should possess a passport, tax receipt, or identification card to prove legal domicile in the United States. Aliens residing or visiting in the United States are subject to special requirements on entering Mexico. Several weeks before starting on their trip, they should write to Sr. Jefe de Población, Secretaria de Gobernación, Mexico, D.F., Mexico, fully outlining their plans, proposed length of stay in Mexico, purpose of the trip, and amount of money they will have available. They should state also whether they are permanent United States residents or temporary visitors, their nationality, whether they are in possession of a properly visaed passport or other identification, and whether they have or can obtain a United States re-entry permit. Generally it takes several weeks to obtain an answer, and applicants are required to post a cash bond with the Mexican immigration office at the border, once permission is granted. Citizens of the Western Hemisphere and British subjects are exempt from these restrictions and may enter Mexico in the same manner as United States citizens, provided they have their passports for identification.

COMMERCIAL TRAVELERS

Entry requirements for commercial travelers to Mexico are given in Chapter XII, page 290.

RESIDENCE IN MEXICO

Persons interested in living in Mexico for extended periods as workers or engaged in business or professions should read the information given in Chapter XII, page 275.

AUTOMOBILE PERMITS

There is no restriction on driving into any of the border towns in Mexico provided the automobile does not remain longer than twenty-four hours. Tourists may encounter some inconvenience, however, on returning to the United States if they have baggage or packages in the car, since they will be subject to inspection by the United States customs authorities. Foreign-made cameras, especially, should be registered with the United States customs before they are taken into Mexico; otherwise heavy duty may be assessed on them when you return to the United States. (See "Cameras" below.)

Automobile permits for stays longer than twenty-four hours and for driving in the interior of Mexico must be obtained from the Mexican customs office at the port of entry. The permit is good for six months and may be extended an additional six months. The cost of the permit is three pesos (about sixty-one cents United States currency). Tourists must bring title, registration certificate, or bill of sale of the car to prove ownership. If the owner is not present on the trip, the driver should be prepared with a notarized written statement giving him permission to drive the automobile. All tires, radio, heater, trailer, and other equipment are listed and must be taken out of Mexico on exit, even though worn out; otherwise duty will be assessed on them. The permit must be kept with the car and returned for cancelation when the car leaves the country. If you plan to leave the country by an exit other than the port of entry, you should so inform the Mexican customs officials at the time of entry.

Automobile insurance and personal accident insurance are not compulsory but advisable. Check with your insurance agent to be sure your United States policy covers you in Mexico. If your agent cannot provide you with insurance in Mexico, you may obtain Mexican insurance at the AAA office in Laredo or El Paso, Texas.

Touring tips and detailed itineraries for driving in Mexico are given in Chapter IV, "Automobile Itineraries," page 39.

BAGGAGE

Your baggage is subject to inspection by the Mexican customs officers at port of entry. However, streamlining of the regulations to encourage tourist travel to Mexico and facilitate the handling of larger numbers of tourists has caused the examination of baggage to be only cursory.

Each tourist may bring into Mexico, duty-free, wearing apparel and personal effects within reason, one pound of tobacco, one hundred cigars, or forty packages of cigarettes.

It is advisable to register foreign cameras, costly furs, and diamonds with the United States customs before entering Mexico to avoid duties on such articles on your return.

CAMERAS

Although the regulations say that each tourist is permitted to bring duty-free one camera and twelve rolls of film, the border inspectors are generally liberal, and one may take a motion-picture camera in addition to one still camera, together with a small supply of film, without question. Professional photographers should arrange for stocks of film to be sent ahead by the manufacturer to dealers in Mexico. However, all common brands and sizes of film are obtainable throughout Mexico.

DOGS

A motorist may take his dog into Mexico without formalities. For tourists other than motorists, a certificate of health is required for the dog, issued by a veterinarian and visaed by a Mexican consul. This should be obtained at the time the tourist card is issued. Most hotels do not admit dogs, and there is a local ordinance in Mexico City prohibiting dogs in hotels unless they have been vaccinated by the

Mexican government. Inquire in advance if your hotel has facilities for caring for your pet.

FIREARMS

All firearms taken into Mexico must be covered by permits that must be obtained from a Mexican consul. Unless you plan to hunt (see page 247), your shootin' irons should be checked on the American side.

RETURNING TO THE UNITED STATES

It has been our experience (once even recently) that a little more knowledge of the United States customs regulations would have saved us several dollars, some chagrin, and useless delay. Few guides we have consulted go into any detail on this subject, and if you stand around a United States customs office very long you will realize that few other returning travelers are aware of the laws and regulations affecting their purchases abroad. We think the United States Customs Office should prepare a summary of these laws and make it available to every American leaving the country. Of course, that would reduce the Customs Office's revenue, but more importantly it would reduce the number of irate citizens who consider the customs officials predatory enemies instead of protectors of our borders.

UNITED STATES CUSTOMS REGULATIONS

1. The person in charge of any vehicle entering the United States must immediately report to the customs officer at the port of entry or the customhouse nearest to the place at which the vehicle crosses the boundary line. Failure to make report as required subjects the person in charge of the vehicle to a penalty of $100 and an additional penalty of $500 for each passenger carried, and any merchandise in a vehicle not reported is subject to seizure and forfeiture.

2. The senior member of a group of passengers who are members of the same family may declare for all and may include servants traveling with them. Residents, see "Grouping of Exemptions" below.

3. Baggage and vehicles must be made ready for inspection. This includes baggage taken out of the United States and returned, even though not opened abroad.

4. Residents must declare in writing (a) all articles acquired abroad for personal or household use of a value in excess of $25 (give prices actually paid or, if some articles were not purchased, their fair value); (b) all articles taken abroad and returned that have received dutiable repairs, alterations, or additions abroad of a value in excess of $25; (c) all articles included in (a) and (b) when the aggregate dutiable value exceeds $25; (d) all articles acquired abroad or changed in condition abroad when any such articles do not accompany them or when any part or all of their baggage is shipped in bond. (See 6 (c) as to duplicate declarations.)

5. Both residents and nonresidents must declare in writing all articles of merchandise, articles purchased for others at their request, and articles for sale or for business purposes.

6. Residents' exemption: (a) A personal exemption from duty for articles valued at not over $100 is allowed each returning resident, including children, but only once in thirty days. (Exemption applies only to articles for residents' personal or household use, and not for resale.) (b) Exemptions do not accumulate, and though the full exemption was not allowed on a previous trip the remainder cannot be claimed on a subsequent trip. (c) Exemptions may include articles not accompanying residents and articles shipped in bond if they are included in written declarations, in duplicate, at time of the resident's arrival. (d) Cigarettes, tobacco, foodstuffs, not more than one hundred cigars, and not more than one wine gallon of alcoholic beverages may be included within the $100 exemption. Compliance with state laws pertaining to the importation of all beverages is necessary whether or not such beverages are free of duty under the $100 exemption. (e) Do not deduct exemption. Customs officer will make this allowance and generally apply it against articles subject to highest rates of duty. (f) In addition to the exemption, resident hunters may bring in free of duty game animals and birds killed abroad by them if for noncommercial use. (Obtain full particulars from nearest United States customs office.)

7. Grouping of residents' exemption: (a) Articles of one resident may not be included in the exemption of another, except that when a husband and wife or a parent or parents and minor or financially dependent children travel together, the articles included within the exemption may be grouped and allowance made without regard to which member is the owner; provided that the group exemption

shall not include servants or anyone who has claimed an exemption within thirty days. For this purpose a "minor" is one under twenty-one years of age. A resident servant, though included in a family declaration, will be allowed his or her exemption separately. All fruits, vegetables, plants, seeds, flowers, and bulbs are absolutely prohibited entry into the United States, except the following: sour limes, pineapples, bananas, and grapes. Cut flowers without seeds are permitted. Cacti and nursery stock of all kinds are prohibited.

Wild Animals and Birds. Not allowed entry into the United States without a permit from the Bureau of Biological Survey, Washington, D.C. If purchased, they should be left on the Mexican side until you have obtained this permit, as United States customs have no facilities available for their detention. Declare them at United States customs upon re-entering the United States, wire Washington advising the Bureau of Biological Survey to answer collect, then with permit recover your animals and birds and bring them across. Furthermore, you need a permit from the Mexican government before wild animals can be taken out of Mexico.

Domestic Animals, Dogs, etc. Domestic animals are allowed entry, subject to quarantine regulations. Furthermore, they must have a permit from the Bureau of Animal Husbandry, Washington, D.C. (Better buy your pooch in the United States and save trouble.)

Canaries, Parrots, etc. Canaries not exceeding five in number may be imported without a permit. Likewise, privately owned birds of the parrot family, not exceeding three in number, may be imported provided they have been in the possession of the accompanying owner for at least two years immediately preceding their importation and providing they also meet other requirements of the regulations provided by the United States Public Health Service. (You can buy parrots in Laredo, Texas.)

Birds of Paradise. The importation of birds of paradise, egrets, osprey plumes and feathers, and heads, skins, etc., of wild birds, raw or manufactured, are prohibited if not for scientific or educational purposes. Eggs of wild birds are prohibited.

The following are absolutely prohibited: lottery tickets and advertisements of lotteries; obscene and immoral articles, books, pictures, films, or publications and seditious matter. Counterfeits of coins, securities, postage stamps, and films of prize fights or pugilistic encounters are prohibited. Insects injurious to agriculture are prohibited. Victor phonograph records likewise are prohibited unless you get written consent of the owner of the Victor trade-mark.

Works of Art. If works of art are of low value, so that they may come within your $100 allowance, there are no particular regulations governing them. If of greater value, and you wish to pass them free of United States import duties, they should be accompanied by an affidavit made by the artist or seller before an American consul. To import them free of duties it is further necessary to send them in bond, at owner's risk and expense, to New Orleans to be appraised.

Antiques and Archaeological Objects. The Mexican government requires that all genuine colonial antiques and archaeological objects have a written permit from the authorities to leave Mexico. The United States government will not pass these things free of duty unless they come within your $100 allowance, or unless they are sent to New Orleans for appraisal at owner's expense.

Zippers. Only three such articles of one kind may be imported by one person. Restriction applies only to articles fitted with slide fasteners having a locking device.

Important Suggestions Regarding Customs. Severe penalties are prescribed for failure to declare and for making false statements as to value, ownership, or use of articles acquired abroad in any manner, and such false statements or failure to declare subject the articles to forfeiture.

Do not give, offer, or promise to give any money or anything of value to customs officers. It will only embarrass them, and may subject you to criminal prosecution.

The examination of baggage will be greatly facilitated if the following rules are followed:

All articles acquired in a foreign country should be packed separately and the original receipted bills presented to the inspector. If the original bills are not available, a carefully prepared list showing the purchase price or value of all articles acquired abroad should be presented to the inspector.

It is important that the returning resident remember that the duties of customs officers assigned to the entry and examination of all articles, free and dutiable, brought into the United States are most exacting and are prescribed by law governing the appointment. With the arrival of large numbers of persons and vehicles at one time, situations arise that become trying to both travelers and customs officials. Therefore, complete co-operation at all times will greatly facilitate the expeditious examination of baggage and effects and accelerate the movement of vehicles. While customs officers are required to be courteous to the public, it must be remembered that they are legally bound to enforce the laws strictly and without favor.

It should also be borne in mind that the examination of baggage after the owner has declared that it contains no dutiable effects or contraband is not a reflection on the owner's honesty or integrity.

U.S. LIQUOR REGULATIONS

A person residing in the United States and returning from abroad may include alcoholic beverages not to exceed one gallon under his $100 allowance, subject to his state's restrictions, if any. Or he may bring in one case of beer, regardless of the size of the bottles. This allowance consists of liquor or beer, not both. For state regulations, see your local police department or state enforcement agency.

U.S. PERFUME REGULATIONS

Some brands of perfumes are prohibited altogether, others are limited to one bottle, while some are unlimited. Labels must be removed or obliterated on certain brands. "One bottle" means one bottle or other immediate container.

If your stay in Mexico is of less than twenty-four hours you must pay duty on all perfume purchased there. Don't depend on the Mexican dealers to give you the correct information regarding United States customs regulations.

MORE PRESCIENCE

CLOTHES

Visitors to Mexico City and the temperate highland regions during the summer should take linens, light wools, and a light topcoat for evenings, early mornings, and drives into the mountains. Clothing such as is worn in the United States during the spring or autumn is appropriate.

For a winter visit one needs much warmer clothing. Sweaters and heavier topcoats will be comfortable for early-morning travel. However, midday in the highlands is generally quite warm, so be prepared to shed your outer clothing.

Mexico City is a much more formal town than most American visitors realize. Sports clothes are not usually worn in the city. Slacks, polo shirts, and sport jackets for men are appropriate attire for Cuernavaca, Taxco, Acapulco, and other resort towns, but in Mexico City a business suit is more correct. Women wear suits a great deal in all seasons, and in the cooler winter months a light coat is often comfortable over the suit. Since central heating is uncommon in Mexico, warm clothes for winter evenings indoors are essential. There are few nights in Mexico City, winter or summer, when one does not need a blanket or two on the bed.

If you plan to visit Acapulco, Veracruz, or Yucatán, you will need tropical-weight cottons, tropical worsted, Palm Beach, or linen clothing. Heavy-soled shoes will be needed if you plan to do any hiking in the mountains or around Parícutin volcano. Low heels will be appreciated for walking along cobblestoned streets of Mexican villages. Do take an umbrella or raincoat if your visit is to be in the summer season.

Women should not wear shorts on the streets of Mexico. It is offensive to the Mexican people, and the authorities have been known to take definite action in prohibiting the practice.

Additional information about clothing will be found in Chapter XII, page 283.

HEALTH

A normally healthy person who can remember and abide by a few simple rules need have no fear of sickness in Mexico. Here are three we think are most important:

1. Never drink water from wayside wells. Pure water will be found at all hotels and tourist courts along the main routes. It is best to avoid drinking water at any other place. Wherever possible, drink bottled water or beer. One may obtain pure bottled water in Mexico City in five-gallon glass bottles delivered anywhere in the city.

2. Eat regularly and well but not too heavily, and be careful about indulging too much in native food and drink at first. All fruits should be peeled before they are eaten.

3. Take it easy! Too much emphasis cannot be placed on moving in a leisurely fashion for the first few days in the higher altitudes. If you are affected by the altitude in the form of headache or nausea or just plain tiredness, rest quietly until you feel comfortable. It generally takes twelve to forty-eight hours to become fully acclimated to living in Mexico City.

For additional information about health conditions in Mexico, see Chapter XII, page 275.

LANGUAGE

The Aztec nation, which dominated the Valley of Mexico at the time of the Spanish Conquest, had extended its sway over only a small portion of the vast territory that now makes up the republic. Consequently, a great part of Mexico at that time was subdivided into small tribal republics and kingdoms, whose people did not intermingle with their neighbors but preserved their own ancient customs and languages. Even today this subdivision of tribes and racial characteristics is apparent throughout the country and gives to the native Indian life of Mexico a color and interest that several hundred years of the white man's civilization have not destroyed. Native tribes differ radically from each other in linguistic characteristics, and no less than sixty-three different Indian languages and dialects are spoken in the republic.

However, Spanish is the official language of Mexico and is spoken by everyone with whom the casual traveler comes in contact. English is spoken in the leading hotels, better restaurants, and many of the shops of Mexico City and other important cities. In fact, throughout most of Mexico a visitor can get along without a knowledge of Spanish. Mexico City has a staff of linguistic police officers, each of whom specializes in some foreign language. They wear miniature flags on their coat sleeves; those speaking English wear American flags.

ACCOMMODATIONS

Since transportation facilities and general conditions affecting travel in Mexico have not reached the same advanced stage of standardization as in the United States, and because in the more remote places good hotel accommodations are often quite limited, the careful planning of a tour is advisable. The traveler who leaves his arrangements to chance may experience difficulties and discomforts that will greatly mar the pleasure of the trip.

The immense increase in popularity that Mexico has enjoyed in the last few years has made the demand for hotel accommodations and tourist facilities greater than the supply. Prospective visitors must, therefore, ascertain in advance that desired accommodations are available. Many American travel agents maintain offices or representatives in Mexico City, and it is strongly advised that you book your travel and hotel services through them. Travel agents operate on commissions paid them by the transportation and hotel companies, so there is no charge for their help in addition to what you would ordinarily pay.

CHAPTER III

MEXICAN ROUTES

A S WE have shown in previous chapters, the topography of Mexico is as complex and varied as its history, or as the multitude of races that have peopled it. From the ribbon of tropical lowlands bordering either coast, the earth rises in a series of terraces culminating in the mountain ranges that parallel the shore. Between them, at an average altitude of nearly 7,000 feet, lies an immense plateau running from the Isthmus of Tehuantepec to the northern boundary.

Successive waves of humanity have broken over the plateaus, crossed the mountains, and reached the coast; others, surging from the sea, have passed the mountains and overrun valleys and plains. All have explored to the north, trafficked with the south, developed civilizations, waged warfare, and extended their boundaries, leaving throughout the country vestiges of their language, religion, science, and art. From this unceasing ebb and flow there arose in the central valleys, on the shores of lakes, and along rivers and the Gulf of Mexico civilizations comparable with those of the ancient East, whence proceeded, according to some archaeologists, the first settlers of America more than ten thousand years ago. The indigenous civilizations left behind them, in the localities where their splendor was greatest, cities and monuments that make up what might be called the Orient of America; this is particularly true of the Toltecs and Aztecs in the central plateau and of the Mayas in the south and southeast.

Later came the "bearded white men" to fulfill the prophecy of Quetzalcoatl. These established their capital on the ruins of the great Aztec metropolis, Tenochtitlán. The extent of the Spanish colonial regime was limited by the same topographical features that

29

had determined the size and importance of native centers. The white flood, although obliterating the cities in its path to such a degree that cathedrals were literally as well as metaphorically erected on the ruins of temples and pyramids, was not strong enough to overcome the indigenous brown currents, which stopped its advance and ended by absorbing it, thus creating a new race.

So modern Mexico is a kaleidoscope of human history; from the capital to the mountains, the traveler will pass from 1948 to 1850, to 1792, to 1500, and thence backward to neolithic times. In the capital itself he will see, cheek by jowl with modern districts, remains of the colonial era and of archaic America. Everywhere he may go the weight of ages will be apparent, giving every detail, every panorama, every hamlet a new significance. Throughout the history of Mexico, its age-long heritage has been growing with the passing of each new epoch. The amalgamation has cost pain and effort, and the depth of human suffering inherent in each change is expressed and reflected in the architecture, the paintings, and the music of each of the great stages of the Mexican past.

These make Mexico the magic land! They are available to American travelers by land, sea, and air from any point in the United States. The visitor has his choice of a number of round-trip combinations and pre-arranged tours; he may travel independently on any of the available services; or he may drive his own automobile.

If the traveler comes from the north, he will traverse by highway, rail, or air a portion of the extensive and sparsely populated plateaus of northern Mexico, passing the mining, railway, stock-raising, and cotton centers of that region. Monterrey, Chihuahua, Torreón, Durango, Saltillo, Zacatecas, and San Luís Potosí are the principal towns serving this area.

The rich and picturesque northwestern coast is covered by rail from the border town of Nogales, or by air through Mexicali. The rail journey through Guaymas, Culiacan, and Mazatlán is climaxed at Tepic and romantic old Guadalajara.

The ascent from either coast offers a bewildering transition from banana fields and palm groves, coffee estates and sugar plantations, gardenias and orchids, over tortuous defiles and along terrifying precipices, to wide fields crisscrossed by straight rows of maguey and corn and beans. The snow-capped peaks of Mexico's most famous mountains—Orizaba, Popocatépetl, and Ixtaccíhuatl—loom over these approaches. You will see them and be thrilled by them whether you come by air, highway, rail, or ocean steamer. The following information will help you choose your *vía de transporte*.

AIRWAYS

One may reach Mexico by air from nearly every point of the compass. The ports of entry, clockwise around the country, are Mexicali, Nogales, Ciudad Juárez (opposite El Paso, Texas), Piedras Negras (opposite Eagle Pass, Texas), Nuevo Laredo (opposite Laredo, Texas), Brownsville (Texas), Matamoros, Mérida, and Tapachula. Domestic lines of the United States connect with Mexican lines through these entry ports. Some lines, in co-operation with Mexican companies, operate direct service to central Mexico from Los Angeles, El Paso, and San Antonio, and to Mérida (Yucatán) from New Orleans and Miami (via Havana, Cuba). Planes entering Mexico through Tapachula come from Central and South America.

Air rates now compare favorably with rail fares, while the traveler with little time will find many advantages in air travel over any other means. With new planes and new schedules being added almost weekly, we suggest you see your local travel agent for the latest information regarding routes and costs. The United States lines most interested in your Mexican trip are Pan American World Airways, American Airlines, United Airways, Braniff International Airways, and TWA (TACA Airways' parent company in the United States). The principal feeder air lines connecting with the main gateways to Mexico are Delta Air Lines, Chicago and Southern Airlines, and Eastern Air Lines.

Air itineraries covering trips to a large number of interesting places in Mexico may be easily arranged by using the information included in Chapter VIII, "Encyclopedia of Places," beginning on page 167. The names of the air lines serving the various towns and the principal connections are shown. For schedules and rates one should make up-to-the-minute inquiry at the Mexico City offices of those lines or at one of the offices or agencies of the above United States lines.

Although visitors entering by train or auto experience little or no inconvenience in the matter of customs inspection or entrance requirements, it is a known fact that air travelers have always been handled with special care by border officials. The customs inspections are more cursory, the tourist entry red tape is shorter, and the courtesy of the officials and attendants is exceptionally respectful.

HIGHWAYS

The main United States highways to Mexico are those connecting with U.S. 81 at San Antonio, Texas. This leads to Laredo, and, after crossing the Rio Grande into Mexico, becomes Carretera Nacional No. 1 (National Highway No. 1). It is also called the Pan American Highway, and so far is the only road from the United States into the central-plateau region around Mexico City.

Other highways enter Mexico from the United States, but these penetrate only short distances into the interior of the country. From left to right across the map, they are: San Diego, California, along the Pacific to Ensenada; Phoenix, Arizona (through Sonoyta, a Mexican border town), to Punta Penasco on the Gulf of California; Nogales, Arizona, to Hermosillo and Guaymas; El Paso, Texas, to Chihuahua; Eagle Pass, Texas, to Saltillo; and McAllen and Browns-ville, Texas, to Monterrey, Saltillo, Torreón, and Durango.

The transcontinental highways are: Tampico through San Luís Potosí to Guadalajara; Veracruz through Puebla, Mexico City, and Morelia to Guadalajara; and Veracruz through Mexico City to Acapulco.

The development of a highway system is a long step forward in the advancement of Mexico. For many years great areas were hampered by lack of good communications, both for the transportation of foodstuffs to market and for the distribution of manufactured products to consumers.

The construction and maintenance of roads is in the charge of the National Highway Authority, a department under the Secretary of Communications and Public Works. Roads are classified as "federal roads," built by the federal government, and "roads in co-operation with the states," built under the act of 1933 providing for equal contributions from state and federal governments, the construction and administrative work being under the local councils for roads.

The surface width of federal roads is ten meters (about 32.5 feet), that of the co-operative roads seven meters. The road network in Mexico is made up of federal roads, which are the truck roads between main marketing centers, fed by the others, which link the principal towns and productive centers within each state.

Almost all of Mexico's 9,810 miles of all-weather highways have been built since 1930. An additional mileage of 35,411 is estimated for dry-weather roads, and an approximate 8,500 miles of various kinds of highways are currently laid out and under construction.

Mexico City is a hub from which the principal all-weather roads radiate to different parts of the republic. The chief road is the Mexican section of the Pan American Highway, which, when completed, will traverse 1,751 miles of Mexican territory from Nuevo Laredo (across the Rio Grande from Laredo, Texas, and 764 miles from Mexico City) to the Suchiate River, which divides Mexico and Guatemala. A transverse highway beginning at Reynosa (across the border from McAllen, Texas) passes through Monterrey and continues westward, through Saltillo, as far as Torreón. This highway will eventually continue to Chihuahua, which is now connected with Ciudad Juárez (across the border from El Paso, Texas) by a paved road 228 miles long.

From the capital a paved road runs east to Puebla (where the Pan American Highway branches off to Oaxaca). A few miles beyond Puebla this road divides, the northern branch leading to Jalapa and Veracruz (282 miles) and the southern to Tehuacán, Orizaba, and Córdoba, beyond which a dry-weather road continues to Veracruz.

The only paved road to the Pacific coast runs south from Mexico City through Cuernavaca, Taxco, Iguala, and Chilpancingo to the popular seaside resort of Acapulco (282 miles).

Mexico City is connected with Guadalajara, 428 miles to the west, by a principal all-weather highway that goes through Toluca and Morelia. Short side roads give access to Pátzcuaro and Uruapan (near the active volcano Parícutin) and to other towns.

The main highways of Mexico, their lengths and surface conditions in January 1948, are shown in the table below.

Pan American Highway (Carretera Nacional No. 1)

Laredo, Texas, to Mexico City	764 miles, all paved
Feeder Roads	
McAllen, Texas, to Monterrey	142 miles, all paved
Monterrey to Saltillo and Torreón	234 miles, all paved
Ciudad Mante to Tampico	96 miles, all paved
Antiguo Morelos to Guadalajara	415 miles, all paved
Ojuelos to Aguascalientes	46 miles, all paved

Ixmiquilpan (Km. 167) to Querétaro,
　Irapuato, and Lagos　　　　　　　　　　237 miles, all paved
Mexico City to Oaxaca (via Puebla)　　　342 miles, all paved
Pacific Highway (Carretera Nacional No. 4)
　Mexico City to Morelia and Guadalajara　428 miles, all paved
　Feeder Roads
　　Guadalajara to Tequila　　　　　　　　42 miles, all paved
　　Quiroga to Pátzcuaro　　　　　　　　　15 miles, all paved
　　Carapan to Uruapan　　　　　　　　　　45 miles, all paved
　　Guadalajara to Chapala　　　　　　　　30 miles, all paved
Acapulco Highway (Carretera Nacional No. 3)
　Mexico City to Taxco and Acapulco　　　282 miles, all paved
　Feeder Roads
　　Tres Cumbres to Zempoala Lakes　　　　12 miles, all paved
　　Buena Vista to Tepoztlán　　　　　　　11 miles, all paved
　　Cuernavaca to Cuautla　　　　　　　　28 miles, gravel road
　　Alpuyeca to Cacahuamilpa Caves and
　　　Dos Bocas　　　　　　　　　　　　　30 miles, all paved
　　Alpuyeca to Tequesquitengo, Jojutla,
　　　Tlalquiltenango, and Tlaltizapán　　　19 miles, all paved
Veracruz Highway (Carretera Nacional No. 2)
　Mexico City to Veracruz (via Jalapa)　　282 miles, all paved
　Feeder Roads
　　Km. 18 to Texcoco　　　　　　　　　　13 miles, all paved
　　Santa Bárbara to Amecameca and Cuautla　47 miles, all paved
　　San Martín Texmelucan to Tlaxcala and
　　　Apizaco　　　　　　　　　　　　　　26 miles, all paved
　　Perote to Teziutlán　　　　　　　　　　24 miles, gravel road
　　Jalapa to Coatepec　　　　　　　　　　12 miles, all paved
　　Puebla to Tehuacán and Córdoba　　　　127 miles, all paved
　　Zacatepec to Nautla (via Zaragoza and
　　　Teziutlán)　　　　　　　　　　　　　122 miles, all paved
Central Highway
　El Paso, Texas, to Chihuahua　　　　　　230 miles, all paved
Miscellaneous Highways
　Mexico City to Teotihuacán Pyramids　　　30 miles, all paved
　Mexico City to Tuxpan, Veracruz (via Pachuca)　217 miles, all paved
　Mexico City to Tepotzotlán　　　　　　　26 miles, all paved
　Mexico City to Desierto de los Leones (via
　　San Ángel)　　　　　　　　　　　　　23 miles, all paved
　Piedras Negras to Saltillo　　　　　　　278 miles, all paved

HIGHWAY ITINERARIES

　Since more tourists travel to Mexico and tour the country in their
own cars than by any other means of transportation, we have out-

lined the automobile itineraries at some length—too much to be included in this one chapter on routes and transportation. Therefore, we have included them as one chapter (Chapter IV, page 39) following this one.

Railways

Mexico has some 14,362 miles of railways, but the service and the condition of the equipment compares very unfavorably with average lines in the United States. First-class passenger coaches frequently are not air-conditioned and are seldom as clean or as comfortable as those north of the border. Second-class passenger coaches are little more than freight cars with hard wooden benches. There is one compensating factor (besides certain appeals to the adventurous): the fares charged on Mexican trains are considerably lower than United States rates. The new system of running through coaches from several United States cities direct to Mexico City now provides, at least on these runs, the accommodations demanded by most American tourists.

The railways of Mexico extend south from four points on the border of the United States where they have railway exchange facilities with United States railways, and north from the Guatemala border, where they connect with the narrow-gauge railways of Central America, as follows:

INTERNATIONAL GATEWAYS

Ciudad Juárez, state of Chihuahua (opposite El Paso, Texas). Exchange facilities with Atchison, Topeka & Santa Fe Railway, Southern Pacific (lines west), and Texas & Pacific Railway.

Nuevo Laredo, state of Tamaulipas (opposite Laredo, Texas). Exchange facilities with Missouri Pacific Lines, Rio Grande & Eagle Pass Railway, and Texas Mexican Railway.

Piedras Negras, state of Coahuila (opposite Eagle Pass, Texas). Exchange facilities with Southern Pacific Lines.

Matamoros, state of Tamaulipas (opposite Brownsville, Texas). Exchange facilities with Missouri Pacific Lines, Port Isabelle & Rio Grande Valley Railway, and Southern Pacific Lines.

Nogales, state of Sonora (opposite Nogales, Arizona). Exchange facilities with Southern Pacific Lines.

Suchiate, state of Chiapas (opposite Ayutla, Guatemala). Exchange facilities (by reloading, since the Central American railways are narrow-gauge) with International Railways of Central America.

RAILWAY ITINERARIES

A large number of interesting side trips can be made by rail from Mexico City. The following table lists the principal towns accessible by rail, the distance from Mexico City (in kilometers, since that is the measurement used by the railways), the scheduled running time, and second-class and first-class fares one way from Mexico City. Round-trip fares are twice the one-way fare less 20 per cent for fifteen-day limit and 10 per cent for thirty-day limit. Lower-berth Pullman, when available, is about 35 per cent of and in addition to the first-class fare. All fares are shown in Mexican pesos. Second-class coaches are crude, dirty, and overcrowded, and the seats are wooden benches. Unless you are a hardy traveler, do not attempt them. And do not attempt to ride in a first-class coach with a second-class ticket!

For additional information such as hotels and sight-seeing in these towns, see page 167.

Station	Kilometers	Time	2nd Class	1st Class
Aguascalientes, Ags.	585	14 hrs., 5 min.	$20.90	$ 37.60
Amecameca, Mex.	59	3 hrs., 47 min.	1.05	1.90
Celaya, Gto.	292	6 hrs., 14 min.	10.40	18.75
Ciudad Juárez, Chih.	1,973	43 hrs., 25 min.	70.45	126.80
Ciudad Victoria, Tamps.				
(via Tampico)	1,206	5 hrs., 48 min.	42.20	75.95
Coatzacoalcos, Ver.	930	28 hrs., 23 min.	33.20	59.75
Colima, Col.	873	19 hrs., 35 min.	31.15	56.10
Cuautla, Mor.	137	3 hrs., 55 min.	2.45	4.40
Cuernavaca, Mor.	120	3 hrs., 58 min.	2.15	3.85
Chihuahua, Chih.	1,613	36 hrs., 2 min.	57.60	103.65
Durango, Dgo.	1,082	26 hrs., 40 min.	38.65	69.55
El Mante, Tamps.				
(via Tampico)	1,163	34 hrs., 36 min.	40.65	73.20
Guadalajara, Jal.	613	12 hrs., 55 min.	21.90	39.40
Guanajuato, Gto.	407	10 hrs., 34 min.	14.55	26.15
Iguala, Gro.	238	8 hrs.	6.35	11.45
Jalapa, Ver.	342	9 hrs.	6.10	11.00
Linares, N.L.	1,170	27 hrs., 6 min.	40.95	73.70
Manzanillo, Col.	968	23 hrs., 10 min.	34.55	62.20

Station	Kilometers	Time	2nd Class	1st Class
Monterrey, N.L.	1,022	23 hrs., 50 min.	35.65	64.20
Morelia, Mich. (via Toluca)	369	9 hrs., 20 min.	13.15	23.70
Nuevo Laredo, Tamps.	1,290	30 hrs.	45.25	81.40
Oaxaca, Oax.	577	15 hrs., 10 min.	14.60	26.25
Pachuca, Hgo.	98	3 hrs., 5 min.	2.65	4.75
Pátzcuaro, Mich. (via Toluca)	430	10 hrs., 45 min.	15.35	27.65
Puebla, Pue.	210	4 hrs., 50 min.	3.75	6.75
Querétaro, Qro.	245	5 hrs., 54 min.	8.75	15.75
Saltillo, Coah.	917	19 hrs., 15 min.	31.90	57.45
San Luís Potosí, S.L.P.	527	10 hrs., 15 min.	17.95	32.30
Tampico, Tamps. (via S.L.P.)	971	22 hrs., 30 min.	33.80	60.85
Tapachula, Chis.	1,351	46 hrs., 10 min.	48.25	86.80
Tehuacán, Pue.	338	5 hrs., 53 min.	6.05	10.85
Toluca, Mex.	74	2 hrs., 15 min.	1.35	2.40
Torreón, Coah.	1,136	25 hrs., 35 min.	40.55	73.00
Uruapan, Mich. (via Toluca)	505	13 hrs.	18.05	32.45
Veracruz, Ver.	473	13 hrs., 25 min.	8.45	15.20

WATERWAYS

MEXICO BY SEA

For those who have the time and for those who enjoy sailing, there are available several delightful cruises to Mexican ports. Arrangements can be made to stop over between ships and visit the interior on extended tours by rail or by chartered automobile. Where a family or a group of three or four persons shares the expenses of such a tour the cost is comparatively reasonable. Although new ships and new cruises are being added and changed frequently, the following list of lines operating to Mexico will be a good starting point for gathering up-to-date information.

Steamship Line	Operates out of	To Mexican Port
Cuba Mail Line	New York, N.Y.	Veracruz
Pacific Cruise Lines	Long Beach, Calif.	Acapulco
Yucatan Line	New Orleans, La.	Progreso

INLAND WATERWAYS

Navigation on Mexican inland waterways is confined for the most part to travel by small vessels on the lakes and coastal estuaries and lagoons and by primitive means on some of the rivers, including the Balsas, Pánuco, and Papaloápam. Plans are reportedly under way to develop inland water transportation, notably by an intercoastal canal-lagoon route between the ports of Tampico and Matamoros, state of Tamaulipas, and the channelization of the river Papaloápam, which flows through a region not served by other means of communication.

The adventurous who want something out of the ordinary should make inquiry at the Mexican Tourist Association offices in Mexico City for information concerning trips on some of the tropic rivers of southern Mexico.

CHAPTER IV

AUTOMOBILE ITINERARIES

THE best way to see Mexico is to drive over the country in your own car. With Mexico's improved new road system and the establishment of adequate service facilities along the principal highways, touring in Mexico can be as comfortable and pleasant as in any part of the United States. The freedom and flexibility of such transportation are obvious.

Capable mechanics will be found in all the larger towns, but automobile parts are frequently scarce and difficult to obtain. Your car should be thoroughly checked, therefore, before you cross over into Mexico.

Trips should be planned so that you will arrive at your hotel before nightfall. You may encounter heavy fogs on some of the higher mountain passes, and though they are not particularly dangerous in the daytime, one should not attempt to drive unfamiliar fog-shrouded roads at night. Night drivers are also cautioned about cattle and livestock on the highways. There are few fences in Mexico and animals are frequently encountered in the roads. In fact, the smooth pavement of a sun-warmed highway is a favorite bed for Mexican cows and burros. Watch out!

Oil and gasoline are sold by the *litro* (liter) in Mexico. It takes 3.8 liters to make 1 United States gallon, or 15 liters to make 4 gallons. Mexican regular gasoline "Pemex" has an octane rating of fifty-seven, which is about ten points below the regular grades of standard gasolines in the United States. An average tour to Mexico City and side trips is about two thousand miles of driving inside Mexico. If you have room, take along a five-gallon can of the best

United States ethyl gasoline and use it at about the middle of your trip. It will help avoid some carbon trouble.

American oils are available in the larger cities of Mexico, but "Mexolub," a good Mexican oil, is available everywhere and is cheaper than imported oils.

Maximum speed limit on the open highway is one hundred kilometers or sixty miles per hour. In towns and villages the limit is forty kilometers or twenty-five miles per hour; in Monterrey, eighteen miles. Most cities have many one-way streets. Signs on each corner (usually on building walls) indicate traffic direction by an arrow; two-way streets have an arrow with two points.

For additional driving tips (in Mexico City) see page 104.

The most important road in Mexico and one of the most extraordinary in the Western Hemisphere is the Mexican section of the Pan American Highway system. This road, when completed throughout Mexico and the other Latin-American nations, will connect all of the New World countries from Alaska to Tierra del Fuego. The Laredo, Texas, to Mexico City portion has been open to traffic since 1936. The Mexico City to Oaxaca portion is now paved (via Puebla), but there is little through traffic beyond Oaxaca. Several portions of the road from Oaxaca to the Guatemalan border are graveled and suitable for rough all-weather travel, a few stretches are paved, and some are simple country roads suitable for dry-weather travel only. There is a wild stretch of about 135 miles on the other end of the route approaching the Guatemala border, where no road exists. We recently covered the Pan American Highway from New York to Guatemala in a jeep, and this last portion of the highway was too difficult even for that sturdy conveyance. We had to turn back and retrace our route to Arriaga, and from there portage via rail to Tapachula.

The greatest inconvenience to travel on the southern portion of the Pan American Highway in Mexico is the lack of gasoline and repair facilities and the nonexistence of hotels—there are practically none of these between Oaxaca and Tuxtla Gutiérrez, and very inadequate in the latter place.

The following chart shows the condition of the Mexican portion of the Pan American Highway as of January 1948. At the present rate of construction it will be several years before this is very much out of date.

Laredo, Texas–Mexico City	764 miles, all paved
Mexico City–Oaxaca (via Puebla)	344 miles, all paved
Oaxaca–Tlacolula	19 miles, all paved
Tlacolula–Tehuantepec	140 miles, all weather
Tehuantepec–Ingenio Santo Domingo	42 miles, all weather
Ingenio Santo Domingo–Mile 258 (from Oaxaca)	57 miles, dry weather
Mile 258–Las Cruces	24 miles, all weather
Las Cruces–Tuxtla Gutiérrez	63 miles, all paved
Tuxtla Gutierrez–Escopetazo	20 miles, all paved
Escopetazo–San Cristóbal las Casas	32 miles, all weather
San Cristóbal las Casas–Comitán	62 miles, dry weather
Comitán–Zapaluta (La Trinitaria)	13 miles, dry weather
Zapaluta–Mile 607 (from Oaxaca)	135 miles, no road
Mile 607–Tapachula	25 miles, all weather
Tapachula–Talismán Bridge	11 miles, all paved

PRINCIPAL ROUTES

LAREDO, TEXAS, TO MEXICO CITY

The first portion of this highway crosses the semiarid desert country of northern Mexico. After leaving Nuevo Laredo, the Mexican town on the other side of the Rio Grande from Laredo, Texas, it runs south in a straight line for almost seventy miles without turning. The ground ascends toward the mountains farther south, but the climb is so gradual that the terrain appears flat. However, a bluish haze soon breaks the line of the horizon and rapidly begins to take shape until the profile of the first mountain range is disclosed to view. From here on the mountains are never out of sight.

Soon after the road meets the foothills it starts up a series of gentle grades and banked though sharp curves to Mamulique Pass, 2,800 feet high. Farther on the road passes a series of odd-looking horizontal mesas, and presently Monterrey, the chief industrial center of Mexico, appears in the distance. Its many smokestacks, church towers, and new buildings appear in miniature by comparison against a background of fantastic mountain shapes rising straight up out of the floor of the valley.

Leaving Monterrey, the road skirts the base of Saddle Mountain, then winds through a broad canyon between parallel ranges of the Sierra Anahuac. Steadily losing altitude, it enters the second zone, a succession of fertile subtropical valleys hemmed in by the ever present mountains. The scanty vegetation of the northern desert gives way here to sugar-cane, cotton, and corn plantations, clusters of trees shading portions of the highway, vegetable gardens and fruit orchards, and flowers in profusion around every dwelling.

Occasionally the road approaches a seemingly impenetrable mountain barrier, then it twists and climbs through heavily wooded narrow canyons, then dips again, reaching lower and lower altitudes.

Extensive orange and lemon groves are left behind, innumerable streams are crossed, and the appearance of mango, aguacate (avocado), and banana trees, as well as a noticeable rise in temperature, indicates that the tropics are at hand. At times the road passes through a forest of tall palms, at others through a wonderland of strange and exotic trees and plants. Drive slowly through this country and you may see flocks of green, yellow, and red parrots cross noisily overhead. Wild orchids and other parasitic plants bloom in the trees beside the highway.

The highway drops down to about ninety feet above sea level, and then, not far away, looms the Sierra Madre Oriental, the mother or central range of Mexico's eastern mountains. Here, within a matter of minutes, the road climbs from near sea level to nearly nine thousand feet! It is the thrill of a lifetime to make this ascent, for the highway is a series of broad, graceful curves easily negotiated in high gear all the way, while the changes in scenery and the breath-taking vistas on every hand are most extraordinary. The vegetation gradually changes as the ascent continues, and at places the road looks out across deep chasms to a perpendicular cross section of a series of climatic zones. The moisture from the hot canyon floors turns to fog and clouds as it rises to higher levels, and the upper panoramas take on a weird, ghostly aspect, strangely quiet and sharply cold.

Finally the road comes out on the vast central plateau. Rolling and nearly level now, it passes between fields of corn and maguey plantations, through small, dirt-colored towns with massive stone churches, and the primitive little homes of farmers and sheepherders. At last it reaches the Valley of Mexico, encircled by high wooded ranges, topped far to the south by the two white volcanoes Popocatépetl and Ixtaccíhuatl. Soon the road enters Mexico City and following one of the oldest streets in the New World arrives at the Zócalo, the heart of the Mexican capital and the official ter-

minus of the Carretera Nacional No. 1 (National Highway No. 1),
the Pan American Highway.

Itinerary. Distance (one way): 764 miles. Road: all paved. Time:
three days, two nights. Hotels in Monterrey, Linares, Ciudad Victoria, El Mante, Tamazunchale, and Zimapán. Service: gasoline and
restaurants are noted below.

Trip may start from San Antonio or Laredo, Texas. If from San
Antonio, leave early in the morning to pass through the Mexican
customs at Nuevo Laredo during the morning hours. The three-hour
drive, Laredo to Monterrey, will bring you to Monterrey in time
for a late lunch and afternoon sight-seeing. Before leaving Laredo,
obtain at the Mexican Consulate a tourist card for each member of
your party, if this has not already been done. Secure an auto permit
at the branch office of the AAA or AMA in Laredo, or at the
Mexican customs upon crossing to Nuevo Laredo. Be sure you have
your state driver's license and car registration certificate. Register at
United States customs in Laredo any articles in your luggage of foreign make or of unusual value (see page 20).

If your time is very limited, the run to Mexico City may be made
in two days by leaving Laredo early, stopping in Monterrey for
brief sight-seeing and lunch, and continuing to Ciudad Valles or
Tamazunchale for the night, arriving in Mexico City during the late
afternoon of the following day. If more time is available, spend an
extra day in the Monterrey region (itinerary, page 190); also an
extra day on a side trip to Tampico or San Luís Potosí while en
route to Mexico City (see itineraries, pages 68 and 70).

The figures on the margin below represent miles from Laredo.

  0 Nuevo Laredo. Altitude, 560 feet. Population, 28,872. Pass
     through customs and then you are "traveling in Mexico"! Leave
     the seals on your baggage in order to avoid possible reinspec-
     tion at two substations farther along the road.

 44 La Gloria. The road to the right leads to Don Martín Dam on
     the Salado River, a seventy-five-mile run; excellent fishing.
     (Gas, restaurant.)

 80 Sabinas Hidalgo. A former mining town. Largest town between
     Nuevo Laredo and Monterrey. (Gas, telephone, telegraph, res-
     taurant.)

100 Mamulique Pass. A few miles south of Sabinas Hidalgo the

road begins the ascent to Mamulique Pass, by which it crosses a spur of the Sierra Madre Oriental. The top of the pass is 2,300 feet above sea level.

124 Ciénaga de Flores. A picturesque village. (Gas.)

146 Monterrey. Altitude, 1,752 feet. Population, 220,000. Capital of the state of Nuevo León. A city of contrasts, being Mexico's biggest industrial and manufacturing center while retaining many buildings and traditions from colonial days. A number of interesting side trips may be made from Monterrey. A trip to Saltillo (see page 77) should not be missed. (Gas, repairs, telephone, telegraph, restaurant, hotel, AMA office.)

150 Huajuco Canyon. A scenic canyon through which the road passes.

166 Villa Santiago. The Horsetail Falls are four miles off the highway to the west. (Gas, restaurant at the Falls.)

195 Montemorelos (just off the highway). One of the largest orange-growing districts of Mexico. An interesting fair takes place here during the second fortnight in July. (Gas.)
The road to the left leads ten miles to General Terán and the hacienda of former President Calles.

228 Linares. Altitude, 1,265 feet. Population, 9,918. The center of an extensive farming and ranching district. Largest town between Monterrey and Ciudad Victoria. (Gas, repairs, telephone, telegraph, restaurant, hotel, AMA office.)
Two picturesque Indian villages, Iturbide and Galeana, can be reached over a forty-three-mile rough dry-weather road from Linares.

258 Villagrán. The center of a mining district. (Gas.)

298 The road to the west goes eleven miles to the Hacienda Santa Engracia, a typical old hacienda operating as a guest ranch.

326 Ciudad Victoria. Altitude, 1,470 feet. Population, 25,825. Capital of the state of Tamaulipas and seat of the Tamaulipas State Agricultural College. Named after Mexico's first president, Guadalupe Victoria. Scenic surroundings, excellent fishing and hunting. (Gas, repairs, telephone, telegraph, restaurant, hotel.)
A road goes from here northeast to Matamoros, opposite Brownsville, Texas. At present parts of it are passable in dry weather only.

347 Tropic of Cancer.

369 Galeana Canyon. A deep canyon with walls covered with tropical verdure.

400 El Limón. A peaceful little village, the lowest town on the route, 197 feet above sea level. (Gas.)

407 Ciudad Mante. Formerly Villa Juárez. Set among extensive sugar plantations. Here is located the largest and most modern sugar mill in Mexico. (Gas, repairs, telephone, telegraph, restaurant, hotel.) The road branching off to the left a mile and a half to the south goes to Tampico (see page 70).

428 Antiguo Morelos. Here begins the steady climb to the big mountains. This is one of the best hunting regions in Mexico. (Gas, repairs, telephone, telegraph, restaurant, hotel.) The road to the right leads to San Luís Potosí and Guadalajara (see page 68).

471 Ciudad Valles. Altitude, 312 feet. Population, 7,240. A railroad center and one of the principal overnight stopping places along the highway. South of Valles the road runs through the lush tropical country of the Huastec Indians. (Gas, repairs, telephone, telegraph, restaurant, hotel, AMA office.) An all-weather road runs ninety miles east to Tampico.

478 El Bañito. Tropical sulphur springs and swimming pool. (Gas, telephone, telegraph, restaurant, hotel.)

483 Pujal. (Gas.)

501 Dry-weather road to the east goes two miles to the Indian village of Tancanhuitz.

514 All-weather road to the west leads thirteen miles, climbing some three thousand feet up a tropical mountainside, to the village of Xilitla.

537 Tamazunchale. Altitude, 394 feet. Population, 2,487. An old town in the heart of the Huastec Indian country, at the foot of the towering Sierra Madre Oriental. The ascent into the Sierra Madre begins just south of here. The first lap is a spectacular climb of five thousand feet in sixty miles. The best time to drive is between nine A.M. and five P.M. to avoid morning and evening fogs. (Gas, repairs, telephone, telegraph, restaurant, hotel.)

556 Chapulhuacan. The village is just off the highway. (Gas, telephone, telegraph, restaurant, hotel.)

596 Jacala. End of the first lap of the climb. You still have to go up

three thousand feet. Good place to stop for lunch. (Gas, restaurant, hotel.)

637 Zimapán. Here you reach the central plateau. Charming colonial town with cobblestone streets and interesting parish church. Founded over four hundred years ago. Notice the huge cypress tree on your left as you enter town; the trunk is forty-two feet around. (Gas, repairs, telephone, telegraph, restaurant, hotel.)

653 Tasquillo. Old capital of the Otomí Indians. A fine old colonial bridge spans the deep gorge of the Tula River just north of town. (Gas.)

660 Highway to Querétaro branches off to the west (see page 71).

665 Ixmiquilpan. Interesting colonial city; sixteenth-century church; and another colonial bridge over the Tula River. (Gas, repairs, telephone, telegraph, restaurant, hotel.)

690 Actopan. Imposing colonial convent with magnificent frescoes, built in 1546, now a rural normal school. (Gas, telephone, telegraph, restaurant.)

705 The road to the left goes five miles to Pachuca. If you wish to detour through Pachuca, you can take this road and rejoin the highway at Colonia, a few miles south.

Pachuca. Altitude, 8,023 feet. Population, 53,354. Capital of the state of Hidalgo. The silver mines of Pachuca date back to before the Spanish Conquest, and this is still one of the largest silver-mining centers in the world. The famous Real del Monte mines, the largest in the district, are six miles from town. (Gas, repairs, telephone, telegraph, restaurant, hotel, AMA office.)

From Pachuca a road continues on through beautiful wild country to Poza Rica and Tuxpan in the tropical region along the shores of the Gulf. You may want to take this road later on a trip out of Mexico City. You can go to Poza Rica, there turn south to Papantla and Nautla, and come out on the main highway between Mexico City and Veracruz. This is a popular two- or three-day circle trip from Mexico City.

707 Hacienda de la Concepción. Highest point on the road, 8,209 feet. The Monument to Mexican-American Friendship is near here.

712 Colonia. The road to the left goes to Pachuca. This is the main road from Mexico City to Pachuca. (Gas, telephone, telegraph.)

731 Tizayuca. (Gas, telephone, telegraph, restaurant.)

747 Venta de Carpio. The road to the left goes to Teotihuacán, twelve miles away, and to the Convent of Acolman (see below). (Gas.)

749 San Cristóbal Ecatepec. Notice here the colonial house known as the "House of the Viceroys" (see below).

755 Santa Clara. The road forks here. The right-hand fork is the new highway into Mexico City; the left-hand fork goes through Villa Madero, near the Shrine of Guadalupe, and thence into the city. Driving will be easier if you take the right-hand fork.

764 Mexico City. Altitude, 7,775 feet. Population (estimated), 2,225,000. Capital of Mexico.

SHORT TRIPS OUT OF MEXICO CITY

Several interesting half-day or day trips can be made from Mexico City. Since the hotel and restaurant accommodations at these places are inadequate or nonexistent, plan to return to your hotel in Mexico City at night, and have the hotel or a good restaurant fix a box lunch for the trip. Sanborn's Restaurant can supply the latter on a moment's notice.

Guadalupe Shrine, Acolman, San Juan Teotihuacán and Pyramids. Distance (one way): thirty miles. Road: all paved. Time: one day (could be made in a half day, with an early start and a late lunch on the return to Mexico City).

The figures on the margin below represent miles from Mexico City.

0 Mexico City. From the Zócalo drive north on Avenida República de Argentina, Jesús Carranza, and Calzada de Guadalupe (different names for the same thoroughfare).

4 Villa Madero. The shrine of the Virgin of Guadalupe is on the main square. In it is the picture of the Virgin that, according to the legend, was miraculously stamped on the cloak of the Indian convert Juan Diego, to whom she appeared. Near the shrine is the Chapel of the Well, at the spring that is said to have gushed forth miraculously at her appearance. On the Hill

of Tepeyac, where Juan Diego saw her, is a chapel built on the spot where she stood. The fiesta of the Virgin, December 3–13, is attended by thousands from all parts of Mexico.

6 Atzacoalco. Drainage works begun in pre-Spanish times and finished during the presidency of Díaz are here.

8 Santa Clara. Junction with the Pan American Highway.

10 Cerro Gordo.

14 San Cristóbal Ecatepec. Here, in the House of the Viceroys, the revolutionary hero José María Morelos was imprisoned. The house has been made into a museum.

17 Venta de Carpio. Leave the Pan American Highway, taking the branch road to the right.

21 Tepexpan. Take the road to the left. The road straight ahead leads to Texcoco.

23 Take the branch road to the right, go one and a half miles to Acolman. One of the finest examples in Mexico of sixteenth-century architecture is the church and monastery of San Agustín Acolman. Return to Mile 23 on the main road and continue north.

30 San Juan Teotihuacán. Two and a half miles from town is the most important archaeological zone in the Valley of Mexico, covering in all eight square miles. See the magnificent Pyramids of the Sun and the Moon, the Temple of Quetzalcoatl, and other temples and temple compounds of extraordinarily beautiful design and decoration. There is also a museum, and in the caves near by is a restaurant (see page 219).

Tenayuca Pyramid and Tepotzotlán. Distance (one way): twenty-five miles. Road: all paved. Time: one-half to one day. Take lunch if full day is planned (see Guadalupe above).

The figures on the margin represent miles from Mexico City.

0 Leave Mexico City by the Pan American Highway to the north (Avenidas Insurgentes and Ramón Guzmán).

3 Leave the Pan American Highway, taking the road to the left (Calzada Vallejo) past the Monument to the Founding of the City.

3.5 Crossroad. To the right is Villa Madero, to the left Atzcapotzalco. Continue straight ahead.

8 Tenayuca Pyramid. Fascinating Aztec pyramid with the serpent

as the predominant decorative motif. The road to the right goes two miles to another, smaller pyramid called Santa Cecilia.

10 Tlalnepantla. Fine sixteenth-century church. The road to the south goes back to Mexico City via Atzcapotzalco and Tacuba. Take the road to the north.

16 Lecheria.

20 Cuautitlán.

25 Take the branch road to the left, which goes one-half mile to Tepotzotlán. The Jesuit church of Tepotzotlán is one of the most perfect examples of Churrigueresque architecture in Mexico and is preserved as a national monument. Begun in 1584, it was not finished until almost two centuries later.

San Ángel and Desierto de los Leones. Distance (one way): twenty-three miles. Road: all paved. Time: one-half to one day (take lunch for full day).

The figures on the margin below represent miles from Mexico City.

0 Take Avenida Insurgentes south out of Mexico City.

8 Villa Álvaro Obregón (formerly named San Ángel and still commonly so called). An attractive residential suburb. See the seventeenth-century church and monastery of the Virgin of El Carmen. Diego Rivera's home is in San Ángel. The road to the east goes along the Pedregal, a great lava field in which prehistoric human remains and artifacts have been found, to the suburb of Coyoacán. The road to the south goes along the west side of the Pedregal to Santa Teresa. Take the road to the west.

16 San Bartolo.

23 Desierto de los Leones (Desert of the Lions), a lovely wooded park containing a seventeeth-century Carmelite monastery, now in romantic ruin, preserved as a national monument. A favorite picnic spot.

Churubusco and Xochimilco. Distance (one way): fourteen miles. Road: all paved. Time: one-half day.

The figures on the margin below represent miles from Mexico City.

0 Leave Mexico City by the Cuernavaca Highway (Avenida Insurgentes and Calzada de Tlálpam).

5.5 The road to the left goes two miles to the quiet town of Ixtapalapa at the foot of the Cerro de la Estrella. A good gravel road goes up the hill. Fine view from the top.

6 Churubusco. The old seventeenth-century Franciscan monastery has been made into a colonial museum. A short distance to the south is the Mexico City Country Club and golf course. The road to the west goes to Coyoacán, suburb of homes and gardens. In Coyoacán see the house that is said to have belonged to Cortés, on the main plaza; the botanical gardens; the museum in a mansion said to have been built by Pedro de Alvarado, companion of Cortés; the parish church and the adjoining Dominican monastery, both built in the sixteenth century.

9 Textitlán.

10 Huipulco. The road to the right goes to Tlálpam, a suburban town, formerly capital of the state of Mexico, on the slope of an extinct volcano; and on to the ancient Pyramid of Cuicuilco on the edge of the Pedregal lava field.

12 La Noria.

14 Xochimilco. The Floating Gardens of Xochimilco were made by the Aztecs. Originally they were floating rafts of woven twigs and reeds covered with soil and planted with flowers, fruits, and vegetables. Through the network of canals around the now stationary islands barges gaily decorated with flowers are poled, carrying holiday groups, while restaurant boats, flower boats, boats of musicians, and many others circulate among them. The road continues east past Xochimilco, then swings north to Chalco, where it meets the highway to Cuautla. Halfway to Chalco a paved road branches to the south. It goes three miles to Milpa Alta, and dry-weather roads go on from there to San Pedro Actopan and San Pablo Ostotepec, all drowsy, pleasant towns with large colonial churches.

Chapingo and Texcoco. Distance (one way): twenty-five miles. Road: all paved. Time: one-half to one day (lunch may be had in Texcoco).

The figures on the margin below represent miles from Mexico City.

0 Leave Mexico City by Calle Moneda and the Puebla Highway.

12 Los Reyes. Sixteenth-century church. Just beyond Los Reyes take the branch road to the left.

22 A dry-weather road to the right leads one mile to Coatlinchan, from which point a foot trail goes three miles to the Idol of Tlaloc, a huge carved monolith believed to represent the god of waters, Tlaloc.

23 Chapingo. The National Agricultural College is located here. See the murals by Diego Rivera in the chapel and main building. A dry-weather road leads southeast three miles to Huexotla, an archaeological site as yet only partially excavated and studied.

25 Texcoco. This was the capital of an Indian kingdom in pre-Spanish days. Here lived the poet-monarch Netzahualcoyotl, on a terraced hill that affords a fine view. From here Cortés launched the boats on Lake Texcoco in which he attacked the city of Tenochtitlán (Mexico City). The town has a sixteenth-century Franciscan church and several colonial mansions.

A dry-weather road goes east from Texcoco to Molino de Flores and San Nicolás Tlaminca, near which are the ruins of Texcotzingo. Another road runs northwest to Tepexpan, on the road to San Juan Teotihuacán.

Other trips commonly made in one day from Mexico City are:

To Puebla and Tlaxcala (see below).

To Cuernavaca, Cuautla, and Amecameca (see page 282).

To Toluca (see page 63).

To Pachuca (see page 46).

MEXICO CITY TO OAXACA

The section of the Pan American Highway between Mexico City and the Guatemalan border is named Carretera Cristóbal Colón (Christopher Columbus Highway). Traffic is at present practicable only as far as Oaxaca; therefore only that part is here treated in detail. For the unfinished Oaxaca-Guatemala section, see page 40.

The main route of the Pan American Highway was originally planned to pass through Cuautla, but since the section between Cuautla and Matamoros is still unfinished, the present route is through Puebla.

Soon after leaving Mexico City the road begins climbing out of the valley, approaching the lofty Sierra Nevada (snow-covered) mountains to the east. It winds upward through eucalyptus and later through cool pine forests, emerging at points to offer gorgeous views of the Valley of Mexico, until it reaches the chilly summit —the continental divide, at this point 10,486 feet above sea level. Then begins the winding descent, with views of the snow-capped volcanoes Popocatépetl and Ixtaccíhuatl.

Texmelucan is well past the mountain range, and from this point on the highway loses altitude so gradually as to be hardly noticeable. Passing through Cholula, the suburb (of Puebla) city of churches, it reaches colonial Puebla, fourth city of Mexico. The trip from Mexico City to Puebla should take about two or three hours. For a description of the points of interest in Cholula and Puebla, see page 53. If you have time, spend a few days in Puebla.

Beyond Puebla there are only small villages and towns, some of them picturesque, but not recommended for overnight stops. The road from Puebla to Oaxaca winds through an extraordinary variety of wild plants and trees. Especially to be noted are the cactus and semiarid desert plants. Note also the desert palmetto and the Indians walking along the highway weaving palm hats as they go to market. Note the changes in color of the soil and rocky cliffs exposed along the highway, especially the bluish-green stone—used in many buildings in Oaxaca.

Itinerary. Distance (one way): 342 miles. Road: route suggested is all paved. Time: driving time one day, but one should plan to arrive in Puebla in time for lunch, spend the afternoon sight-seeing in Puebla and overnight there, then drive on to Oaxaca the next day. Counting one day in Oaxaca and environs (see page 192) and one day to return, this could be an easy four-day trip or a rushed three-day trip. Hotels in Puebla and Oaxaca.

The figures on the margin below represent miles from Mexico City.

  0 Calle Moneda leads east from the Zócalo to the Puebla Highway.

12 Los Reyes. Sixteenth-century church. The branch road to the left just beyond Los Reyes leads to Texcoco (see page 51). (Gas.)

16 Ayotla. Eighteenth-century church. (Gas.)

18 Santa Bárbara. The branch road to the right goes to Ameca-meca and Cuautla (see page 57). (Gas.)

20 Zoquiapan. Here begins the climb over the Sierra Nevada. (Gas.)

39 Puerto del Aire. Continental divide at 10,486 feet. Breath-taking views of the volcanoes at turns of the road.

40 Río Frío. In olden days this was a bandit hangout. Much of the charcoal for Mexico City comes from here. (Gas, restaurant.)

44 La Venta. Early nineteenth-century colonial bridge. (Gas.)

57 San Martín Texmelucan. Colonial Franciscan and Carmelite monasteries. Tuesday is market day. (Gas.)
A paved branch road to the left goes fifteen miles to historic Tlaxcala. Altitude, 7,386 feet. Population, 3,261. Capital of the state of Tlaxcala. In its Franciscan church, founded in 1521, were baptized four Tlaxcalan chiefs, allies of Cortés. Besides this church you will want to see the church of Ocotlán and the near-by ruins of Tizatlán with their remarkable ancient frescoes. Today Tlaxcala is noted for serapes and woolen cloth woven by the Tlaxcalan Indians. (Gas, repairs, telephone, telegraph, restaurant, hotel.)

66 Huejotzingo. Interesting sixteenth-century Franciscan church and monastery of fortress-like construction; fine murals and frescoes. It is now kept as a museum. A good place to buy serapes, both local and brought in from other sections. (Gas.)

76 Cholula. Once the center of the Toltec kingdom. The famous Church of Los Remedios is built on the top of an ancient pyramid. At the foot of the pyramid is the Royal Chapel, with sixty-three domes. The countryside around is dotted with ornate churches, of which two are especially remarkable—San Francisco Acatepec and Santa María Tonanzintla. (Gas.)

85 Puebla. Altitude, 7,091 feet. Population, 150,000. Fourth largest city of Mexico and capital of the state of Puebla. The distinctive *poblana* architecture of the colonial period gives a most unusual and charming aspect to the city. The cathedral and several other churches, the hidden convent of Santa Mónica, and some of the old mansions should not be missed. Visit some of the factories where the famous Talavera tiles and pottery are made. (Gas, repairs, telephone, telegraph, restaurant, hotel, AMA office.)

104 Atlixco. A textile center in a fertile valley. (Gas.)

125 Matamoros. Here the route via Cuautla joins the Puebla route. The road to the right is the one to Cuautla. It is passable only in the dry season between Matamoros and Jonacatepec (twenty-five miles); from Jonacatepec to Cuautla (fifteen miles) it has all-weather surface. (Gas.)

155 Tehuitzingo. (Gas.)

179 Acatlán. Eighteenth-century church. (Gas.)

193 Petlalcingo. Just south of here the road enters the state of Oaxaca. (Gas.)

219 Huajuapan. Sixteenth-century church. (Gas, restaurant, hotel.)

245 Tamazulapan. Sixteenth-century church with fine paintings and sculpture. (Gas.)

266 Yanhuitlan. Sixteenth-century Dominican monastery. (Gas.)

276 Nochistlán. (Gas.)

320 Huitzo. (Gas.)

342 Oaxaca. Altitude, 5,128 feet. Population, 33,867. Capital of the state of Oaxaca. Set in the warm semitropical Oaxaca Valley. The city is distinctively colonial. The native handicrafts are renowned, especially serapes, linens, and pottery. Market day is Saturday. In the surrounding country live the Zapotec and Mixtec Indians, who retain many colorful traditions. The pre-Columbian ruins of Monte Albán and Mitla are among the most interesting and beautiful in all of Mexico. (Gas, repairs, telephone, telegraph, restaurant, hotel, AMA office.)

A 180-mile road is being built to connect Oaxaca with the Pacific port of Puerto Ángel. It is passable at present as far as Ejutla, thirty-five miles from Oaxaca.

MEXICO CITY TO ACAPULCO

This is one of the most popular tours in Mexico, since it includes the pleasant resort town of Cuernavaca and picturesque old Taxco.

Leaving Mexico City, the road crosses ten miles of level land before starting the climb to El Guarda Pass, almost ten thousand feet high and generally chilly. It continues south through the mountain range to Tres Cumbres. Stop here for a good view of the Valley of Mexico. From this point the road descends five thousand feet into the warm semitropical valley of Morelos and Cuernavaca.

Between Cuernavaca and Taxco the road dips into a warm and

arid valley, then climbs into the mountains again to reach Taxco, 5,609 feet high.

Beyond Taxco the land becomes hot and dry again. From Iguala to Mexcala the highway crosses a succession of valleys and low ranges, and just beyond Mexcala the road enters the scenic Cañada del Zopilote (Buzzard Canyon), through which it rises to 4,500 feet at Chilpancingo. From this point it descends gradually to the coast.

Itinerary. Distance (one way): 282 miles. Road: all paved. Time: actual driving time, one day, but Cuernavaca and Taxco are two "musts" that no visitor to Mexico should forego, and an extra day for each place should be scheduled—even if limited vacation time necessitates omitting Acapulco. Hotels in Cuernavaca, Taxco, and Acapulco.

The figures on the margin below represent miles from Mexico City.

0 Leave Mexico City via Avenida Insurgentes and the Calzada de Tlálpam; or (from the Zócalo) south on Cinco de Febrero, left on Calzada de Chimalpopoca, and right on San Antonio.

6 Churubusco (see page 50).

10 Huipulco. Road to the left goes to Xochimilco. Take the right-hand fork.

11 Tlálpam (see page 50). South of Tlálpam begins the sixteen-mile climb into the mountains. Fine views of the volcanoes Popocatépetl and Ixtaccíhuatl and of the Valley of Mexico at every turn. (Gas.)

23 El Guarda. Highest point on the road, 9,869 feet.

32 Tres Cumbres. From this point, about fifteen miles north of Cuernavaca, the road drops five thousand feet into the semi-tropical Valley of Morelos. The paved road to the right leads to the Lakes of Zempoala, twelve miles away. (Gas, restaurant.)

44 Buenavista. Road to the left leads to the interesting Indian village of Tepoztlán (eleven miles). See the sixteenth-century monastery and the Pyramid of Tepozteco.

46 Cuernavaca. Altitude, 5,043 feet. Population, 14,500. Capital of the state of Morelos and one of Mexico's most popular resorts, as it has been since the days of the Aztecs. See the Palace of Cortés, with some of Diego Rivera's best-known murals; the cathedral, founded by Cortés in 1529; the Borda Gardens; the

Pyramid of Teopanzolco; San Antón Falls; Maximilian's hunting lodge at Acapacingo. (Gas, repairs, telephone, telegraph, restaurant, hotel, AMA office.)

A road to the east goes twenty-eight miles to Cuautla via Yautepec.

62 Alpuyeca. (Gas.)

The road to the right leads to the Pyramid of Xochicalco and continues on several miles to the Caverns of Cacahuamilpa.

The road to the left goes to the co-operative sugar refinery at Zacatepec. The same road goes on to Lake Tequesquitengo and the Tehuixtla sulphur baths.

71 Puente de Ixtla. An old Indian village. (Gas, restaurant.)

101 Taxco. Altitude, 5,609 feet. Population, 4,963. Probably the most picturesque town in Mexico. An old silver-mining town on a steep mountainside, it has been declared a national monument in order to preserve its distinctive charm. It is especially interesting on market day, Sunday. The best silver work in Mexico is done in Taxco and sold in its many small shops. (Gas, repairs, telephone, telegraph, restaurant, hotel.)

123 Iguala (just off the highway to the west). Here the highway has descended into the real *tierra caliente* (hot country), at an altitude of 2,400 feet. Mexico's Plan of Independence was proclaimed in Iguala in 1821. See the large plaza shaded by tamarind trees, and the parish church. A refreshing swim can be had in an unusual pool just off the road. Inquire at the gas station. (Gas, repairs, telephone, telegraph, restaurant, hotel.)

156 Mexcala. Here you cross the Río Balsas, one of Mexico's largest rivers, and enter the twenty-two-mile-long Zopilote Canyon.

190 Chilpancingo. Capital of the state of Guerrero. Quiet and attractive mountain town. (Gas, repairs, telephone, telegraph, restaurant, hotel.)

198 Petaquillas. The road to the left leads to the Grottos of Juxlahuaca.

223 Buenavista. (Gas.)

231 Tierra Colorada. From here the road descends into the tropical lowlands of the Pacific coast.

244 Puente del Río Papagayo. Bridge over the Papagayo River. Presently the road crosses the old stone bridge over the Sabanao River and you get your first view of the Pacific.

282 Acapulco. Altitude, sea level. Population, 9,993. In colonial days this was Mexico's most important Pacific port, situated on one of the finest natural harbors in the world. Today it is a tropical vacation spot, with sumptuous resort hotels, several beautiful beaches, facilities for fishing, boating, golf, and other sports. (Gas, repairs, telephone, telegraph, restaurant, hotel, AMA office.)

MEXICO CITY TO CUAUTLA

This tour uses a road that passes at the very foot of the volcanoes Popocatépetl and Ixtaccíhuatl. The trip can be combined with one to Cuernavaca in a scenic circle drive, with a stopover in Cuautla or Cuernavaca, or both.

Itinerary. Distance: fifty-six miles to Cuautla; forty-eight miles to Cuernavaca; and twenty-eight miles from Cuernavaca to Cuautla. Road: paved from Mexico City to Cuernavaca and from Mexico City to Cuautla, but gravel all-weather between Cuernavaca and Cuautla. Time: one day driving time for the circle tour, but one should plan to remain overnight in Cuautla or Cuernavaca. The best two-day plan is to stop in Amecameca for a visit to the Santuario de Sacramonte, then lunch in Cuautla, thence to Cuernavaca for overnight; sight-seeing in Cuernavaca the next morning and lunch in Cuernavaca, then return to Mexico City in the afternoon. Take time on the Cuautla-Cuernavaca road to visit the old monastery near Yautepec.

Figures on the margin below represent miles from Mexico City.

0 Leave Mexico City by the Puebla Highway (east on Moneda from the Zócalo).

18 Santa Bárbara. The Cuautla and Puebla roads separate here. Take the right-hand fork.

23 Chalco. Ancient Aztec town. Interesting old Franciscan church. The road to the south goes to Xochimilco. Take the left-hand fork to the east.

33 Tlalmanalco. The Franciscan monastery here merits a visit. The road branching to the left leads three miles to the San Rafael paper mills. Attractive picnic spots are to be found in the surrounding woods.

37 Amecameca. On the site of an Aztec town, at the foot of the two volcanoes Popocatépetl and Ixtaccíhuatl. On a hill on the

outskirts of town stands the shrine called Santuario de Sacramonte, from which there is a fine view of the volcanoes. Sunday is market day. Excursions to the top of the volcanoes begin at Amecameca, where horses and guides are available. (Gas, repairs, telephone, telegraph, restaurant, hotel.)

39 Branch road to Ixta-Popo Park. This road goes sixteen miles up the forested slope of Popocatépetl. The area between the two volcanoes has been designated as Ixta-Popo National Park. (Restaurant, hotel in the park.)

45 Ozumba (just off the highway to the east). Nearest town to the volcano Popocatépetl. Paintings of unusual interest are to be seen at the old Franciscan church. The picturesque gardens of Chimalhuacan and the Falls of Chimal are near by.

50 Nepantla. The Mexican poetess Sor Juana Inés de la Cruz was born here in 1651.

63 Cuautlixco. The all-weather road to Cuernavaca runs west from here, passing through Yautepec. It is twenty-seven miles to Cuernavaca through beautiful mountain country.

65 Cuautla. Altitude, 4,254 feet. Population, 6,431. A popular resort in a warm semitropical valley. Two and one half miles south of town are the outdoor hot sulphur baths of Agua Hedionda. (Gas, repairs, telephone, telegraph, restaurant, hotel.) The road to the east goes to Matamoros on the Puebla–Oaxaca highway (see page 52). It is all-weather surface as far as Jonacatepec; from there to Matamoros it is in construction, passable only in the dry season.

MEXICO CITY TO VERACRUZ

Although little publicized, this is one of the most outstanding trips in Mexico. There are two routes, and the trip from Mexico City to Veracruz can be made in one day of easy driving, but it should be broken with overnight stops in Puebla or one of the other recommended points en route.

The two routes begin at Mexico City and continue together to twenty-five miles beyond Puebla, where they fork, one going via Jalapa and the other via Orizaba. Both are paved all the way with the exception of a forty-eight-mile stretch of gravel on the Orizaba route.

The first portion of the road goes over the mountains to Puebla (see page 53) and thence through the semiarid cactus-covered country to the point where the two routes separate.

Beyond the fork the Jalapa route continues through this dry land and over the sandy plain on which stand the towns of Limón and Perote. Here are good views of Cofre de Perote volcano. Then begins the descent into the tropical Valley of Jalapa. Quickly one feels the change in temperature and the landscape changes suddenly from arid plain to the lush gardens of Jalapa. Beyond Jalapa the road drops 4,500 feet more through tropical jungles, coffee plantations, and orange groves to the coastal lowland.

The Orizaba route, after leaving the fork, continues on the high tableland to the Garci-Crespo mineral springs, near Tehuacán. Here it turns east to drop three thousand feet through subtropical forests, coffee plantations, and orchards into the Orizaba region, with striking views of snow-covered Orizaba volcano throughout the descent. From Orizaba the road drops another thousand feet through a beautiful tropical canyon, past flower-embowered Fortín, to Córdoba. No one should pass up the opportunity to spend a day or several days at Fortín. Beyond Córdoba the road drops gradually three thousand feet more to sea level, passing through a number of small tropical villages before arriving in Veracruz.

Itinerary. Length: via Jalapa, 282 miles; via Orizaba, 290 miles. Road: via Jalapa, all paved; via Orizaba, all paved except forty-eight miles of all-weather gravel between San Juan de la Punta and Paso del Toro. Hotels in Puebla, Jalapa, Orizaba, Fortín, Garci-Crespo, and Córdoba. Service: gasoline and restaurants are noted below.

The figures on the margin below represent miles from Mexico City.

0 The Mexico City to Puebla itinerary is on page 52.

85 Puebla.

94 Amozoc. Quaint Indian village famous for its handicrafts, particularly inlaid silver spurs and miniature toys. Sixteenth-century Franciscan monastery. (Gas.)

105 Tepeaca. Imposing sixteenth-century Franciscan monastery in the main plaza; house in which the viceroys used to stay when traveling between Veracruz and Mexico. Notable onyx quarries. (Gas.)

109 Here the road forks.

The Jalapa Route

114 Acatzingo. Old parish church with valuable paintings; ruined Franciscan monastery. (Gas.)

144 Zacatepec. The road to the left goes to Teziutlán and Nautla (see page 46). (Gas.)

157 Alchichica. Near the town is the extinct volcano in the crater of which lies Alchichica Lake. Through this section one has fine views of snow-capped Orizaba (Aztec name, Citlaltepetl) off to the south. Towering to 18,320 feet above sea level, it is the third highest peak in North America.

172 Perote. Interesting old town at the foot of the extinct volcano Cofre de Perote. The sandy plain is now left behind and the road runs through pine woods. (Gas, repairs, telephone, telegraph, restaurant, hotel.)
The gravel road to the left goes (twenty-four miles) to Teziutlán.

185 Las Vigas. Here begins the descent into the Valley of Jalapa. (Gas.)

201 Banderilla. A large botanical garden, the Jardín Lecuona, famous especially for orchids, is located here.

205 Jalapa. Altitude, 4,541 feet. Population, 46,825. Capital of the state of Veracruz. Though an ancient town, it has only recently become a popular resort. It has a mild climate, a profusion of flowers and fruits, and picturesque white colonial buildings with red-tiled roofs overhanging narrow, steep cobblestone streets. (Gas, repairs, telephone, telegraph, restaurant, hotel, AMA office.) A road leads south twelve miles to the tropical town of Coatepec, and on to Teocelo.

240 Rinconada. The descent from Jalapa has been gradual but continuous. This place is only 500 feet above sea level. (Gas, restaurant.)

245 Tamarindo.

247 Puente Nacional. Interesting old colonial bridge. A road, not always passable, runs north to the pre-Spanish ruins of Cempoala, and on to the Gulf coast beach of Chachalacas.

273 Tejería. Airport. (Gas.)

282 Veracruz. Altitude, 23 feet. Population, 71,720. Historic city

founded by Cortés in 1519. Main port of entry into Mexico by sea. Old buildings on narrow streets contrast with modern, open construction. Visit the sixteenth-century Fortress of San Juan de Ulúa, on an island in the bay, and also the Island of Sacrifices. Swimming and sun-bathing on smooth safe beaches, fishing, and boating are popular sports. Mocambo and Boca del Río, along the coast just south of the city, are the two most popular beaches. (Gas, repairs, telephone, telegraph, restaurant, hotel, AMA office.)

THE ORIZABA ROUTE

118 Tecamachalco. Picturesque village. Sixteenth-century Franciscan church. (Gas.)

157 Garci-Crespo. One of Mexico's foremost mineral-springs resorts, with excellently appointed hotel, mineral baths, swimming pool, and golf course. (Gas, telephone, telegraph, restaurant, hotel.)

Tehuacán. Altitude, 5,497 feet. Population, 16,278. This town is only a mile and a half farther south. Good bargains in Indian handicrafts can be had here. (Gas, repairs, telephone, telegraph, restaurant, hotel, AMA office.)

169 After a steady climb the road reaches an altitude of 7,545 feet. At this point it crosses into the state of Veracruz and starts down through the spectacular forest-covered Cumbres de Acultzingo (peaks of Acultzingo), which divide the plateau from the hot country below. The road is often foggy in the early morning and late afternoon.

180 Acultzingo. Beautiful panoramas of the valley below and the peak of Orizaba looming above it.

191 Ciudad Mendoza. Noted chiefly as a textile center. (Gas, restaurant.)

192 Nogales. Another textile center.

193 Río Blanco. Still another important textile center. (Gas, repairs, telephone, telegraph, restaurant, hotel.)

197 Orizaba. Altitude, 4,211 feet. Population, 47,910. Set in the lush vegetation of the tropical Maltrata Valley, below the snowy peak of Orizaba. Enjoys a delightful climate and is a popular resort. It has some of the largest cotton mills in Mexico and the

Moctezuma Brewery. Don't miss seeing the Tuxpango power plant. Lovely surroundings for excursions. (Gas, repairs, telephone, telegraph, restaurant, hotel, AMA office.)

208 Fortín. Famous for its tropical fruits and beautiful flowers. Gardenias, camellias, orchids, and azaleas grow here in profusion. In the surroundings are sugar-cane fields, coffee plantations, and orange groves, shaded walks, running streams, and brilliant tropical birds. Excellent resort hotel. (Gas, telephone, restaurant, hotel.)

212 Córdoba. Altitude, 2,697 feet. Population, 17,865. The Treaty of Córdoba, establishing Mexican independence, was signed here in 1821. (Gas, repairs, telephone, telegraph, restaurant, hotel.)

230 San Juan de la Punta. Here the paved road ends.

278 Paso del Toro. Ferry across the river. The delay is seldom more than fifteen minutes or so. From here into Veracruz the road is paved. (Gas, telephone, restaurant.)
A road runs southeast thirty-two miles to Alvarado, on the Gulf coast.

283 Boca del Río. One of the favorite beaches of Veracruz. Restaurants here specialize in sea food cooked in Veracruz style. Ferry across the river. (Gas, telephone, restaurant.)

287 Mocambo. Another popular beach, with one of Veracruz' most lavish resort hotels. (Gas, repairs, telephone, restaurant, hotel.)

290 Veracruz. (See page 60 for additional information.)

MEXICO CITY TO GUADALAJARA

The route to Guadalajara offers some exceptional scenery and much of the local color for which Mexico is famous. The highway goes over one high, pine-crested range to the Toluca Valley and then another one to reach the Zitácuaro Valley. The popular spa of San José Purua is not far from the town of Zitácuaro. Near the summit of the next range, at an altitude of 9,179 feet, is the lookout known as Mirador de las Mil Cumbres (Thousand Peaks Lookout), from which one can see a magnificent panorama of range after range of mountains.

The descent to Morelia is a succession of beautiful views and hairpin turns. Quiet colonial Morelia is a good overnight stop and a pleasant place in which to spend any number of days. A short distance farther on, and a few miles off the main highway, is Pátzcuaro, spread out on a slope overlooking Lake Pátzcuaro. Here is the center of the colorful Tarascan Indian country. Another branch road a few miles beyond leads to Uruapan and the famous Parícutin volcano.

Just before the approach to Guadalajara the highway skirts Lake Chapala, the largest and one of the most beautiful lakes in Mexico.

Itinerary. Distance (one way): 428 miles. Road: all paved. Time: two days, one night. The trip could be made in one day of actual driving, but if you have not been over the road before plan to stop overnight in Morelia or Pátzcuaro. For minimum sightseeing plan to spend three days as follows: one hour at Toluca, and evening and night in Morelia; morning and early lunch in Pátzcuaro; afternoon at Parícutin and evening in Uruapan; third day continue to Guadalajara. This is a tight schedule. Hotels in San José Purua (off the main highway near Zitácuaro), Morelia, Pátzcuaro (off the main highway), Uruapan, and Guadalajara.

The figures on the margin below represent miles from Mexico City.

0 Leave Mexico City via the Paseo de la Reforma, Calzada Tacubaya, and Calzada Madereros.

15 La Venta. The road to the left leads to El Desierto de los Leones (see page 49). The mountain climb begins a short distance beyond La Venta.

20 Las Cruces. Summit of the pass, 10,381 feet high.

23 Hidalgo Memorial, commemorating a victory of the revolutionary leader Father Hidalgo over the Spanish army in 1810.

30 Lerma. The highway has now crossed the Cruces Range and entered the Toluca Valley. (Gas.)

40 Toluca. Altitude, 8,793 feet. Population, 43,429. Capital of the state of Mexico. Toluca's Friday market is one of the largest and most colorful in Mexico. Indians from all over the Toluca Valley crowd into town to sell baskets, hats, serapes, shawls, pottery, and other handicraft goods. (Gas, repairs, telephone, telegraph, restaurant, hotel, AMA office.)
A road to the right leads six miles north to the prehistoric ruins of Calixtlahuaca.

46 The road to the left goes through the town of Zinacantepec and then up to the summit of the Nevado de Toluca, 13,621 feet

high. The crater of this extinct volcano holds two lakes, named for the sun and the moon. Magnificent view from the summit; on clear days the Pacific coast can be discerned through binoculars.

72 San Agustín. Off the road to the right is Villa Victoria, at the foot of an old Aztec fortress. (Gas.)

102 Zitácuaro. Altitude, 6,398 feet. Population, 11,434. Historic old city noted for its wood carvings. (Gas, repairs, telephone, telegraph, restaurant, hotel, AMA office.)

115 The road to the left leads four miles to the hot springs of San José Purua, one of the country's most popular resorts. Attractive modern hotel, swimming pool, private baths.

120 Tuxpan. Seventeenth-century church. (Gas.)

132 Ciudad Hidalgo. Old Tarascan town. Sixteenth-century church. (Gas.)

152 Mil Cumbres. Altitude, 9,179 feet. In Atzimba National Park. Magnificent view over an infinitude of mountain peaks.

161 Highest point, 9,469 feet. Road to the left winds around to the summit of Cerro Garnica, another splendid lookout. From this point the road gradually loses altitude as it curves around the mountainsides, at last descending into the valley surrounding Morelia.

195 Morelia. Altitude, 6,234 feet. Population, 47,600. Capital of the state of Michoacán. One of the early centers of Spanish culture in Mexico, Morelia has figured prominently in Mexican history and is one of the most aristocratic of the old colonial towns. See the cathedral and several other colonial churches; the Government Palace; the museum; San Nicolás School, founded in 1540 in Pátzcuaro and moved to Morelia in 1580; the house where Morelos was born, now a museum; and the old aqueduct. Morelia is a good place to buy Tarascan handicraft goods, such as lacquer work, wood carving, weaving, etc. (Gas, repairs, telephone, telegraph, restaurant, hotel, AMA office.)
An all-weather road runs north from Morelia to Salamanca (see page 72).

221 Quiroga. Sixteenth-century town founded on the site of an important Tarascan center near Lake Pátzcuaro. Noted for its lacquer work. (Gas.) From Quiroga a branch road runs south fifteen miles along the shores of the lake to Pátzcuaro. It passes

first through Tzintzuntzan, formerly the capital of the Tarascan kingdom, now only a small village. See the sixteenth-century church and monastery.

Pátzcuaro. Altitude, 6,934 feet. Population, 9,557. One of Mexico's most distinctive and charming colonial towns. Built on higher ground back from the lake, it retains many of its sixteenth- and seventeenth-century churches and mansions, and is the scene of a market every Friday to which come Indians from all of the lake villages. Take a lake excursion to the fishing village built on the steep slope of the island of Janitzio, and to some of the lake-shore Tarascan villages. Note the graceful "butterfly" fishing nets used by the Indians. (Gas, repairs, telephone, telegraph, restaurant, hotel.)

250 Zacapu. An old Indian settlement, now a typical provincial town. Near by are many archaeological sites. (Gas.)

267 Carapán. (Gas.)

From Carapán a branch road runs south forty-five miles to Uruapan.

Uruapan. Altitude, 5,285 feet. Population, 20,583. Known formerly as a lush garden spot, Uruapan now is often blackened by the ashes of Parícutin volcano only a few miles away. Parícutin sprang up in a cornfield on February 20, 1943. Within a week it was five hundred feet high, within three months a thousand feet, and now it is a huge cone of over fifteen hundred feet, belching smoke and ashes. The road to the volcano branches off from the highway at Capacuaro, about thirty miles south of Carapán, and runs twenty-five miles or so to the town of San Juan Parangaricutiro. From here you can go by horse across the lava fields to the volcano. You would do well to hire a car in Uruapan to make this trip so as not to take your car into the volcanic ash. Overalls and hats can be rented at the hotels in Uruapan. (Gas, repairs, telephone, telegraph, restaurant, hotel.)

290 Zamora. Altitude, 5,140 feet. Population, 15,447. Attractive town in a fertile valley. Good hotel. (Gas, repairs, telephone, telegraph, restaurant, hotel, AMA office.)

293 Jacona. The mountains have been left behind for a while, and the road is level and straight. Two sixteenth-century churches. (Gas, telegraph, restaurant.)

307 A road to the right leads two miles to Chavinda, a picturesque Indian town.

320 Guaracha. Formerly a hacienda. The typical old hacienda house is now an industrial school for boys. (Gas.)

325 Jiquilpan. An interesting village with an active market. (Gas, telegraph, restaurant.) A road runs from Jiquilpan southwest sixty miles to Tamazula. This road will eventually be pushed through to Colima and the Pacific coast towns of Tecomán and Manzanillo.

332 Sahuayo. Agricultural town. Good sixteenth-century church. (Gas.)

342 Columatlán. A quaint fishing village on Lake Chapala. From here on the road borders the lake shore, passing through several more fishing villages. (Gas.)
Lake Chapala is the largest lake in Mexico, and a favorite resort, famous for mild climate, lovely countryside, interesting Indian fishing villages, and facilities for swimming and fishing. Most of the popular resort hotels are in the neighborhood of the town of Chapala, on the other side of the lake.

409 The road to the left is the highway to Barra de Navidad, a new beach resort on the Pacific, and to Manzanillo. The road is passable for only one hundred miles, as far as Autlán; the rest is under construction.

428 Guadalajara. Altitude, 5,199 feet. Population, 255,000. Capital of the state of Jalisco and second largest city of Mexico. Distinguished colonial city of flower-filled parks and plazas, gems of colonial architecture, and old-style mansions with open patios. Famous for its gay music and the *jarabe tapatio*, the Mexican "hat dance." See the cathedral and several other colonial churches, the Government Palace, the state museum, the Hospicio with its twenty-six patios and its Orozco frescoes in the chapel, and the Degollado Theater. On the outskirts of town are the potters' villages of San Pedro Tlaquepaque and Tonalá, and Zapopan with its fine Franciscan church, and the two-thousand-foot-deep river gorge known as Barranca de Oblatos. Farther afield are the Juanacatlán Falls and Chapala, most popular of the lake resorts. (Gas, repairs, telephone, telegraph, restaurant, hotel, AMA office.)

GUADALAJARA TO TEPIC

The west-coast highway running north from Guadalajara to Nogales, Arizona, is open to traffic for a few miles at either end but impassable for long stretches in between. It is open north of Guadalajara as far as Tepic, but only about one third of this distance is paved; the rest is all-weather gravel. The road passes through some spectacular mountain scenery and a variety of climates.

Between Tepic and Guaymas, approximately 750 miles, the route is little more than a trail, impassable even in the dry season. The road is paved from Guaymas to Nogales (see itinerary, page 80).

Itinerary. Distance (one way): 145 miles. Road: paved to Tequila (42 miles); all-weather gravel from Tequila to Tepic (103 miles). Time: one day. Hotels in Tequila and Tepic.

The figures on the margin below represent miles from Guadalajara.

0 From the center of Guadalajara drive west on Avenida Juárez and follow Tepic and Tuxpan signs (turning right).

35 Amatitlán. (Gas, telephone, telegraph, restaurant, hotel.)

42 Tequila. Picturesque town in a little valley. The paved road ends here. The road has been across level country to this point. Here begins the rough barranca country of jagged cliffs and deep gorges lush with tropical vegetation. (Gas, repairs, telephone, telegraph, restaurant, hotel.)

55 Magdalena. (Gas, telephone, telegraph, restaurant, hotel.)

82 Plan de Barrancas.

95 Ixtlán del Río. The most forbidding part of the barrancas is now past. (Gas, repairs, telephone, telegraph, restaurant, hotel.)

102 Ahuacatlán. (Gas, telephone, telegraph, restaurant, hotel.)

125 Santa María del Oro. (Gas.)

145 Tepic. Altitude, 3,000 feet. Population, 17,547. Capital of the state of Nayarit. A quiet colonial town, one of Mexico's most charming for old-time architecture and way of life. The city lies in a fertile rolling district of ranches and maguey plantations, and the climate, at 3,000 feet elevation, is mild. For the Sunday market the Cora and Huichol Indians come from the mountains, wearing attractive traditional costumes. (Gas, repairs, telephone, telegraph, restaurant, hotel.)

In the dry season it is possible to continue on from Tepic thirty-five miles to Santiago Ixcuintla, but the trip is not recommended. There is also a dry-weather jungle road to the port and beach of San Blas.

GUADALAJARA TO ANTIGUO MORELOS

This road, running from Guadalajara to a point some distance north of Mexico City on the Pan American Highway (see itinerary from Laredo to Mexico City, page 41), makes it possible to drive back to the United States from Guadalajara without returning through Mexico City. The route crosses the central plateau of Mexico, staying at altitudes of from 5,000 to 7,000 feet, until within about fifty miles of Antiguo Morelos, when it descends abruptly to 500 feet. The cactus and maguey-covered land between Guadalajara and San Luís Potosí is the region of the colorful *charro* (Mexican cowboy). The road is part of a transcontinental highway that will eventually extend from Barra de Navidad on the Pacific to Tampico on the Gulf of Mexico. The section between Barra de Navidad and Guadalajara is not finished. The road is open from Guadalajara as far as Autlán (125 miles), but from there to Barra de Navidad (85 miles) it is still in construction. The section from El Mante (on the Pan American Highway) to Tampico is open to traffic (see itinerary, page 70).

Itinerary. Distance (one way): 415 miles. Road: all paved. Time: two days, one night; actual driving time, one day. Hotels in San Luís Potosí. Service: gasoline and restaurants as noted below, and at Aguascalientes (off the highway to the north of Lagos de Moreno or Ojuelos de Jalisco).

The figures on the margin below represent miles from Guadalajara.

0 From downtown Guadalajara go east on Avenida Heroes (Tlaquepaque road).

5 San Pedro Tlaquepaque. Most of the famous pottery of Guadalajara is made in the pottery factories of Tlaquepaque and in near-by Tonalá.

17 Puente Grande. A fine colonial bridge. Guadalajara's power plant is located here. (Gas.)

23 Zapotlanejo. (Gas, repairs, telephone, telegraph, restaurant, hotel.)

48 Tepatitlán. A town in the Jalisco highlands. Stock raising and cultivation of maguey are the principal activities. (Gas, repairs, telephone, telegraph, restaurant, hotel.)

66 Valle de Guadalupe. (Gas, restaurant, hotel.)

85 Jalostotitlán. Noted for its cleanliness and well-kept cobblestone streets. (Gas, telephone, telegraph, restaurant, hotel.)

95 San Juan de los Lagos. Quiet colonial town with narrow streets. Note the colonial bridge as you enter town. In the principal church is the image of the Virgin of San Juan de los Lagos, whose four festivals every year—in January-February, May, August, and December—are attended by thousands of pilgrims. San Juan is also famous for its November 20–December 20 fair, which has been held every year since the seventeenth century. (Gas, repairs, telephone, telegraph, restaurant, hotel.)

120 Lagos de Moreno. This is where the Mexico City–Durango highway crosses (see page 71). To the south is León, to the north Aguascalientes. If you wish to visit Aguascalientes, you might turn north on this road, and return to the main highway by the paved road from Aguascalientes to Ojuelos de Jalisco farther on. (Gas, repairs, telephone, telegraph, restaurant, hotel.)

167 Ojuelos de Jalisco. The road to the left goes forty-six miles to Aguascalientes. (Gas, telephone, telegraph, restaurant, hotel.)

182 Villa de Arriaga. (Gas, telephone, telegraph, restaurant, hotel.)

220 San Luís Potosí. Altitude, 6,156 feet. Population, 77,161. Capital of the state of San Luís Potosí. It was an extraordinarily rich mining center in the colonial period, and its importance is still due principally to the mines in the district. Several colonial churches of interest, especially the cathedral and the Carmen Church. (Gas, repairs, telephone, telegraph, restaurant, hotel, AMA office.)

250 Villa Hidalgo. (Gas, restaurant.)

360 Ciudad del Maiz. Beyond this point begins the descent from the central plateau to the coastal lowlands. (Gas, telephone, telegraph, restaurant, hotel.)

396 A road to the left goes eight miles to El Salto, a waterfall.

415 Antiguo Morelos. On the Pan American Highway. (Gas, repairs, telephone, telegraph, restaurant, hotel.)

EL MANTE TO TAMPICO

This is part of the proposed Tampico–Barra de Navidad highway, which will cross the country from the Gulf of Mexico to the Pacific. This portion of the road runs through the warm tropical lowlands lying along the Gulf. See page 68 for an itinerary covering the portion from Guadalajara to Antiguo Morelos.

Itinerary. Distance (one way): ninety-six miles. Road: all paved. Time: two and a half hours. Hotels in El Mante and Tampico.

The figures on the margin below represent miles from El Mante.

0 Ciudad del Mante (the name is generally shortened to "El Mante"). Formerly Villa Juárez. On the Pan American Highway, just eighteen miles north of Antiguo Morelos. Take the Pan American Highway to the south. (Gas, repairs, telephone, telegraph, restaurant, hotel.)

1.5 Leave the Pan American Highway, taking the road to the left.

18 Magiscatzín. Ferry across the Guayalejo River. (Gas, telegraph.)

35 González. (Gas, telegraph, restaurant, hotel.)

45 Manuel. (Gas, telegraph, restaurant, hotel.)

83 Altamira. Colonial church and monastery. (Gas, telegraph, restaurant, hotel.)

96 Tampico. Altitude, 11 feet. Population, 82,895. Seven miles from the Gulf of Mexico on the Pánuco River, in a rich oil region. Although it is a very old city, its aspect is modern, because of the building that went on during the wildcat oil boom of the first two decades of this century. Besides being an oil center, it is a vacation resort, with excellent bathing, golf, hunting, and deep-sea fishing. (Gas, repairs, telephone, telegraph, restaurant, hotel, AMA office.)

Tampico is connected with the Pan American Highway by another road, from Valles, sixty miles south of El Mante. This road, ninety miles long, has all-weather surface.

MEXICO CITY TO DURANGO

This is an interesting trip for hardy travelers who don't mind a little dust. It is the Central Highway, which, when completed, will run from Mexico City to Ciudad Juárez, across the border from El Paso, Texas. At present it is passable from Mexico City to La Zarca, about 150 miles north of Durango, and from Chihuahua to Ciudad Juárez. The road between La Zarca and Chihuahua, some 250 miles, has not been constructed.

The route follows the Pan American Highway north from Mexico City to Ixmiquilpan, then turns west into one of the most picturesque and historic regions of Mexico—the fertile Bajío, an extensive depressed plain in the great central plateau of Mexico. The land is rolling, fertile, and intensively cultivated. The three colonial cities of Querétaro, San Miguel Allende, and Guanajuato in this region are among the most interesting in Mexico. Beyond León the Bajío is left behind, and the road continues across drier country. North of Aguascalientes it enters the dry mountain country around Zacatecas. From that point on it is a desert road running north through the dry and dusty land of northern Mexico.

The condition of this road as of January 1948 was as follows:

Mexico City–Ixmiquilpan	Paved
Ixmiquilpan–Lagos	Paved
Lagos–Zacatecas	All weather
Zacatecas–Fresnillo	Paved
Fresnillo–Saín Alto	All weather
Saín Alto–Nombre de Dios	Dry weather
Nombre de Dios–Durango	All weather

For an itinerary covering the highway between Chihuahua and Ciudad Juárez, see page 79.

Itinerary. Distance (one way): about 660 miles. Road: see table above. Time: two days, two nights; preferably three days, two nights. Hotels in Querétaro, Aguascalientes, San Miguel Allende (thirty-two miles off the main road), and Guanajuato (fifteen miles off the main road). Service: as indicated below.

The figures on the margin below represent miles from Mexico City.

0 Mexico City. Follow the Pan American Highway north.

101 Ixmiquilpan. On the Pan American Highway. (Gas, repairs, telephone, telegraph, restaurant, hotel.)

106 Kilometer Mark 167. Here the road to Querétaro leaves the Pan American Highway.

135 Huichapan. (Gas, telephone, telegraph, restaurant.)

159 Cazadero. A road runs south from here to Toluca. The first few miles are no more than a trail; the rest is all-weather road.

165 San Juan del Río. Noted for basketwork. The Trinidad opal mines are in the vicinity. (Gas, telephone, telegraph, restaurant.)

196 Querétaro. Altitude, 5,948 feet. Population, 33,563. Capital of the state of Querétaro. A colonial town of rare charm. See the many colonial churches, in a variety of architectural styles. Emperor Maximilian was imprisoned in the Church of La Cruz. See also the federal monastery; the house of the Corregidora, the Spanish official's wife who was a ringleader in the early days of plotting for independence from Spain; and the aqueduct. The "Hill of the Bells," where Maximilian was shot, on the edge of town, is now surmounted by a chapel built by the Hapsburgs. (Gas, repairs, telephone, telegraph, restaurant, hotel.)

A road goes from Querétaro to San Miguel Allende (see page 75).

216 Apaseo. (Gas, telephone, telegraph, restaurant.)

231 Celaya. Altitude, 5,850 feet. Population, 22,766. An old city on the level Bajío plain. Notable especially for the works of the architect and decorator Francisco Eduardo Tresguerras, a native of Celaya, who lived from 1765 to 1833. Of his works see the Carmen Church, the chapel in which he is buried in San Francisco Church, the Independence Monument, and the bridge over the Laja River. *Cajetas de Celaya* are boxed sweets made of milk and sugar, famous all over Mexico. (Gas, repairs, telephone, telegraph, restaurant, hotel.)

A road goes from Celaya to San Miguel Allende (see page 74).

256 Salamanca. (Gas, repairs, telephone, telegraph, restaurant, hotel.)

An all-weather road runs south seventy-five miles to Morelia, on the Mexico City–Guadalajara highway. It is an interesting drive passing the small lake of Yuriria, and crossing the middle of Lake Cuitzeo on a causeway built in colonial times.

268 Irapuato. Altitude, 5,888 feet. Population, 32,377. An old city in one of the richest parts of the Bajío, and a growing industrial center. The strawberries of Irapuato are famous. (Gas, repairs, telephone, telegraph, restaurant, hotel.)

An all-weather road runs southwest from Irapuato fifty miles to La Piedad, passing through Abasolo (site of the hot springs of La Caldera) and Pénjamo. From La Piedad a road runs south to Carapán, on the Mexico City–Guadalajara highway, but it is not recommended.

292 Silao. The distinctive serapes of the Guanajuato region are made in this city. (Gas, repairs, telephone, telegraph, restaurant, hotel.)

An all-weather road runs east fifteen miles to Guanajuato (see page 75).

302 The branch road here goes five miles to the hot springs of Comanjilla. (Hotel at Comanjilla.)

312 León. Altitude, 6,183 feet. Population, 74,155. Largest city in Guanajuato State, a flourishing industrial center. (Gas, repairs, telephone, telegraph, restaurant, hotel, AMA office.)

338 Lagos de Moreno. This is where the Guadalajara–Antiguo Morelos highway crosses the Central Highway. (Gas, repairs, telephone, telegraph, restaurant, hotel.)

389 Aguascalientes. Altitude, 6,165 feet. Population, 82,234. Capital of the state of Aguascalientes. An attractive colonial city in a fertile area of fields and gardens, known for the thermal springs that give it its name, and for the prehistoric system of tunnels underlying the city. (Gas, repairs, telephone, telegraph, restaurant, hotel, AMA office.)

414 Rincón de Romos.

430 San Francisco los Adame.

445 Ojocalientes. (Gas.)

466 Zacatecas. Altitude, 8,187 feet. Population, 21,846. Capital of the state of Zacatecas. A historic mining town with some fine colonial architecture. It is still wealthy from its silver mines, and it is an agricultural and cattle-raising center as well. From the Church of Los Remedios on the ridge known as La Bufa an over-all view of the city in its mountainous setting can be had. (Gas, repairs, telephone, telegraph, restaurant, hotel.)

503 Fresnillo. Altitude, 7,377 feet. Population, 24,614. Another important silver-mining town. (Gas, repairs, telephone, telegraph, restaurant, hotel.)

518 Rancho Grande.

546 Sain Alto.

576 Sombrerete.

596 Suchil.

625 Nombre de Dios. (Gas.)

641 Areral.

660 Durango. Altitude, 6,209 feet. Population, 33,412. Capital of the state of Durango. An old city dating from the sixteenth century. The outstanding feature is the Cerro del Mercado, just north of the city, a solid hill of iron, probably the largest single iron deposit in the world. (Gas, repairs, telephone, telegraph, restaurant, hotel.)

The highway continues north another 150 miles to the town of La Zarca. Beyond that point it is not advisable to attempt to drive, for there are only unmarked trails between La Zarca and Chihuahua.

A road runs northeast from Durango to Torreón (see page 78).

ANTIGUO MORELOS TO SAN MIGUEL ALLENDE, GUANAJUATO, AND SILAO

This is an interesting side trip that can be made from either the Pan American Highway (Laredo–Mexico City route) or the Mexico City–Durango road. When the dry-weather road between San Miguel Allende and Dolores Hidalgo is open for traffic, one may make a circle tour—Querétaro, San Miguel Allende, Dolores Hidalgo, Guanajuato, Silao, Irapuato, Celaya, and return to Querétaro. Otherwise, both San Miguel and Guanajuato are available by separate detours from the main highway.

Itinerary. Distance: round trip, Querétaro through the towns listed above and return to Querétaro, 216 miles; one way, Querétaro to Silao via Dolores Hidalgo, 120 miles; one way, Querétaro to Guanajuato via Celaya and Irapuato, plus detour to San Miguel Allende, 144 miles (see page 71 for itinerary covering these towns). Road: paved from Pan American Highway through Querétaro to Irapuato (detour to San Miguel Allende all-weather gravel); from Irapuato, through Silao and Guanajuato, to Dolores Hidalgo, all-weather gravel; and dry-weather road from San Miguel Allende to Dolores Hidalgo (get information on this road before leaving Querétaro). Time: minimum, two days, one night. Hotels in Querétaro, San Miguel Allende, Guanajuato, Irapuato, and Celaya.

The figures on the margin below represent miles from Kilometer Mark 167 on the Pan American Highway.

0 Kilometer Mark 167 on the Pan American Highway is 106 miles from Mexico City. For itinerary of towns between this point and Querétaro, see page 71.

90 Querétaro (see page 72).

126 San Miguel Allende. Altitude, 6,400 feet. Population, 9,030. Set among rolling green hills, it is considered by some the city of purest colonial style in Mexico. See the old churches, each with a shady plaza in front; the great houses of colonial aristocracy, with coats of arms carved over the doorways; the home of the revolutionary hero Ignacio José de Allende, whose name has been added to the original name of San Miguel. The School of Arts and Crafts, which attracts artists from both Mexico and the United States, occupies one of the old convents. Just out of town is the lovely church of Atotonilco. (Gas, repairs, telephone, telegraph, restaurant, hotel.)

157 Dolores Hidalgo. In this little town Father Miguel Hidalgo y Costilla, on September 16, 1810, raised the *Grito de Dolores*, the battle cry that launched Mexico's war for independence from Spain. See the little parish church where Hidalgo rang the bells to call the people to hear his cry for independence, and the house in which he lived. (Gas, repairs, telephone, telegraph, restaurant, hotel.)

An all-weather road goes east from Dolores Hidalgo twenty-eight miles to San Luís de la Paz and on forty miles farther to Xichú.

195 Guanajuato. Altitude, 6,835 feet. Population, 23,521. Capital of the state of Guanajuato. An old silver-mining town of extraordinary wealth, picturesquely set among mountains honeycombed with mines. The streets are narrow, steep, and tortuous, overhung by balconied windows. Some are so steep that they are built as stairways. See the magnificent churches and mansions built with the fabulous wealth of colonial mineowners; the Alhondiga de Granaditas, where in the war for independence the royalists of Guanajuato held out until the door was set afire by a patriot boy (a statue of whom now dominates the city); the Juárez Theater, representing the lavish era of

Porfirio Díaz at the end of the last century. The Church of La
Valenciana, just out of town, is considered one of the most
perfect colonial churches in Mexico. (Gas, repairs, telephone,
telegraph, restaurant, hotel.)

210 Silao. On the main highway. (Gas, repairs, telephone, telegraph, restaurant, hotel.)

MATAMOROS TO MONTERREY

This road is an alternate route for entering or leaving Mexico, and
is especially convenient for motorists entering Mexico from southeast Texas. One may cross the border at Brownsville, opposite Matamoros, or at Hidalgo (near Pharr and McAllen, Texas), opposite
Reynosa. The highway passes through the subtropical country of
the lower Rio Grande valley.

Should you enter Mexico via Reynosa and plan to leave via
Nuevo Laredo, or vice versa, it is important that the Mexican immigration authorities at the border be so advised at the time and place
of entry, in order that necessary records can be sent to the immigration office at point of exit.

Itinerary. Distance (one way): 200 miles. Road: all paved. Time:
half a day. This is a fast road, but watch out for cattle on the highway. Hotels in the Texas towns and Monterrey.

The figures on the margin below represent miles from Matamoros.

0 Matamoros. Altitude, 26 feet. Population, 15,699. Border town
opposite Brownsville, Texas. Leave the customs seals on your
bags until after you pass the inspection substation beyond Reynosa. From Matamoros to Reynosa the road parallels the Rio
Grande, or Río Bravo, as it is called in Mexico.

60 Reynosa. Altitude, 125 feet. Population, 9,412. Border town
opposite Hidalgo, Texas. Hidalgo is the border station for the
towns of Pharr and McAllen. (Gas, repairs, telephone, telegraph, restaurant, hotel.)

79 El Jabilí. (Gas.)

120 General Bravo. (Gas, telegraph, restaurant.)

128 Villa China. (Gas, restaurant.)

An all-weather road runs southwest through General Terán to
Montemorelos on the Pan American Highway south of Monterrey.

178 Cadereyta. An old town on the Santa Catarina River in a fertile agricultural region. (Gas, telephone, telegraph, restaurant, hotel.)

185 Juárez. (Gas.)

200 Monterrey. Junction with the Pan American Highway (see page 44). (Gas, repairs, telephone, telegraph, restaurant, hotel, AMA office.)

MONTERREY TO TORREÓN

This is a continuation of the Matamoros-Monterrey highway, and the scenery en route is much the same. The highway will eventually run all the way from Matamoros to Mazatlán, on the Pacific coast. It is possible now to continue on past Torreón as far as Durango; but between Durango and Mazatlán the road has not yet been constructed. This is a good straight road on which one can make good time, but watch out for livestock, as this is open range country.

Itinerary. Distance (one way): 234 miles. Road: all paved. Time: five hours. Hotels in Monterrey, Saltillo, and Torreón.

The figures on the margin below represent miles from Monterrey.

0 Monterrey. Exit on Avenida Bolívar (a one-way street).

3 The road to the left goes twelve miles up to Chipinque Mesa, a mountain resort at an altitude of 4,000 feet. Attractive cabin camp on the mesa.

9 Santa Catarina. A road to the left leads two miles to Huasteca Canyon, a deep rocky gorge with sheer walls eroded into striking formations.

The highway begins here the ascent to the tableland.

13 The road to the right takes you seventeen miles to García Caves.

44 Ramos Arizpe. (Gas, restaurant.)

54 Saltillo. Altitude, 5,212 feet. Population, 49,700. Capital of the state of Coahuila. Although it is an old town, it retains few colonial buildings besides the cathedral. Because of the pleasant dry climate at this altitude, Saltillo has become popular as a summer resort, with good hotels and facilities for golf, tennis, swimming, hunting. Saltillo serapes have for centuries been considered Mexico's finest, but they are difficult for the casual tourist to pick up, the good ones being quickly bought by col-

lectors from Mexico City. (Gas, repairs, telephone, telegraph, restaurant, hotel, AMA office.)

A road to the south leads eleven miles to Diamante Pass, which affords beautiful views.

A road to the north goes to Piedras Negras, on the border (see below).

136 Paila. A road to the left goes sixteen miles to the quiet colonial town of Parras, birthplace of Francisco I. Madero. (Gas.)

191 San Pedro. (Gas, repairs, telephone, telegraph, restaurant, hotel.)

234 Torreón. Altitude, 3,741 feet. Population, 6,600. This is the center of one of Mexico's most interesting social experiments—the communally owned and co-operatively worked La Laguna lands, which were made arable by a large-scale government dam project. The town is neat and modern. In the vicinity are two attractive colonial towns, Gómez Palacio and Lerdo. (Gas, repairs, telephone, telegraph, restaurant, hotel, AMA office.)

The road to Durango is about 158 miles long. About half of it is rough dry-weather road; the rest has all-weather surface. It goes first to Lerdo, then runs southwest through Cuéncame, Yerbanis, and Villa Madero to Durango.

PIEDRAS NEGRAS TO SALTILLO

This road offers another alternative to the Laredo-Monterrey route, crossing the border at Eagle Pass, Texas, and running south to Saltillo, where it meets the Monterrey-Torreón road. The route crosses the northern Mexican desert. From Piedras Negras to Hermanas it is fairly level, staying between 1,200 and 1,400 feet above sea level. At Hermanas it begins to gain altitude, reaching 5,244 feet at Saltillo. The trip is easily made in a day. There are no good hotels for overnight stops en route.

Itinerary. Distance (one way): 278 miles. Road: all paved. Time: six hours.

The figures on the margin below represent miles from Piedras Negras.

0 Piedras Negras. Altitude, 722 feet. Population, 15,663. Just across the Rio Grande from Eagle Pass, Texas. (Gas, repairs, telephone, telegraph, restaurant, hotel.)

4 Villa de Fuente. (Restaurant.)

26 Nava. (Gas, telephone, telegraph.)

34 Morelos. (Gas, telephone, telegraph, restaurant.)

77 Nueva Rosita. (Gas, repairs, telephone, telegraph, restaurant, hotel.)

81 Agujita. (Gas, repairs, telephone, telegraph.)

85 Sabinas. A road to the left goes to Don Martín Dam on the Salado River. Not recommended. (Gas, repairs, telephone, telegraph, restaurant, hotel.)

125 Hermanas. Beyond here begins the gradual climb up to the plateau country. (Gas, telephone, telegraph, restaurant.)

157 Monclova. No towns of any importance beyond here. Be sure you have enough gasoline to take you to Saltillo. (Gas, repairs, telephone, telegraph, restaurant, hotel.)

165 Castaño. (Gas, restaurant.)

278 Saltillo (see page 77). (Gas, repairs, telephone, telegraph, restaurant, hotel, AMA office.)

CIUDAD JUÁREZ TO CHIHUAHUA

This is the northern section of the Central Highway (see page 70). It runs straight and level across the desert and the plateau grazing lands of the state of Chihuahua, the largest state of Mexico.

Itinerary. Distance (one way): 230 miles. Road: all paved. Time: five hours.

The figures on the margin below represent miles from Ciudad Juárez.

0 Ciudad Juárez. Altitude, 3,752 feet. Population, 48,881. Border city across the Rio Grande from El Paso, Texas. (Gas, repairs, telephone, telegraph, restaurant, hotel.)

28 Samalayuca. (Gas, telegraph, restaurant.)

46 Candelaria. (Gas, restaurant.)

80 Villa Ahumada. (Gas, telegraph, restaurant, hotel.)

112 Moctezuma. (Gas, telegraph, restaurant, hotel.)

138 Gallegos. (Gas, restaurant.)

180 Encinillas. (Gas.)

202 Terrazas. (Gas, telegraph, restaurant, hotel.)

230 Chihuahua. Altitude, 4,634 feet. Population, 56,805. Capital of the state of Chihuahua and the most important city in the north of Mexico. It is the center of a rich silver-mining and ranching district. Off to the west rise the high mountains of the Sierra

Madre Occidental. The eighteenth-century cathedral and the tower in which Hidalgo awaited his execution are of special interest. Well worth a visit are the Santa Eulalia Mines and the large modern smelting plants a few miles out of the city. (Gas, repairs, telephone, telegraph, restaurant, hotel.)

NOGALES TO GUAYMAS

This is the northern section of the Pacific Highway (see page 67). It is much used by United States tourists who run down to Guaymas for fishing or for relaxation in the excellent resort hotel set on a desert-bordered bay not far from Guaymas. The country traversed by the highway is cactus desert, level, but with low desert mountain ranges always in view.

Itinerary. Distance (one way): 268 miles. Road: all paved. Time: one day; or two days with overnight stop in Hermosillo. Hotels in Hermosillo, Guaymas, and Playa de Cortés (suburb of Guaymas).

The figures on the margin below represent miles from Nogales.

  0 Nogales. Altitude, 3,867 feet. Population, 15,453. Border town opposite Nogales, Arizona. (Gas, repairs, telegraph, restaurant, hotel.)

 45 Imuris. (Gas.)

 58 Magdalena. (Gas, restaurant, hotel.)

 75 Santa Ana. (Gas.)

 90 Casa Blanca. (Gas.)

145 Pinto. (Gas.)

180 Hermosillo. Altitude, 693 feet. Population, 30,000. Capital of the state of Sonora, on the Sonora River, surrounded by orange, date, and other fruit groves. Good hunting. (Gas, repairs, telephone, restaurant, hotel.)

    A road runs west to Kino Bay, on the Gulf of California, where fishing is excellent. The almost extinct Seri Indians, who live on Tiburon Island, are often seen around Kino Bay.

268 Guaymas. Altitude, 9 feet. Population, 20,360. A desert resort on a beautiful land-locked bay in the Gulf of California. The big resort hotel is four miles northeast of the town on the Gulf. It is open from November 1 to the middle of July. Excellent deep-sea fishing, surf and pool swimming, hunting. (Gas, repairs, telephone, telegraph, restaurant, hotel.)

    In the dry season it is possible to drive as far as Navojoa, about

130 miles south. The road goes through the Yaqui Indian country, then through the country of the Mayo Indians. Alamos, inland from Navojoa, set among bold desert mountains, is an unusually picturesque colonial town. It was once a silver center, but is now almost abandoned. Inquire in Guaymas about the condition of the road before starting out.

CHAPTER V

MEXICO CITY

TWO mountain chains sweep from beyond Mexico's northern boundary southeast as far as the Isthmus of Tehuantepec. The land between these cordilleras is a plateau shaped roughly like a triangle. At the southeast apex of the triangle a depression, sixty miles by forty, constitutes the fertile Valley of Mexico. This valley, over 7,000 feet above sea level, hemmed in on the southeast by the precipitous heights of Popocatépetl and Ixtaccíhuatl, and on the southwest by Ajusco, benefits from a plentiful water supply and an invigorating climate from which extremes of heat and cold are absent. All the year round the atmosphere is springlike, the mean temperature being 58 degrees.

BACKGROUND

At the present time archaeologists are patiently groping to reconstruct the history of the peoples inhabiting the plateau before the coming of Europeans. The Toltecs, worshipers of the feathered-serpent god Quetzalcoatl, and builders of pyramids at Teotihuacán and Cholula, were succeeded by many tribes of Nahua Indians who filtered in from the north. Of these the last to arrive were the Aztecs. They had to fight to get land, and in so doing developed warlike qualities that by the fifteenth century were winning them ascendancy in the shifting confederacy of independent Nahua tribes distributed throughout Mexico. Having established themselves on two islands in Lake Texcoco in the heart of the Valley of Anáhuac (as they called the Valley of Mexico), the Aztecs created land by partially filling in the lake. Thus the city of Tenochtitlán grew up, sprawling out over the made land and intersected by a network of canals.

Three masonry causeways connected it with the mainland; a dike seven miles long dammed the lake and prevented its flooding the city; and two aqueducts brought drinking water from the heights of Chapultepec to a population of perhaps a hundred thousand. (In colonial times one of these aqueducts was rebuilt to a length of 904 arches and continued to be used. Its ruined remains may still be seen on Avenida Chapultepec.) Ignorant though they were of the uses of the wheel, and unequipped with any but human draft animals, the Aztecs nevertheless constructed dwellings of red or white-washed stone and a paved market place surrounded by colonnades where were sold products from different parts of Mexico—slaves, animals, gold and jade ornaments, pottery, textiles, cacao, vanilla, rubber, and feather mosaics. At the meeting point of the three causeways an eight-foot wall surmounted by carved serpents enclosed the forty temples built in honor not only of the Aztec gods, but also of the gods of conquered tribes. Dominating them was a pyramid nearly a hundred feet high crowned by the temple to the Aztec god Huitzilopochtli.

It was in November 1519 that Hernán Cortés led a force of four hundred men into the Valley of Anáhuac. Bernal Díaz del Castillo, one of the soldiers, wrote an account of the conquest, telling how, when from the pass below snow-covered Popocatépetl they beheld the valley filled with shining lakes "and many cities and villages built in the water and other great towns on dry land and that straight and level causeway going toward Mexico [City], we were amazed and said that it was like the enchantments they tell of in the legend of Amadis, on account of the great towers and temples and buildings rising from the water, and all built of masonry. And some of our soldiers even asked whether the things that we saw were not a dream." On November 8 they pressed with difficulty along the crowded causeway leading into Tenochtitlán, the lake beside them being filled with houses and with canoes. The Aztec king, Moctezuma II, coming forth to meet them richly robed, descended from his litter and stood supported by four chieftains under a green feather canopy embroidered with gold and silver and pearls. Cortés in turn dismounted from his horse and the two chiefs clasped hands.

This meeting of white man and Indian was the prelude to a death struggle that lasted nearly two years. Cortés very nearly lost everything on the night of June 30, 1520, when he and his men tried to slip away secretly from the hostile city. The fleeing Spaniards were massacred and their forces all but annihilated by the Aztecs. At the end of the terrible rout Cortés sat down and took stock of his losses under an ahuehuete tree that still stands, a reminder of that sorrowful night. The next May Cortés returned with new recruits and laid siege to the city. The end came on August 13, 1521. On that day the last section of Tenochtitlán was seized, and Cuauhtemoc, Moctezuma's heroic successor, was made prisoner.

The Spaniards set to work rebuilding the city, filling in the lake and erecting Christian churches with the broken remains of the Aztec temples. In a comparatively short time Mexico City, the capital of New Spain, could show a grandeur in keeping with its position as head of the wealthy first viceroyalty. Uppermost with the Spanish conquerors were two motives—the desire for riches and the determination to Christianize the Indians. The Crown granted large tracts of land to Cortés, his followers, other early conquerors, and the Church. By 1572 the Church was the largest private property owner, with valuable holdings scattered throughout the viceroyalty. In Mexico City alone something like a hundred churches adorned with carvings, paintings, and statuary attested to the Church's wealth and power, and festival days were splendid with processions of richly robed clergy and nobles winding through the streets escorting the sacred images.

Government was administered by the viceroy and an *audiencia* or tribunal at Mexico City, besides various other bureaucratic officials, all of whom were required to be peninsular Spaniards. The *creoles,* persons of pure Spanish blood born in the New World, were excluded by law from all but subordinate political posts; while they could and did grow rich through the ownership of silver mines and haciendas worked by the Indians, and while they imitated the *gachupines* (Spaniards) as much as they could, they lacked the salutary experience of either working themselves or exercising political responsibility.

The first great outward change came when the Spanish monarchy, to which Mexicans had professed allegiance for almost three hundred years, suffered an eclipse. In 1808 Charles IV abdicated, and he and his son Ferdinand VII were imprisoned by Napoleon, who set his brother Joseph on the Spanish throne. Gachupines and creoles, while disagreeing on all other points, united in refusing to acknowledge the usurper. The Mexican War of Independence began in September 1810, when the learned and humanitarian parish priest of Dolores, Manuel Hidalgo, rang the village church bell and with the "Grito de Dolores" called on his Indian parishioners to overthrow gachupín tyranny. Years of guerrilla warfare followed. Independence was achieved in 1821 when for a brief time Agustín de Iturbide succeeded in holding together many opposing parties. The capital witnessed the extraordinary spectacle of Iturbide's coronation as first emperor of Mexico in 1822, and a couple of years later, after Iturbide had abdicated, it rejoiced over the inauguration of Guadalupe Victoria as first president of the Republic of Mexico.

During the first century of independence, Mexico City was the stage for the enactment of many dramatic scenes. In 1829 the capital gave a hero's welcome to that opportunist and international meddler, Santa Ana, after he had defeated an invading Spanish army at Tampico. Thereafter he was by turns in and out of favor for thirty years. In 1846, when war broke out between Mexico and the United States, he was recalled from exile to lead the Mexican armies. The 1850's were times of civil war caused by the social revolution known as the Reform. Its dominating figure was a pure-blooded Zapotec Indian, Benito Juárez, who as president promulgated the liberal constitution of 1857. Years of struggle had, however, exhausted both the national treasury and the patience of foreign creditors, so that in 1862 they decided on forcible intervention. Napoleon III sent an army to prepare the way for Maximilian of Austria, who in 1864 entered Mexico City as emperor. For three years he and the Empress Carlota ruled their turbulent domains with spendthrift grandeur. Evidences of their short unhappy reign survive in the Paseo de la Reforma and the Zócalo, which they beautified with plantings of trees and flower beds, and at Chapultepec, where they spent large sums rebuilding and refurnishing the castle. In 1867 Napoleon withdrew the French troops and the liberals under Juárez captured Maximilian and his native supporters. Juárez, after ordering the execution of the Emperor, became president once more, but his death in 1872 cut short efforts at social reconstruction. The regime of Porfírio Díaz, which lasted from 1876 to 1911, brought many outward improvements to the capital. Drainage of the Valley of Mexico was effected, reducing the danger of recurrent floods and pestilences; railroads were built, industry was promoted, and new and imposing buildings gave Mexico City the appearance of a modern cosmopolitan urban center. Unfortunately these changes chiefly benefited foreign investors and a few favored Mexicans; they did not help the neglected rural Indians, who needed land and education, or the industrial workers, whose wages failed to increase with the rise in the cost of living.

A revolt that was an explosion of pent-up forces no longer to be denied began in 1910. It continued, interrupted at times by shattering civil war; Mexicans think of the "Mexican Revolution" as still going on. By the term they mean that policies in regard to foreign investments, the role of the Church, land distribution, transportation, and the provision of education and housing adapted to the people's needs are still being shaped and altered. The period since 1917, when the present constitution was adopted, has been marked by the constant practical application of the principles that inspired the movement.

Sight-seeing

Mexico City, shaped by 450 years of fascinating history, has, according to recent estimates, a population of about 2,225,000 in the metropolitan area. The older part, to the east of the Zócalo, although containing many solid colonial structures of admirable proportions, is now a poor and relatively obscure quarter. Office buildings, fine hotels, and splendid stores have established themselves along the great avenues, Tacuba, Cinco de Mayo, Francisco I. Madero, and 16 de Septiembre, between the Zócalo and the Alameda, while residential buildings have spread from the Paseo de la Reforma district westward beyond Chapultepec Park to Chapultepec Heights. On the south side the newest ideas in workers' housing have recently been executed by the municipality.

Zócalo (SOH-cah-loh), sometimes called the Plaza de la Constitución, is at the eastern end of the main business district. This wide plaza has been the center of national life and the scene of historical events since the time when it was the heart of the Aztec capital. Moctezuma's palace, the Teocalli or Great Temple, a forum, and other buildings stood here before the Conquest, and the Spaniards used some of the same materials when they built the present cathedral and National Palace. It was here that the world-famous

Aztec calendar stone was found. Make the Zócalo your starting point for sight-seeing.

Palacio de Justicia (Palace of Justice). Occupies a position on the southeast corner of the Zócalo. Completed in 1941, it is of modern colonial architecture and contains frescoes by José Clemente Orozco.

Catedral (Cathedral—see also page 98 below). Occupies the north side of the Zócalo. Probably the largest church in Mexico, it was built on the site of the earliest Christian church on the continent (1525). It was begun in 1573 and finished in 1667. The exterior is a composite of Doric, Ionic, and Corinthian architecture, richly ornamented. It was designed by the Spanish architect Manuel Tolsá. It is 374 feet long and 198 feet wide and has two towers, each 204 feet high. One of the bells weighs 27,000 pounds; the clapper is eight feet in length and weighs 500 pounds. The vaulted roof is supported by twenty Doric columns 179 feet in height. The cathedral contains marble altars, statuary, wood carvings, silver railings, and priceless tapestries and paintings. There are two Murillos, one in the chapel and the other in the choir. Adjoining the cathedral is the Sagrario (Sanctuary) Metropolitano, built in 1750, in the highly decorated Churrigueresque style, now housing an ecclesiastical museum. The cathedral is open all day, every day, including Sundays and holidays. On the east side of the cathedral is the monument to Fray Bartolomé de las Casas. The inscription reads: "Stranger, if you love virtue, pause and do honor; this is Fray Bartolomé de las Casas, protector of the Indians."

Aztec Ruins. Opposite the northeast corner of the cathedral, at the corner of Guatemala and Seminario Streets, is an excavation that has revealed the foundations of an ancient Aztec structure, believed to have been a part of the Teocalli, or Great Temple, of the god of war. The snake's head seen here may have been a part of the Coatepantl, or wall of snakes' heads that surrounded the Teocalli.

Palacio Nacional (National Palace). A huge structure covering four blocks on the east side of the Zócalo, on the spot where Moctezuma's palace one stood; built between 1692 and 1698 of early colonial architecture after an earlier structure built by Cortés had been destroyed by fire. It was the official residence of the viceroys from 1698 until the establishment of the Republic, and since then has housed the offices of the president and other government offices.

Additions have been made from time to time, the latest being the third floor in 1927. Guides are available to conduct visitors through the complicated series of corridors, rooms, and patios. The historical murals within the central entrance on the walls of the main staircase are the work of Diego Rivera. The Independence Bell, which was tolled by the revolutionary priest, Father Miguel Hidalgo y Costilla, on the night of September 15, 1810, to call the people to arms (see page 86), now hangs over the central doorway. Annually at eleven P.M. on September 15 the bell is tolled by the president of the Republic in a dramatic re-enactment of the Grito de Dolores. Outstanding among the many salons are the great banquet hall, furnished during the reign of Maximilian and notable for the carved paneling of the ceilings and walls; the state reception room; and the magnificent ballroom. The building is open from nine A.M. to one P.M. except Mondays. On Sundays some of the private rooms, which are closed to visitors during the week, may be seen.

Museo Nacional (National Museum). Back of the National Palace at 13 Calle Emiliano Zapata, formerly called Calle Moneda. Previously the viceregal mint, this building now contains one of the finest archaeological museums in the world. The exhibit includes stone images, monoliths, and sculptures; precious relics from the Mixtec tombs at Oaxaca; relics of the Aztec, Mixtec, Zapotec, Toltec, and Tarascan races; the Aztec calendar stone, weighing thirty tons (more accurate than European calendars of the same period); an Aztec sacrificial stone and the mysterious Palenque Cross. Relics of more recent times include armored suits of the conquistadors; old maps, books, and documents of the Conquest; relics of the colonial and imperial periods; an extensive exhibit from Maximilian's time, including his carriage, and historical paintings. Among the other interesting exhibits are the collections of ceramics, antique furniture, jewelry, and native arts and handicrafts. The museum is open Monday through Friday nine A.M. to two P.M., Sunday ten A.M. to one P.M., closed on Saturdays and holidays; admission fifty centavos.

Palacio Municipal (City Hall). Stands on the southwest corner of the Zócalo at 16 de Septiembre and 5 de Febrero Streets. Built in 1724, it houses the government offices of the Federal District and contains valuable archives and portraits of the rulers of Mexico. Open eight A.M. to two-thirty P.M. and four to six P.M.

Monte de Piedad (National Pawn Shop). On the Avenida Cinco de Mayo near the northwest corner of the Zócalo. Founded in 1775 by the Conde de Regla, who made a fortune in the Pachuca silver mines, it was established for the public benefit as a place where the poor could get loans on personal property at low rates of interest. Unredeemed articles may be bought cheaply at periodical auctions and daily sales. Open eight A.M. to two-thirty P.M. and four to six-thirty P.M. weekdays; nine A.M. to two P.M. Saturdays: The building is of colonial architecture and stands on the site of a viceregal palace built by Cortés.

Escuela Nacional de Bellas Artes (National School of Fine Arts, formerly the San Carlos Academy). Housed in a seventeenth-century building at No. 22 Calle de la Academia, two blocks east of the Museum. It has a splendid art gallery (the "Metropolitan" of Mexico); paintings include works of Murillo, Rubens, and other old masters. Free, open daily ten A.M. to one P.M., including Sundays, but closed on holidays.

Casa del Conde de Santiago (House of the Count of Santiago). Located at 30 Pino Suárez. Erected shortly after the Conquest. This is a private residence, but the exterior, of pink *tezontle* with massive carved doors, is interesting.

Hospital de Jesús Nazareno (Hospital of Jesus of Nazareth). Located at No. 117 Calle San Salvador, at Pino Suárez. The oldest continuously functioning hospital in the Americas, founded by Cortés in 1524. It contains relics of Cortés and his personal files and is said to stand on the spot where Cortés and Moctezuma first met.

Biblioteca Nacional (National Library). Occupies a corner at Calle Isabel la Católica and Avenida Uruguay; housed in a building that was formerly the church of a monastery of San Agustín, built in 1667. It is under the direction of the National University, and besides its 200,000 volumes contains many ancient documents, some of the first books printed on the continent, and books in Indian languages dating from the sixteenth century. Free, open ten A.M. to five P.M., Saturdays ten A.M. to two P.M.

Universidad Nacional (National University). Located at Justo Sierra 16. This is the administrative building of the university; the several colleges are located in different sections of the city. This building contains the Anfiteatro Bolívar (Bolivar Amphitheater) with frescoes by Diego Rivera and Fernando Leal. The original university, known as the Royal and Pontifical University of Mexico, was founded in 1553 and was closed after a long and distinguished career about the middle of the nineteenth century. Sixty years later the present National University of Mexico took its place. Open nine A.M. to two P.M.

Escuela Nacional Preparatoria (National Preparatory School). Located at San Ildefonso 43. It occupies a spacious structure in the baroque style, built in 1749 as the Jesuit School of San Ildefonso. It has a fine collection of modern art, including frescoes by Orozco, murals by Leal, and paintings by Jean Charlot. In the Salon "El Generalito" are carved choir stalls with Biblical scenes by Indian artists, which came from the old San Agustín monastery, now the National Library.

Secretaría de Educación Pública (Ministry of Public Education). North of the Zócalo at the corner of Avenida República de Argentina and Calle Luis González Obregón. A modern building famous for its murals by Rivera and Orozco, symbolizing the struggle of the Indian from slavery to freedom. Open weekdays nine A.M. to six P.M., closed Sundays.

Plaza de Santo Domingo. A colorful plaza three blocks north of the Zócalo on Avenida República del Brasil. On the west side are the *portales,* or arcades, where professional typists, letter writers, artisans, fortunetellers ply their various trades. Facing the plaza at Venezuela Street is the Church of Santo Domingo, first church established by the Dominicans in Mexico (1526). The present building, erected in 1737, is an excellent example of baroque architecture with a Churrigueresque interior. Near by at the northeast corner of Brasil and Venezuela Streets is the *Escuela Nacional de Medicina* (National School of Medicine), which occupies the old Inquisition Building, where the tribunal and prison were located. Open all day.

National Express Office. Located at Avenida Isabel la Católica and Calle Donceles. An old colonial building, formerly the home of the counts of Heras. Note the interesting Churrigueresque façade and arch.

Iglesia de San Francisco (Church of St. Francis). On Avenida Madero, almost directly across from Sanborn's. Begun in 1525 with money granted by Cortés, it was long the center of Catholicism in America and headquarters of the powerful Franciscan order. Open all day, including Sundays and holidays.

Casa de los Azulejos (House of Tiles). At Avenida Madero 4. Dates from about 1596 and was one of the finest colonial mansions in the city. The exterior is entirely covered with blue and white Puebla tiles, producing a unique effect. The Chinese bronze balustrade and the colonial fountain inside are also of interest. It houses Sanborn's drugstore, tearoom, and gift shop. Ask one of the clerks for a free booklet describing the house and its history in detail.

Near by, at Avenida Madero 17, is the Iturbide Palace, occupied by Emperor Agustín de Iturbide from 1821 to 1823. It was built in the eighteenth century by a wealthy Mexican nobleman and was one of the most extravagant of the colonial residences. It is now occupied by a curio store.

Correo Mayor (Main Post Office). Corner of Tacuba and Teatro Nacional. Although a comparatively modern building (1904), it is the city's finest example of antique Spanish architecture. It was designed by the Italian architect Adam Boari in the plateresque style with Indian details. Open all day. Near by, on the corner of Cinco de Mayo and Teatro Nacional, is the *Banco Nacional de Mexico* (National Bank of Mexico), open nine A.M. to one P.M. and three-thirty to four-thirty P.M., on Saturdays nine A.M. to noon.

Palacio de Bellas Artes (Palace of Fine Arts). At the east end of the Alameda, facing Avenida Juárez. Begun in 1905 and dedicated in 1935, this ornate structure was built at a cost of 35,000,000 pesos. It is a blend of Mayan, Mixtec, and classical architecture, designed by Adam Boari and completed by Federico Mariscal. Because of its enormous weight and the soft character of the underlying soil, the building has settled several feet since its construction. It contains the national theater, auditoriums, and art galleries. The colored glass curtain in the theater is famous. It depicts the volcanoes Popocatépetl and Ixtaccíhuatl and was made by Tiffany at a cost of $47,000. Open daily except Monday, ten A.M. to one P.M. The glass curtain may be seen only on Tuesdays and Thursdays and at performances.

The Alameda. This is the city's beautiful central park, located west of the Palace of Fine Arts between Avenidas Juárez and Hidalgo. It has been a park since 1592 and in early days was the scene of burnings by the Inquisition. Many of the great ash, elm, and eucalyptus trees are from two to three centuries old. It contains the Juárez Monument, one of the finest in America.

Vizcaínas Convent. Calle Vizcaínas near San Juan de Letrán. A magnificent baroque building, dating from 1751.

El Caballito (Statue of Charles IV). In the circle at the junction of Paseo de la Reforma and Avenida Juárez. An equestrian statue, cast as a single block of bronze, it weighs thirty tons. It was the work of Manuel Tolsá, the Spanish sculptor, and was cast in Mexico in 1803.

Plaza de la República. The first circle west on the Paseo de la Reforma from El Caballito. Contains the Monument to the Revolution.

Statue of Columbus. Located in the second circle of the Paseo de la Reforma, at Avenida Morelos. It was the work of Charles Cordier, a Frenchman.

Statue of Cuauhtémoc (or Quauhtemotzín), last of the Aztec emperors. Paseo de la Reforma at Lucerna. Cuauhtémoc, the greatest hero of the Aztecs, was tortured by Cortés in an unsuccessful attempt to force him to reveal the hiding place of the royal treasure. Sometimes on August 1, the anniversary of this event, the Indians hold a memorial service around the statue and perform native dances. The statue is the work of Miguel Morena, Mexican sculptor.

Monumento Independencia (Independence Monument). In the center of Paseo de la Reforma at Florencia. This beautiful column, 150 feet high, was begun in 1901 and finished in 1910 at a cost of 537,000 pesos. At the top is a winged statue of Victory. The central figure at the base of the monument is that of Miguel Hidalgo; others are of Morelos, Guerrero, Mina, and Nicolás Bravo.

American Embassy and Consulate. Avenida Insurgentes 105 at Calle Niza.

Chapultepec Park and Castle. At the end of the Paseo de la Reforma. The castle is on top of a hill about two hundred feet high, which affords a magnificent view of the city and the Valley of Mexico. This was the site of the ancient seat of the Aztec emperors. The present castle was begun in 1783 by the Viceroy Galvez but was not completed until 1840, when it was fortified and made the home of the Military College. It was attacked and taken by the Americans in 1847, when it was defended only by the young cadets from the college. Maximilian made the castle his royal residence in 1866 and Carlota designed the lovely formal gardens. It was for a while the official home of the president of Mexico. The interior contains many relics of Maximilian and Carlota; the furnishings of her bedroom and of the drawing room were given by Napoleon III and the tapestry coverings of chairs and sofas are copies of Gobelin tapestries in the Louvre. The stained-glass skylight over the great stairway bears the arms of the eighteen rulers of Mexico from the Aztecs to Maximilian.

The castle was the scene of the meeting of the Inter-American Conference on Problems of War and Peace, held in Mexico City, February and March 1945. Here on March 6, 1945, the conference adopted the security measures embodied in the instrument known as the Act of Chapultepec. The Museum of History now forms a part of the general exhibits at Chapultepec Castle. Admission charge includes guide service.

The park is one of the oldest natural parks in America. Many of its old ahuehuetes (a kind of giant cypress) are centuries old, and some stand two hundred feet high. One of the oldest is the Tree of Moctezuma, which is forty-four feet in circumference. Near it is the monument to the young cadets who died defending the hill against American forces in 1847. The Don Quijote Fountain memorializes Cervantes' literary hero, whose story is pictured in the tiles of the seats. The park is a popular rendezvous for people of all classes, particularly on Sunday morning, when band concerts are given. There are bridle paths and beautiful drives, athletic fields, children's playgrounds, a lake for boating, and zoological and botanical gardens.

Los Piños (The Pines), the residence of the president of Mexico, is located at the southwest section of Chapultepec Park.

ENVIRONS OF MEXICO CITY

Points of interest within a few miles of Mexico City and easily reached by car or bus in an hour or so are listed here, together with suggestions for combining them on circle trips.

Shrine of Our Lady of Guadalupe (gwah-dah-LOO-peh). Four miles north of the Zócalo at Villa Gustavo A. Madero. This, the most sacred shrine in Mexico, was erected to Our Lady of Guadalupe on the spot where, according to legend, she converted an Indian's *tilma,* or cloak, into a beautiful cloth with a vivid image of the Virgin. The cloth, or *ayate,* hangs over the main altar in a frame of pure gold enclosed by a solid silver railing. Thousands of pilgrims from every part of Mexico visit this shrine annually from

about December 9 to 18 for the fiesta, which is a combination religious and tribal ceremonial (see page 260). The church is a gem
of colonial architecture, originally built in 1695, but altered many
times since. Near the shrine is the Chapel of the Well, where, the
legend states, a spring burst from the rock at the spot where the
Virgin stood.

San Juan Teotihuacán (sahn-hoo-AHN teh-oh-tee-wah-CAHN).
Situated thirty miles northeast of Mexico City. Put this on your
"must" list and plan your trip for the morning. Teotihuacán is the
site of one of the most important archaeological discoveries on the
North American continent, a zone covering eight square miles containing majestic pyramids, temples, and courts constructed many
centuries ago by the Toltecs, who preceded the Aztecs in the Valley
of Mexico. The pyramids are at least a thousand years old, and
some of the structures may date from the archaic civilization that
preceded the invasion of the Toltecs. For more description of the
ruins, see page 219.

On the way to or from Teotihuacán, a short side trip (1.3 miles)
may be made to Acolman. The church and monastery of San Agustín Acolman, begun in 1539 and completed in 1560, constitute one
of the best examples of very old ecclesiastical structures in Mexico.
The façade is designed in the plateresque style with some Italian
Gothic influence. Along the upper corridor of the patio are frescoes
depicting the life of St. Augustine.

Tenayuca Pyramid (teh-nah-YOO-cah). Nine miles north of the
city. An outstanding example of Aztec construction, 140 feet square
and 50 feet high, noted for the plumed serpents of stone that adorn
three sides of its base. There are fifty-two snakes on each side, cor-
responding to the Aztec cycle of fifty-two years. At the foot of the
stairway on the west side is a carved frieze of skulls, and inside is a
fresco with similar carvings. Several tunnels cut through the pyramid have revealed still earlier structures. A guide is provided and
a small museum is near by.

Pyramid of Santa Cecilia. Two miles beyond Tenayuca is the
Pyramid of Santa Cecilia, smaller and not completely excavated. It
is of the same epoch and construction (Aztec) and is decorated
with carved human skulls.

Tepotzotlán (teh-poh-soht-LAHN), twenty-six miles north and
west of Mexico City, has a church and monastery that have been

designated a national monument. The monastery, an austere building, was founded by the Jesuits in 1584 as a school for the sons of Indian nobles. The church, completed in the eighteenth century, is considered to be Churriguera's masterpiece. Its façade of cut stone, gilded altarpieces, polychrome chapel, and formal colonial garden are its best features. There are many fine paintings, some by Villalpanda and Cabrera. Note the multiple, superimposed bell towers.

Los Remedios (lohs reh-MEH-dee-ohs). Just beyond Naucalpan is an unusually interesting shrine where an elaborate festival to the Virgin of Los Remedios is held the first week in September (see page 268). The image of the Virgin was one of the first brought to Mexico by the Spaniards.

Villa Álvaro Obregón (vee-yah AHL-vah-roh oh-breh-GOHN). Formerly called San Ángel, eight miles south of the Zócalo. A suburb of fine homes. The Church of El Carmen dates from 1615 and has tiled domes, carved doors, Churrigueresque altarpieces, and paintings. In a crypt beneath one of the chapels are a number of well-preserved mummies. A monument to General Obregón, president from 1920 to 1924, stands at the end of Calzada de Nueva, on the spot where he was killed. Diego Rivera's home is opposite San Ángel Inn. The latter was formerly a seventeenth-century monastery.

El Pedregal (peh-dreh-GAHL). A basaltic lava stream covering about fifteen square miles beginning three or four blocks south of the Church of El Carmen in Villa Obregón. The eruption of Xitli, probably the last lava flow in this area, took place about 5000 B.C. Excavations at the quarry of Copilco have revealed human remains and examples of primitive craftsmanship of an archaic people believed contemporaneous with those who built the Pyramid of Cuicuilco (see page 97). Tunnels excavated beneath the lava cap have revealed well-preserved skeletons. The tunnel entrance is about one-half mile from town. Do not venture farther into the Pedregal without a guide.

El Desierto de los Leones (deh-see-AIR-toh deh lohs leh-OH-nehs). Located eighteen miles southwest in a beautiful national park of rugged, pine-forested mountains. Interesting ruins of an old Carmelite monastery built in 1606. Its underground passages and cells, aqueduct, and chapel are of interest.

Ixtapalapa (ees-tah-pah-LAH-pah). Six miles southeast of Mexico City at the foot of Cerro de la Estrella (Hill of the Star). On the top of this hill the Aztecs lighted their new fires at the beginning of each cycle of fifty-two years. A good gravel road (two miles) leads to the summit. The natives speak Aztec.

Churubusco (choo-roo-BOOS-coh). Six miles south of the Zócalo. An interesting old Franciscan monastery (1678) of Spanish colonial architecture, surrounded by lovely gardens, and now maintained as a colonial museum with relics of the battle between Mexicans and Americans that took place here August 13, 1847. Just south of the village is the Mexico City Country Club, oldest golf club in the republic.

Coyoacán (coh-yoh-ah-CAHN). Six miles south. The first seat of Spanish government. Here Cortés built a palace, now the Municipal Palace, where it is said he had Cuauhtémoc, the Aztec emperor, tortured in an attempt to obtain the Aztec treasure. Here also he is said to have poisoned his Indian wife, Malinche. Also of interest are the Church of San Juan Bautista (1583), the Dominican monastery (1530), and Casa de Alvarado, home of one of Cortés' aides, now a museum.

Xochimilco (soh-chee-MEEL-coh). Situated about fourteen miles southeast of Mexico City. It was once the home of Aztec nobles, and the Indians still speak Aztec among themselves. Xochimilco is a lake dotted with "floating islands," so called because the islands originally were rafts covered with earth and vegetation. Eventually these became stationary and now seem to be natural islands. Flower-decked boats carry visitors around the waterways. On Sundays the village is at its gayest. The Church of San Bernardino dates from the sixteenth century.

Tlálpam (TLAHL-pahm). About ten miles south of the Zócalo is a suburban town of beautiful homes on the slope of the extinct volcano Mount Ajusco. Of interest is the Church of San Agustín de las Cuevas (1532) with a Churrigueresque altar and paintings by Cabrera.

Pyramid of Cuicuilco (kwee-KWEEL-coh). About one and one-half miles west of Tlálpam is one of the most important archaeological finds ever uncovered, for it is undoubtedly the oldest man-made structure in the Western Hemisphere. Scientists have estimated its age at nine thousand to ten thousand years, certainly more than seven thousand years, which is the approximate length of time since the last eruption of Xitli. The lava that flowed during this eruption engulfed the pyramid to about half its height. Much of the lava has been blasted away, revealing the structure to its foundations. The original pyramid was a truncated cone, 369 feet in diameter and 60 feet high, and was enlarged twice until the diameter was 387 feet.

Chapingo (chah-PEEN-goh). Two miles south of Texcoco is Chapingo, seat of the National Agricultural College. In the main building and chapel are frescoes by Diego Rivera. Two miles southeast is Coatlinchán. From this point a three-mile hike leads to the *Idol of Tlaloc*, rain god of the Toltecs and Aztecs. It weighs several hundred tons and lies face upward in a ravine. It is one of the archaeological mysteries of Mexico. East of Chapingo, at Huexotla, are a great wall and traces of temples and pyramids dating from Aztec days.

Texcoco (tess-COH-coh). This place, located twenty-five miles northeast of Mexico City, was the site of an ancient Aztec kingdom. At the time of the Conquest the waters of Lake Texcoco reached this far, and a tablet at the entrance to town marks the spot where Cortés launched his ships in the siege of the Aztec capital. Five miles east of Texcoco, on top of Texcotzingo Hill, was the summer palace of the Indian king and poet Netzahualcoyotl. The hill was originally laid out in terraces or hanging gardens, with a flight of several hundred steps. Near the top of the hill are two broken idols.

ART AND ARCHITECTURE

Mexicans, being intensely responsive to color and form, have in every age lavished their superlative skill in the plastic arts upon the decoration of their capital city. Nowhere in the Western Hemisphere, probably, is there a city more profusely illustrative of the organic artistic growth of its people. Throughout the colonial epoch the Church gathered to itself those artistic talents that since independence and the Revolution have been given over to the creation of public buildings and their adornment.

In view of the multitude of churches in Mexico City, it is possible to cite here only a very few as examples of the kind of work found. The cathedral is built in the form of a cross with fifteen chapels adjoining the nave and apse. The choir is celebrated for its entrance grille of a special tombac (a gold, silver, and copper alloy), procured from Macao, China, in 1730. Within the choir enclosure are beautifully carved stalls and two organs encased in carved cedar surmounted by sculptured angels. Set against the choir and facing the south entrance doors, the carved gilt retable above the Altar of Pardon is hung with paintings by Baltazar de Echave. Both this retable and that above the Altar of Kings (behind the high altar) are excellent representations of the style originated by the Churriguera family of Salamanca. The Church of El Sagrario, next to the cathedral, is one of three in the capital executed in that same style. Like the retables, it seems the product of a wayward inventiveness, spawning numberless delicate variations of form without stint, almost without order. A façade of the same sort may be seen at La Santísima Trinidad, which is conspicuous for its lantern dome of glazed tiles and red *tezontle;* and two Churriguera altars in the great baroque church of Santo Domingo give an idea of the splendor of the entire building when the Dominican order was at the height of its power. Once among the very richest in a city famous for the wealth of its church, San Agustín has likewise a Mudejar tile-covered dome. In 1867 President Juárez converted the building to the use of the National Library, which he established with the nucleus of collections taken from the university, the cathedral, and other ecclesiastical foundations. It is now directed by the National University, and besides later works in English and in the romance languages it contains early Indian writings, rare books, and paintings concerned with Indian life, and some examples of the first printing in America.

The social revolution that began in Mexico after 1910 brought with it a great flowering of art. In the late twenties and the early thirties of this century a large number of native artists produced an abundance of fresh work in lithography, oils, and especially fresco painting. A few of the frescoes have been mentioned in the description of the capital; these are but a sample of the great outpouring of artistic expression. To foreigners the name of Diego Rivera is most widely known; in Mexico he is one, perhaps the greatest one, of a group of some twenty-five artists that includes such men as José Clemente Orozco, Carlos Mérida, David Alfaro Siqueiros, Jean Charlot, Rufino Tamayo, Fernando Leal, and Francisco Goitia. Rivera's work immediately conveys a sense of energy akin to that of a natural force like water or fire, along with an effortless abundance. The spectator becomes aware that here is a painter who is master of every technique he tries. In his case the framework of Catholicism that served the colonial painters is replaced by a social philosophy reflected in every painting. In Orozco the torment and fervor that imbued the colonial religious painters have been transferred from Catholicism to humanity; again and again the vast sweeping gestures of his subjects indicate a colossal horror and despair. The strength of the new school shows itself in a very wide variety of expression, but there are certain points in common. These men are revolutionists in that they are rebelling against the picturesque and the sentimental of the nineteenth century, and the decorative prettiness of the eighteenth. Theirs is an art of harshness and violence, from which serenity is absent. For their subjects they choose the Mexican people (rarely the Mexican landscape), for their colors they hark back to the reds and yellows and browns of Indian pottery, and their forms, impressive for their solidity and lack of detail, are reminiscent of Aztec sculpture.

Along with the revolution in painting has gone a similar architectural transformation. In 1926 José Villagrán García set out to teach a brilliant group of students in the National Academy the principles of functionalism in architecture. His ideas were carried further by his followers Juan O'Gorman and Juan Legarreta, whose primary purpose was to produce architectural forms that should be adapted to use. Decoration for its own sake, other than color, was excluded, although certain decorative effects incidental to the meeting of planes and the massing of volumes could not be avoided. Such an architecture proved eminently suitable in hospitals, schools, restaurants, and other buildings where it was necessary to accommodate large numbers of people, as well as for low-cost housing developments. In 1935 Juan O'Gorman founded the School of Construction, which treats architecture entirely as a branch of engineering. Meanwhile Legarreta had obtained an appointment as government architect, and for a time during the early 1930's the functional approach was dominant in all official building. Inevitably then reaction set in, and a cry arose that the international characteristics of the new style were driving out all that was distinctively Mexican. By distinctively Mexican the critics referred to the colonial of earlier periods, forgetting that this had itself come into being not as a purely native development, but as a foreign importation. Although the first fervor of the new style has thus received a check, and its use in Mexico City has been largely confined to the southern quarters, its vigor will undoubtedly enable it to survive transient criticism when it achieves its ideal of suitability to local conditions.

EDUCATION

In 1562 the Franciscan Pedro de Gante opened San José de Belén, a school for Indians, in Mexico City. In 1551 the first university to open its doors in America, the Royal Pontifical University, was founded by royal decree, and started functioning two years later. The Colegio de San Ildefonso was started in 1572. These and other early institutions of learning under the patronage of the Church were the beginnings of Mexico's educational system. By the end of the colonial epoch their teaching had become narrow and formalized, and their effectiveness was further dissipated by the troubled times of the nineteenth century.

The revolution that began in 1910 found itself faced with the need to evolve a new theory of education and to bring into existence buildings, equipment, and a trained corps of teachers. Since the country is predominantly agricultural, naturally the greatest effort has been made to teach the rural inhabitants to live better and improve their environment. A parallel endeavor aims at providing opportunities for city dwellers. Two ideas underlie the entire program of urban education. The Ministry of Education, which prescribes the curriculum for practically all schools, both public and private, desires to enable the workers to earn a living; it also intends to guide their choice of careers into those fields that will be most useful to the nation. It tries to avoid the overcrowding of certain careers, especially medicine and the law, and to encourage students to prepare for positions that will eventually develop national raw materials and make Mexico economically more self-sufficient. Care is therefore exercised to place the greatest possible emphasis on the practical rather than the cultural aspect of the courses offered.

City children are expected to undergo six years of primary instruction. Thereafter the student is presented with eight choices, designed to suit the widest possible diversity of economic and psychological conditions. The available types of postprimary school are secondary, military or naval, prevocational, university pre-preparatory, specialized vocational training, agricultural, music and plastic arts, and normal training. It is of course possible to take an unskilled or semiskilled job upon completion of three years of postprimary instruction. The secondary schools, however, each prepare students to take further training in one of the following specialized branches: library work, physical education, nursing, military or naval training, university preparatory, social service, normal training, and agriculture. If instead of attending a secondary school for three years, the student desires to go on to a prevocational institution in Mexico City, he will probably attend one of the schools leading to the Instituto Politécnico Nacional. After three years at prevocational school, where his abilities will have been ascertained by scientific tests, the student may enroll in a course of from four to six years in one of the seven departments of the Polytechnic Institute.

If, on the other hand, the pupil has an academic career in view, after primary school he will first attend the university pre-preparatory school for three years, follow with two years at the Escuela Nacional Preparatoria, and end with two to five years at the Universidad Nacional Autónoma. Although the university is the stronghold of learning in the traditional branches of law, social sciences, medicine, and arts and letters, it also contains departments covering almost all other fields of knowledge. Since 1920 the university has conducted a school for foreigners during six weeks of the summer, and included such subjects as languages, history, education, economics, sociology, and art. The school offers the degree of Master of Arts in Spanish and has effected a mutual arrangement with certain United States universities in regard to the recognition of academic credits.

Plentiful opportunities for study of the fine arts are provided in Mexico City. After primary school, music students may attend either the National Conservatory, the National Music School (connected with the university), or the Night Music School. Art students may receive instruction at the National School of Plastic Arts of the university, or at the Studio School of Plastic Arts of the Ministry of Education. A school of the dance is held in the Palacio de Bellas Artes, and elsewhere a special school is given over to the arts of bookmaking.

All of the numerous learned and cultural societies in Mexico City cannot be mentioned here. The Seminary of Mexican Culture, the International Institute of Iberian and American Literature, and the Athenaeum of Mexican Science and Art all publish literary, artistic, and scholarly reviews. A scientific journal is published by the Antonio Alzate National Academy of Science, and others are published by the Institute of Biology, the Institute of Hygiene, and the Institute of Health and Tropical Diseases; these latter organizations possess laboratories where serums are prepared and research is undertaken, and these are described in their published monographs. The Pan American Institute of Geography and History, of which all the American republics are members, has headquarters in Tacubaya, on the outskirts of Mexico City. It sponsors research expeditions, and besides numerous monographs publishes two reviews, the *Bibliographical Bulletin of American Anthropology* and the *Review of American History*.

SUGGESTIONS

If you are taking your first trip to Mexico, get a guide, for the first few days at least. Licensed guides (employ no other) carry identification and credentials from the Asociación Mexicana de Turismo (Mexican Tourist Association—a federal agency), and their fees are usually 25 pesos (about $5) per day for showing you around the city and slightly more for trips outside. You will be expected to pay for lunch and transportation and, in the case of trips away from the city, their hotel expenses. If you use your own car, get a guide who is a competent driver and leave yourself free to enjoy as much as you can; be sure he has a license to drive, or you may both land in traffic court.

If you have a week to spend in Mexico City and vicinity, then we suggest three days in the capital, two days at Taxco and Cuernavaca, and two days in Puebla and environs. If you can squeeze in another day, then take in Toluca and points en route.

If you have ten days, then a good division of time would be three days in Mexico City, one to Toluca, two in Puebla, and four days for a trip to Acapulco with stopovers in Cuernavaca and Taxco. If there is additional time, the Toluca trip should be extended to Morelia and Pátzcuaro.

The automobile itineraries on page 39 were designed to help you plan your trip before you begin it. If you are traveling by train or bus, use the other information given in Chapter III. In any case, make a schedule and try to follow it. You will find greater satisfaction in the money and time you spend. The following is an example of the way in which you can design your own schedule.

Sunday. This is the best day for the market at Lagunilla, located several blocks north of the Avenida Madero district; everything under the sun is offered for sale, and cheap—but watch out for gyps. Just before noon drive through Chapultepec Park and watch the bridle paths for *charros* in costume. The best time to visit Xochimilco is also Sunday forenoon. Drive out by way of the Viga Canal and Churubusco, take a ride in one of the flower-decked boats, and have lunch from one of the floating "restaurants." There is a fast trolley service direct from the Zócalo on Sunday mornings. Bullfights begin at four P.M. on Sundays, so there is plenty of time for these earlier trips.

Monday. Sight-seeing at museums and about town in the forenoon, with a trip to Guadalupe shrine, Acolman convent, and San Juan Teotihuacán pyramids in the afternoon.

Tuesday. Tlaxcala, Cholula, and Puebla for the night.

Wednesday. Sight-seeing in Puebla during the forenoon and return to Mexico City in the afternoon.

Thursday. Cuernavaca, and Taxco for the night.

Friday. Sight-seeing in Taxco during the forenoon and return to Mexico City in the afternoon.

Saturday. Cover any places missed on Monday, or make a trip to Tenayuca Pyramid and Tepotzotlán Convent, or the Desierto de los Leones. The latter place could be visited en route to Toluca. However, if you plan to visit Toluca try to arrange your trip on a Friday, as this is the big market day of the week.

For more details covering the above places, see the index.

TRAFFIC REGULATIONS

Mexican traffic regulations are, generally speaking, the same as in the United States. It is obligatory that brakes be in good working condition and that car be equipped with horn, speedometer, muffler, rear-view mirror, and tool kit.

Arm signals for turns are the same as those specified in California and New York traffic regulations. To make turns when there is an officer on duty, wait for his signal. Wherever you find the word *siga* painted on the pavement alongside the curb, it means you can turn right on a red light.

Avenida (Avenue), *Calle* (Street), *Calzada* or the abbreviation *Calz.* (Boulevard), *Camino* (Road), and *Carretera* (Highway) are words you will see on street, and highway signs. *Tránsito* (Traffic), when shown on an arrow on corners of buildings or painted on the pavement, show direction of traffic. Mexico City has numerous one-way streets—look for the arrow at the corner, usually high up on the side of a building.

Note that the same street may change its name every few blocks. Some streets have as many as five names. The equestrian statue of Charles IV (locally called *El Caballito*—the Little Horse), located in the circle or *glorieta* where Avenida Juárez and the Paseo de la Reforma join, is the geographic and traffic center of Mexico City. The traffic flow around the statue is fairly easy to understand.

However, it is difficult to explain satisfactorily the traffic in the Zócalo. Our advice is to avoid the Zócalo until someone has put you wise to its complicated system. It is easy to cross if you are leaving the city for Puebla, for instance. Enter the Zócalo from Madero and cross it between the cathedral and the park. You will note three lanes of traffic: the left is for Avenida Argentina (running north from the Zócalo toward Guadalupe, Teotihuacán pyramids, and Laredo); the middle lane for Moneda and Emiliano Zapata (continuing east from the Zócalo—the Puebla road); and the right lane for the Palacio and circling the Zócalo. If you hit this latter lane, circle the Zócalo and make the correct exit lane on your return.

If you employ a chauffeur, be sure that he has a license to drive, or both he and you may be fined.

When you park in the downtown section of Mexico City you will be approached by a *cuidador,* or one who looks after parked cars. It is well to pay a small tip for this service.

When leaving the city for any outside trip, study a map (highway map sources are listed on the map in the envelope in the back of the book). Usually a route can be found leaving the city without passing by or through the Zócalo and the congested downtown traffic. Below are the principal exit routes.

Laredo Road (Pan American Highway north). From the downtown district, take Avenida Argentina north from the east side of the Zócalo; the name changes to Avenida Carranza after a few blocks. From the Reforma district, take Calle Ramón Guzmán (a continuation of Avenida Insurgentes) north from the Paseo de la Reforma; the name changes to Mejia after a few blocks, then jogs left and right to become Calle Encino.

Puebla Road (eastbound for Puebla, Veracruz, or Amecameca). From the downtown district, take Avenida Moneda running east from the cathedral; the name changes to Emiliano Zapata after a couple of blocks. From the Reforma district, Hotel Geneve, and Hotel Waldorf, take Avenida Chapultepec (passing the Waldorf) to Arcos de Belém to San Juan Letrán; turn right on the latter street to Cuauhtemotzin; turn left and continue out to Calzada Balbuena; turn left and follow Balbuena to the first right turn around the park; when you have passed the park you will be on the Puebla road.

Taxco Road (southbound for Cuernavaca and Acapulco). From the downtown district, take the narrow street (Cinco de Febrero) beginning at the southwest corner of the Zócalo and continue south to Calzada de Chimalpopoca, and thence left to San Antonio Abad, then right. The latter street later becomes Calzada de Tlálpam and then the road to Cuernavaca. From the Reforma district, take Avenida Insurgentes and follow it all the way out.

Toluca Road (westbound for Morelia, Pátzcuaro, and Guadalajara). Follow the Paseo de la Reforma west to its end, turn left into Calzada Tacubaya, then shortly bear right along the south edge of Chapultepec Park. Or you can take the right fork at the end of La Reforma and pass through the park and the exclusive residential section of Lomas de Chapultepec (Chapultepec Heights).

Tepotzotlán Road (northwest to Tlalnepantla and Tenayuca Pyramid). From the downtown district, follow Avenida Hidalgo west along the Alameda park; the name changes to Avenida Alvarado, then Avenida San Cosme, then Calzada Mexico Tacuba; continue through Tacuba on main traffic lines. Or, also from the downtown district, drive north from the Alameda on Avenida Serdan (on the east side of the Palacio de Bellas Artes), and thence into Santa María la Redonda, then left and right into Avenida Lerdo. From the Reforma district take any street north to Calzada Mexico Tacuba, turn left, and continue with main traffic lanes.

TRAVEL AGENCIES

Your local travel agent or transportation company office, or the
Travel Division of the Pan American Union in Washington, D.C.,
will assist you with your travel plans, and you may find that they
have a correspondent or office in Mexico City to give you further
service on arrival there. Many people are under the impression that
for assistance given them by travel agents there is an additional
charge. Travel agencies make their money on the 10- or 15-per-cent
commission they receive from the transportation companies, hotels,
resorts, and sight-seeing companies. There is no charge for their
service, and your ticket should cost you no more or less when purchased through a licensed travel agency than if you bought it at the
transportation company's office. Travel agents base their recom-
mendations on the time at the traveler's disposal, with due regard
to the traveler's desires in the matter of expenditures. Furthermore,
travel agents relieve their clients of much work in attending to a
number of formalities in connection with tourist cards and other essential documents, assisting with baggage, language problems, hotel
reservations, currency problems, and shopping suggestions. This, of
course, applies to your home-town agency. There may be some var-
iance in this practice when you buy service from a travel agency
in Mexico City, since many of them are not agencies but actual
transportation companies. Be sure to ask for published rates and
never accept only a verbal quotation for any travel service.

Formerly, new travel agencies blossomed with every spring in
Mexico City, and like the flowers they died when the frost of off
season hit them in the autumn. A few old, long-established offices
like Wagon Lits–Cook and Wells Fargo stayed on and have continued to prosper. But it was only after the government began to
take an interest in the tourist business that the annual crop of mush-
room offices gave way to more reliable concerns. We cannot vouch
for all of the following, or that all of them will still be in business
when you need their services, but as of January 1948, these were
among the best of those authorized by the federal government.

Aguirre's Guest Tours, Cinco de Mayo 805.

Albertsen–López Mexico Guest Tours, Avenida Madero 73 (Hotel Majestic 510-A).

Cartan Travel Bureau, Paris 21 (across from Hotel Reforma).

Central de Hoteles y Turismo, Avenida Morelos 45, Room 306.

David Velasco Travel Service, at Hotels Majestic and Ontario.

De la Paz Travel Bureau, Iturbide 18 (in the lobby of Hotel de la Paz).

Garza Travel Service, Londres 118.

Geneve Travel Bureau, Londres 130 (in lobby of Hotel Geneve).

Inter American Travel Service, Avenida Niños Heroes 139 (Hotel Posada del Sol).

Mexican Travel Association, Cinco de Mayo 23 (fifth floor, Room 7).

Oxford Travel Bureau, Ignacio Mariscal 155.

Pan American Travel Service, Arcos de Belem 73; and Avenida Chapultepec 316.

Ramírez Sightseeing Tours & Travel Bureau, Danubio 39.

Reforma Travel Bureau, in Reforma Hotel lobby.

Regis Travel Service, Avenida Juárez 77.

Sita (Society for International Travel), Niza 50 (Office 207, second floor).

Victory Tours De Luxe Travel Service, Paris 21 (across from Hotel Reforma).

Wagon Lits–Cook, Avenida Juárez 88.

Wells Fargo & Co. Express, Madero 14.

HOTELS AND APARTMENTS

Hotel and apartment rates in Mexico City fluctuate very little from season to season, but they have experienced a general and gradual rise since 1940. Even so, most rates are still about 10 per cent lower than they are in the United States for the same accommodations and service. In line with the government policy to do everything possible to increase tourist trade, many hotels reduced their rates late in 1947. However, some of these had been guilty of gouging and deserve no halos for their saintliness. The government and the AMH (Asociación Mexicana de Hoteles) exercises some control over prices and quality of service, and rates are supposed to be posted in every room, but to avoid misunderstanding ask the rate when you register. If you plan a long stay it is also customary to ask to see the room.

You should experience no difficulty through changing rates, but the quality of the service and accommodations do change. Once we wrote a friend highly recommending a hotel at which we had enjoyed a pleasant and comfortable week. A year later our friend went to Mexico and, entirely on our advice, stopped at that hotel. He was awakened during the night by a light knock on his door, which, when opened, disclosed a pretty *mujer del calle* looking for a "customer." Fortunately for our own reputation, he discovered the next day that the hotel had changed hands since our visit the previous year and the new *propietario* was less impeccable than his predecessor.

Mexico City is one of the world's large cities, and like all great metropolises it has many hotels and many kinds of hotel service. It would be difficult (and risky!) to recommend any one hotel in such a city, even if we knew your financial circumstances. Our safest ground, therefore, is to give you a list of those we feel reasonably sure will pass a fair inspection. The rate and location, then, should be the factors determining your choice. Hotels that are members of the Asociación Mexicana de Hoteles are indicated by (AMH), and members of the American Automobile Association by (AAA). Although the latter membership does imply merit, we know from experience that membership in the AMH does not always guarantee satisfactory accommodations. The listing here, whether or not the establishment is a member of one of these organizations, is approval after our personal inspection or the recent recommendation of other travelers.

The rates shown in the table below (in Mexican pesos) are based on the European plan, or rooms without meals, unless otherwise specified. These are daily rates; weekly and monthly rates frequently offer considerable savings. *Pensiones* or *casas de asistencia* (boardinghouses), inexpensive apartments, and furnished rooms are advertised (often in English) in the classified advertisement sections of the Mexico City daily press and the various free weekly tourist publications.

Among the following hotels the newest is the Hotel Prince, located in the downtown district. It opened in 1947. The massive new Hotel Prado, whose opening was postponed many times because of delays in construction, was finally scheduled to open in January

Name	Address	Single	Double	Rooms
Altamira Apts. (AMH)	Independencia 101	$16–35	$35–45	30
Avenida (AMH)	San Juan de Letrán 38	8–14	11–20	70
Belpra (AMH)	Ponciano Arriaga 22	8–10	15–20	21
Bernal Díaz	Bernal Díaz 19	10–14	12–16	
Calvín	José Azueta 33	20–30	30–40	28
Canada and Annex	Cinco de Mayo 47	6–15	12–30	200
Carlton (AMH)	Ignacio Mariscal 132	10–25	30–45	100
Casa Blanca	García Lorca 7	6–12	10–14	57
Casa del Viajero	Basilio Badillo 34	20–30	25–40	44
Castilla	Uruguay 12	7–11	14–20	130
Castle View Apts. (AMH)	Ganges 44	15–25	30–45	14
Cuba Apt. Hotel	Cuba 69	15–25	20–35	40
Chapultepec (AMH)	Ave. Chapultepec 171	15–20	25–35	50
Danky (AMH)	Donato Guerra 10	10–50	15–50	25
De Cortés (AMH)	Ave. Hidalgo 85	15–37	25–42	26
De la Paz (AMH)	Iturbide 18	15–25	22–35	60
De Soto Arms (AMH)	Ramón Guzmán 96	15–20	25–50	30
Edison Mo-Tel	Calle Edison 106	10–12	12–15	38
Emporio (AMH)	Paseo de la Reforma 124	15–25	20–30	65
Fidelia Apts. (AMH)	Glorieta de los Insurgentes 473		600	20
Fornos	Revillagigedo 92	8– 8	12–16	50
Fortín	Sahagun 28	8– 9	12–14	40
Geneve (AMH)(AAA)	Londres 130	12–20	36–42	450
Gillow (AMH)	Isabel la Católica 17	10–18	20–40	150
Guadalupe Courts (AMH)	Arequipa 918, Tepeyac, Insurgentes		From 10	12
Guardiola (AMH)	Ave. Madero 5	12–35	16–45	75
Hipodromo	Insurgentes 287	8– 9	10–14	40
Hollywood Apts. (AAA)	Calle Edison 51	12–18	14–20	20

Name	Address	Single	Double	Rooms
Hunter (AMH)	Villalongín 12	$10–15	$18–20	28
Isabel (AMH)	Isabel la Católica 63	7–12	10–18	70
La Joya Apts.	Balderas 90	8–10		14
L'Escargot (AMH)	Filadelfia y Oklahoma	15–25	20–40	33
Lincoln (AMH)	Revillagigedo 24	15–20	25–30	100
Los Angeles Courts	Insurgentes 786		10–18	22
Luma	Orizaba 16	30–60	30–70	100
Majestic (AMH)	Ave. Madero 73	18–25	25–35	100
Mancera	Venustiano Carranza 49	7–20	10–28	54
María Cristina (AMH)	Lerma 31	18–25	20–30	100
Mil Flores	Calle Cano 22	10 Up, American plan		14
Montecarlo (AMH)	Uruguay 69	5–8	10–16	70
Montejo (AMH) (AAA)	Paseo de la Reforma 240	16–23	16–29	60
Ontario (AMH)	Uruguay 87	14–18	30–35	88
Oxford	Ignacio Mariscal 155	15–20	25–30	100
Palace Apts. (AMH)	Gómez Farías 6	40–50	50–60	10
Pánuco	Ayuntamiento 148	7–12	12–15	70
Paris Mansión	Paseo de la Reforma 119	10–20	12–25	30
Polanco	Edgar Allan Poe 8	16–18	20–24	50
Polly Apartments (AMH)	Zaragoza y Orozco	19	30	30
Posada de San Ángelo (AMH)	Pl. del Carmen 17, San Ángel		20–30	20
Posada del Sol	Ave. Niños Heroes 139	18–25	25–35	450
Prince	Luis Moya 12	18–36	28–45	150
Reforma (AMH)	Paris y Paseo de la Reforma	25–50	45–55	250
Regis (AMH)	Avenida Juárez 77	10–18	15–30	300
Ritz (AMH) (AAA)	Avenida Madero 30	14–24	24–34	150
Roosevelt (AMH)	Ave. Insurgentes 287	25–35	30–45	100
San Ángel Inn (AMH)	Palmas 50, Villa Álvaro Obregón		From 10	14

Name	Address	Single	Double	Rooms
Shirley Courts (AMH) (AAA)	Villalongín 139	$12–16	$10–18	50
Tivoli (AMH)	Ramón Guzmán 6			11
Toledo (AMH)	López 22	From 90	14–20	35
Vendome (AMH)	Balsas 37		From 90	
Waldorf	Calle Chapultepec 316	15–25	25–30	80
Washington Apts. (AMH)	Plaza Dinamarca 42	17	50	35
Windsor (AAA)	Santa Veracruz 67	20–30	20–45	113

1948. It is near the heart of the business and shopping district, on Avenida Juárez, facing Alameda Park, close to the Palace of Fine Arts. Its managing director told the writer that rates for many of his hotel's six hundred rooms and fifty suites will be less than those now being charged by other first-class hotels in Mexico City.

CHAPTER VI

COLONIAL GEMS

THE principal scenic interests in Mexico are architectural. They can be divided into three distinct classifications. They are the strange and mysterious ruined temples built by the civilizations that inhabited the country before the arrival of the Spaniards; the colonial churches, palaces, and homes that were superimposed on the land by the Spanish conquerors; and the functional skyscrapers and ornate homes of modern Mexico. Of them all, perhaps the most picturesque and understandable are the colonial gems, varying from Churrigueresque to Gothic in architecture, found in nearly every city, town, and village. By the fortunate circumstance of location, climate, or natural resources, some of these are lavish expressions of their builders. Many have been enriched by historical association, and time has mellowed them all. For the traveler earnestly desirous of visiting the best and getting the most out of Mexico, we suggest a trip to one or more of the following colonial towns. This chapter is intended to be an intimate guide to the principal points of interest in those selected few that, in our opinion, offer the greatest pleasure in picturesque colonial treasures. Other information, such as facts on transportation and hotels, is included in Chapter VIII, page 167. Detailed itineraries of the routes are given in Chapter III (airways and railways) and Chapter IV (highways).

CUERNAVACA

For centuries previous to the conquest of Mexico, the ancient Tlahuicas prospered in Cuauhnahuac, on the site of what is now Cuernavaca. They developed a high civilization, erecting pyramids

115

and palatial dwellings, vestiges of which remain today as testimonials of their skill and ingenuity.

After bloody fighting the Tlahuicas succumbed to Cortés, the Spanish conqueror, who went on to Tenochtitlán, the capital of the Aztecs, which he took in 1521. In gratitude for his achievements, the king of Spain granted Cortés the greater part of the state of Morelos, and in 1530 he returned to Cuauhnahuac to assert his rights over his lands and subjects. Cuauhnahuac became Cuernavaca because the Spaniards found difficulty in pronouncing the Indian name. Cortés introduced the *encomienda* system, a type of economic organization similar to the feudal system. Friars followed the sword with the cross. The conquerors introduced Christianity, colonial architecture, sugar cane, silkworms, new handicraft techniques, and new ways of mastering the land.

The epic saga of the Spanish invasion lives on today in the many buildings, palaces, churches, aqueducts, and mills dating from the sixteenth century that may still be seen in Cuernavaca and its environs.

But the period of Spanish domination and construction was also one of oppression. Its progress was stained with the blood of stoic, resentful Indians who bore the brunt of a civilization in which they could not share. During the colonization, anger seethed but was repressed. In 1810 it boiled over in a revolutionary flood. In the region around Cuernavaca, José María Morelos was the outstanding leader in the fight for freedom. Cuernavaca, like the rest of Mexico, experienced the lightning shifts from independence to monarchy, anarchy, dictatorship, reformism, and constitutionalism. The brief reign of Carlota and Maximilian left a memorable imprint on Cuernavaca, for it was here that the puppet monarchs of the French intervention spent the few happy hours of their ill-fated Mexican careers.

Palace of Cortés. Cortés built a palatial mansion with beautifully decorated salons, galleries, and gardens, the splendor of which was a symbol of his own magnificence. Though the interior has changed, the imposing exterior of the palace has remained intact and is a good example of early colonial architecture. The Diego Rivera murals that occupy an outdoor wall on the rear veranda were the $10,000 gift of the late United States ambassador Morrow. They provide a striking comment on the Conquest by one of Mexico's great painters.

Cathedral. The Cathedral of Cuernavaca, the oldest in America, has been altered little in the four hundred years since its construction. The ancient, weather-beaten structure, with its high tower and low dome, was built for military as well as for religious purposes. Its grim, massive lines suggestive of a medieval fort and the naïve stamp of Indian decoration are typical of early Franciscan architecture.

The first Franciscan monks arrived in Cuernavaca in 1529 and in that same year began building the Monastery and Chapel of San José. Open-air mass was held from the roof of the latter for thousands of Indian converts, and it was in this very chapel that Cortés himself attended mass.

Pagan Mexico and Christian Spain meet on the charming façade of the Chapel of the Third Order, a sixteenth-century chapel decorated with native plant and animal designs in the primitive style.

Borda Gardens. When José de la Borda, in the early days of the eighteenth century, had amassed a fortune estimated at forty million pesos, he built a mansion in Cuernavaca in the ornate classic style. It was a tropical Versailles that Marie Antoinette herself might have enjoyed. The clear waters of two exquisite pools reflected the white of graceful swans. In the patterns of a formal garden, fruits and flowers spilled their radiance over ordered paths. When Carlota and Maximilian visited the place in 1864 they were enchanted with its elegance and beauty. It became the imperial residence during a period of regal splendor, gay parties, French fetes and masques. The Empress Carlota and the ladies of her court swam in the tepid waters of the artificial lake. Only a little of the original splendor remains today, but the Borda Gardens are worth a visit.

Hotels and Living. The Cuernavaca hotels range in architecture from remodeled sixteenth-century convents and mansions to modern, up-to-date edifices. Some of the older buildings retain their original woodwork, stone masonry, and tiling. Interiors are variously decorated and the style may be colonial, modern Mexican, California Spanish, or modern. They provide generally good accommodations and service. Some have inner gardens, swimming pools, private baths, European and American cuisine, and room telephone service.

Two recently constructed hotels are located a brief distance from the center of town in the midst of rolling country; they are equipped with tennis courts, swimming pools, and facilities for all outdoor sports, including horseback riding.

The Country Club, to which the manager of your hotel may secure your temporary admission, was built by a group of residents to provide a social and recreational center. Its tiled bar, graceful ballroom, and airy rooms have a cosmopolitan atmosphere that is at once elegant and simple, reminiscent of the more select casinos of the French Riviera. The swimming pools are set in floral arbors and the well-laid-out golf course is popular with golf enthusiasts. The club is a meeting place for visitors and for the international set that has taken up permanent residence in Cuernavaca. There is also much informal entertaining within the gardens and salons of the many elegant private homes. The sidewalk tables of the Continental-style cafés that line the plazas provide another popular rendezvous.

Since it is possible to live in Cuernavaca on a limited income, a steadily growing foreign colony is spending several months of the year or establishing permanent homes in Cuernavaca. The village and its environs offer many varied attractions. There are hunting, fishing, golfing, hiking, and swimming. There are numerous archaeological and historic sites, and the flora of the region is a botanist's delight. The importance of doing nothing becomes apparent in Cuernavaca, where a stroll through the streets or an afternoon idling in the plaza is its own excuse for living. See page 181 for a complete list of hotels and their rates.

Market and Crafts. The market place is busy and colorful. Gay stalls of fruit, flowers, vegetables, fish, and meat mingle with displays of brilliant native basketry and serapes. Gaily painted rush-bottom chairs, terra-cotta pottery the color of the sun-baked earth, and huaraches are typical local handicrafts. The Indians come to market on burro and on foot, emerging from the mountains with heavy burdens of native produce.

Excursions Near By. Forty minutes' drive from Cuernavaca at the base of high granite mountains lies the primitive, unspoiled village of Tepoztlán. On the crest of a peak overhanging the village is the Pyramid of Tepozteco, built centuries before the advent of the Spaniards, in honor of Ometotochtli, the god of pulque. A two-hour climb through dense foliage leads to the summit, from which the Spaniards once hurled his image. When the idol did not break, the monks destroyed it with hammers. Only then did the simple villagers accept the credo of the conquerors and the destruction of their own pagan divinity.

Oaxtepec is another village in this region. The many clear springs and streams watering the town, the sixteenth-century church in the foundations of which is embedded a fragment of Ometotochtli's image, and the vestiges of an ancient Aztec botanical garden endow Oaxtepec with a unique and special charm.

Xochicalco, or "The House of Flowers," is a short drive from Cuernavaca. It consists of the remains of a fortified town and a mysterious pyramid decorated with sitting priests encoiled by the symbolic serpents of the Aztecs. The subterranean passages beneath it still bear traces of the paintings that once adorned them.

The Pyramid of Teopanzolco is a five-minute drive from Cuernavaca. The deep ravine separating the pyramid from the town divides the ancient from the modern culture. The view from Teopanzolco's summit is not much changed from that which pagan priests once gazed upon. From the summit one may gaze miles eastward to the imposing snow-capped volcanoes that dominate the valley, Popocatépetl and Iztaccíhuatl.

Ten minutes from the center of Cuernavaca is the San Antón Waterfall. The falls drop one hundred feet over a sharp declivity, forming a deep pool before continuing on through a gorge. A walk cut into the rock behind the falls enables one to see them from behind. Wild orchids cling to the perpendicular trees whose roots pierce the surrounding boulders.

On a ledge above the waterfall is the tiny potters' village of San Antón, where the fine skill of pottery making has been handed down from father to son for generations.

When Maximilian wearied of the gaieties of the Borda Gardens, he found seclusion at Acapacingo, a short distance from the imperial residence in Cuernavaca. A quaint chapel surrounded by flowering trees faces the tiled gateway of this rural retreat, which bears the inscription "Antigua Casa del Emperador Maximiliano."

Cortés planted the first sugar cane grown in America and established the first American refinery at Tlaltenango, two miles from Cuernavaca. Part of the aqueduct constructed to bring water to the mill can still be seen. An inscription on it reads: "Hernán Cortés, Conqueror of the great Tenochtitlán."

By contrast near-by Zacatepec is one of the most modern sugar refineries in the world and symbolizes the achievements of the new Mexico. It was established with government financing and is co-operatively run by Mexican workers.

Las Estacas is located on the Yautepec River about thirty miles from Cuernavaca. The royal palms, mangoes, oranges, limes, and aguacates with which the place is overgrown make it an idyllic picnic spot.

The seven lakes of Zempoala are set in rugged mountains back of Cuernavaca at 10,000 feet above sea level. The nearest lake is a forty-minute drive from Cuernavaca. The air is crisp with the clean fragrance of pines, *ocotes*, herbs, and wild flowers. This alpine region of Mexico is an excellent site for brief or extended fishing and camping trips.

During the dry season it is sometimes possible to see the belfry of the sunken cathedral in the mysterious waters of Lake Tequesquitengo, an hour's drive from Cuernavaca in the opposite direction from the Zempoala Lakes. This spot is noted for large-mouth bass, dove, quail, and deer.

Chapultepec Springs with its icy swimming pool, lush foliage, and old Cortés aqueduct is enjoyable for a day's outing in the sun.

The Cacahuamilpa Caves contain a series of domes and palaces wrought by nature to rival the architectural achievements of the Indians and Spaniards. The endless labyrinth has been only partially explored. More than fifty forms of stalactites and stalagmites, among them the "Tule Tree," which is some 217 feet high, achieve strange decorative effects in this mansion under the earth. Two streams flowing from beneath the caves unite at their entrance to form the Amacuzac River.

Cuautla is an hour's distance from Cuernavaca on the way to Puebla. The red *tavachin* trees that line its main streets are symbolic of the city's bloody past. Zapata's body is interred in Cuautla, and many crucial battles of the Revolution were waged here. Today the town is a peaceful, sunny resort mainly noted for its warm sulphur baths.

In sunny Yautepec village on the Cuernavaca–Cuautla road Cortés established the first silkworm industry in the Western Hemisphere. Today its partially explored pre-Columbian ruins constitute Yautepec's main attraction for travelers.

GUADALAJARA

Guadalajara was founded in 1530 by Spanish aristocrats and adventurous nobles, who built palatial residences and cultivated the refined customs and traditions of the motherland. Established originally as a base for exploration and conquest on the west coast, it soon outgrew its rival, Santiago de Compostela. It was from this severely religious yet gay and worldly community that some of the founding fathers of the California missions went forth to convert the heathens in the North American wilderness.

A few years after Guadalajara was settled, it was made the capital of a rich and fertile region long known as the Kingdom of New Galicia. The city thrived and prospered, and by 1810 its population had reached sixty thousand. During the following decades Guadalajara suffered the desolation and stagnation of the War of Independence, but with peace, prosperity returned. With the appearance of the first American locomotive on April 16, 1888, the city's importance as a commercial and industrial center was assured. Since then it has followed a steady line of progress, but it has never outgrown its charming Old World atmosphere.

History has laid a gentler hand on Guadalajara than on most Mexican cities, permitting it to pursue its own aristocratic, slightly remote destiny, an island of culture and tranquillity in a land of abrupt changes.

Location. Guadalajara is one of the cleanest, brightest, and most healthful of Mexican cities. It is located 428 miles (by highway) northwest of Mexico City at an elevation of 5,000 feet. Capital of the state of Jalisco, it is the second largest city in Mexico with a population of 255,000. It is a trade and rail center, and, as the terminal of the Southern Pacific west-coast route, is a natural stopover for visitors traveling to Mexico City from that direction.

Climate. Spring is the predominant season in Guadalajara, but there is nearly always sparkling sunlight and a fresh, invigorating tang in the air. The climate varies little throughout the year. Because of its climate, the city is becoming known as a health resort, for the atmosphere is exceptionally dry from September to June.

April and May are warm but the remainder of the year is generally delightful.

Main Plaza. The main plaza is a parklike promenade in the center of the city, flanked by the mellow old buildings of the Government Palace and cathedral and by adjacent arcades where regional candies, drinks, knickknacks, and handicrafts are displayed. Ancient, odorous orange trees weave a green and gold border around the square, which is laid out as an old-fashioned garden. Frequently in the evenings a military band plays popular Mexican music.

Elements of Spanish, Moorish, and Hellenic architecture form a curious blend in the old Government Palace, constructed in 1643. The loopholes and fortress-like windows were built to withstand a siege, and its carvings, finely adorned clock towers, grillework, and iron balconies have a graceful airy lightness. It was in this building that Hidalgo conceived and wrote part of his famous Declaration of Independence, and fittingly enough, as one ascends the central stairway, it is the figure of Hidalgo that one notices first in the mural background that Orozco has so magnificently painted.

Cathedral. The bizarre Cathedral of Guadalajara is the most outstanding example of the transitional style of architecture in the republic. Begun in 1618, it has undergone a series of subsequent reconstructions lasting through three centuries that has resulted in a building that includes Gothic, Tuscan, Arabic, Mudejar, Corinthian, Byzantine, and Doric features. The combined effect achieves an unexpected harmony that is extravagant, sumptuous, and strange.

Church of Santa Mónica. This graceful little church is unique. The carved stone grapes of the elaborately decorated façade have been warmed by centuries of Guadalajara sun to a rich heavy voluptuousness.

Museum and Public Library. The museum and library are housed in an ancient seminary building that, constructed in 1700, is one of the finest examples of architecture of this period on the American continent. This old building, with its long, tranquil lines, has a secret, elusive beauty. In the flowering arched patio where ancient trees and shrubs weave a fragrance of the past are several Indian carvings and sculptures of pre-Conquest Mexico. Here in the late afternoons, beneath time-stained arches, gather the elderly wise men of the town to discuss life, letters, and politics. With typical Guadalajaran graciousness they invite the passing visitor to join a discussion that is often learned and brilliant, thus affording the traveler a treasured insight into one of the most refined and typical of local pastimes, the fine art of conversation.

The museum itself contains a collection of outstanding Spanish and Mexican paintings, as well as a fine display of popular arts and regional costumes.

Church and Garden of San Francisco. Thousands of birds have built their nests in the ancient nooks and crannies of San Francisco's moss-covered towers. The bustling modern thoroughfare below provides an interesting contrast to this mid-sixteenth-century church, in the richly carved façade of which is embedded the finest of early Spanish craftsmanship. The dreamy, Old World garden on which the church faces is a charming reminder of Guadalajara's gracious past.

Church of Our Lady of Aranzazu. The medieval atmosphere that pervades many of the Guadalajara churches is most strikingly revealed in the Church of Our Lady. Its curious old belfry bears the weight of more than three centuries, and the whole building appears to brood darkly over a past at once beautiful and grim.

Penitentiary. Guadalajarans consider their modern fortress-like penitentiary one of the most notable sights of the city. The enormous structure appears to have been designed to accommodate the entire community, should occasion arise.

Temple of San Agustín. Facing the Degollado Theater is a sturdy, ancient edifice whose single nave rises from a quaint, groined arch of seventeenth-century workmanship. The massive, impressive architecture of the Temple of San Agustín is typical of the city's older structures.

Santuario de San José de Gracia. A brilliant red sandstone belfry and a gleaming blue and white tiled Mudejar dome rise above the severe façade of San José. The interior, richly decorated with gold leaf, silver-plated columns, and an elaborate main altar, reflects the sumptuous splendor of this colonial city.

Church of Jesús María. A stone-paved atrium bordered by fragrant orange trees leads to this attractive church, the entrances to which are adorned with quaintly carved stone figures. The church is dedicated to the much venerated "Most Holy Virgin of the Thunderbolt," who, during a terrific thunderstorm in the year 1807, was seen to move from her accustomed position, smile, and wink one eye, thus saving the church from destruction by lightning.

San Felipe, Sanctuary of Our Lady of Guadalupe. The combination of Carmelite belfries, remarkable buttresses, unique façade, modern French dome, and Spanish simplicity of the main structure of Our Lady of Guadalupe produces a curious effect.

Mexicaltzingo Church. This unpretentious Indian church facing the market place is favored by the native population, which feels more at home in its simple, time-worn interior than in the more imposing churches of the town.

Here barefoot Indians wrapped in brightly colored serapes and blue *rebozos* throng the aisles, bringing their humble offerings of field flowers and little corn cakes to San Juan Bautista, to whom the church is dedicated.

Market and Crafts. The Indian Market of Mexicaltzingo has the choicest fruits and flowers of the region—golden papayas, blood-red pomegranates, and all the luscious tropical fruits of the near-by Oblatos Canyon are here in abundance. There are huge piles of gleaming pottery, delicate handmade lace and linens, blue hand-blown glassware, clay toys, dolls, and amusingly painted animals from the near-by potters' villages and huge painted vases.

Mural Art. Clemente Orozco is one of Mexico's famous mural painters. For four years this one-armed artist secluded himself from the world, creating a vast series of panels and domes in Guadalajara's most important public buildings. As a result, painters and art lovers are beginning to make pilgrimages to Guadalajara in order to study and admire some of the greatest fresco painting of modern times.

The decoration of the huge dome of the University of Guadalajara deals with the universal character of man, depicting him as sage, constructor, dialectician, creator, and rebel. Orozco has treated this classic theme in the grand tradition of the greatest painters of all time, with painting that is novel and audacious yet solidly traditional. The wall of the main lecture hall in the same building contains a brilliant, incisive mural denouncing false educators.

The Hospicio is an Orozco triumph in a completely different vein. It is more restrained, less tragic, and more decorative than the work in the other Guadalajara buildings. The panels, painted in clear, fresh colors, deal with the epic subject of Mexico's early history and with episodes from the life of Bishop Cabañas, founder of the Hospicio. The great dome takes for its theme the merging of the four natural elements; the flaming central Promethean character is surrounded by four magnificently painted figures representing Fire, Water, Earth, and Air.

As one enters the seventeenth-century Government Palace of Guadalajara and stands at the foot of the stairway, the enormous head of the patriot-priest Hidalgo looms out of the curved upper wall. Hidalgo is the central figure of a vast fresco that depicts contemporary religion, militarism, betrayal, and the homeless refugees of the world.

Hotels. When the visitor enters the doorways of most Guadalajara hotels, he steps back three centuries into the aristocratic splendor of colonial Mexico. Nevertheless, they generally offer good service and cuisine, private baths, Simmons beds, and room telephone service. (For a complete list of hotels, see page 184.)

Excursions Near By. From Guadalajara the visitor may undertake numerous interesting trips ranging from half-day to four-day excursions.

Twenty minutes from the center of town the ground drops precipitously two thousand feet, as though a broad knife had cut a gash in the earth. This is Barranca de Oblatos. A turbulent river flows beneath large overhanging rocks at the bottom of the canyon, and midway between the river and the plateau the almost vertical earth is divided into flourishing patches of cultivated land. Fruits that could not be grown in the higher altitude of the plain above thrive on these miniature farms. The gorge is like a brilliant cornucopia of tropical fruits.

A half hour out of Guadalajara rise the arresting spires of seventeenth-century Zapotán. The unusual plateresque façade of the church for which the suburb is famous has an Old World grace. The brilliant dome is decorated in the Mudejar style with colored tiles formed into a Greek key pattern. In the flagged atrium of the church Indians from throughout the state gather on October 4 each year to perform primitive dances at a solemn religious fiesta and to sell their fine handicrafts.

The picturesque ancient potters' village of San Pedro Tlaquepaque is twenty minutes from Guadalajara. Here, in factories that are really the patios of private homes, one may watch Mexico's finest pottery being made.

The old Indian capital of Tonalá is another center of fine pottery making. Tonalá and Tlaquepaque are noted for their blue-gray and buff tableware adorned with finely drawn designs and for their natural terra-cotta pottery decorated in flower and animal motifs. Charming vases, toys, animals, and figurines are also made in Tonalá. In this sleepy village young and old bend their heads to the wheel.

For over three centuries the old Spanish town of Tequila has maintained its precarious position on the edge of a ravine down which clear, tumultuous waters rush. This charming rural village, an hour's drive from Guadalajara, is finely flavored by tradition and liquor, for it is the original home of Mexico's national maguey drink, the famous, hard-hitting tequila.

Chapala, the largest and one of the loveliest of Mexican lakes, is thirty miles distant from Guadalajara on the boundary between Jalisco and Michoacán. Its perpetual Indian-summer climate provides a winter haven for Mexicans, foreigners, and an international assortment of wild fowl. Chapala is the fisherman's, huntsman's, and bird lover's paradise. Ducks float on the water's surface and sandpipers skim the banks of small lagoons. The Santiago River, which issues from the lake, is alive with great blue herons, reddish egrets, and mallards.

From Chapala the traveler may visit many of the Indian villages situated on the shores of the lake. In the little fishing ports of Jocotepec, La Palma, Ajijic, and Tizapán life maintains its tranquil, dignified pre-Conquest rhythm. Each has its stretch of white sandy beach that serves as a harbor, its main street, and its fleet of time-stained fishing smacks.

The small island of Mezcala, a few miles from Chapala village, is of special interest to visitors because of its historic background. For five years during the War of Independence it withstood the attack of powerful royalist forces and later served as an isolated penal colony. Now an ancient caretaker and his wife are the sole occupants of the castle-like ruin that still clings valiantly to the crest of a hill.

Just off the road to Chapala, about twenty miles southeast of Guadalajara, are the falls of Juanacatlán, seventy feet high and worth a visit.

Guanajuato

The Tarascan Indians called it Guanaxhuato, which meant "Hill of Frogs." No one is certain of the reason. Some say it was because the creatures abounded in the warm clefts of the mountain slopes. Others claim that when the Tarascans came to this part of the Sierra, they found stone idols in the shape of frogs, which they proceeded to worship as their own gods. And still others point to the two jutting peaks on the hill called Mecco and insist they look like frogs.

Stand on one of the hills above the city and you see that Guanajuato is crowded into a fold of the mountains. The long winding slope of its main street runs along the floor of the fold itself. The rest of the city steeply climbs the mountainsides.

As you look down upon the multicolored mass of roofs and patios and plazas, you wonder how anyone could have chosen so unlikely a place to build a city. It sits behind its mountain walls like a Shangri-la hiding from discovery.

The reason is silver and gold—primarily silver. The mother vein was discovered in 1550, and since that time Guanajuato has supplied the world with about two thirds of its silver. The city is undermined by a maze of tunnels and shafts. Gone now are the bonanza days when to say you were from Guanajuato was as good as proclaiming yourself a millionaire. A few mines are still working, however. You can visit them by making arrangements with the office manager of the Agencia de Minería on Sopeña Street, a block from Plaza Unión.

Village Streets. Guanajuato's main street, Calle Hidalgo, is a winding avenue, broad and narrow by turns and evenly paved with flagstones, that meanders up the long slow slope from the railroad station to the Jardín de la Unión. From it stem the twisting, climbing *callejones,* or lanes, some so narrow that your outstretched arms touch the houses on either side, some so steep that the roof of one house is on a level with the door of its neighbor. Callejon del Beso (Lane of the Kiss) one of them is called, because a couple walking it together are thrown into each other's arms. Another is so steep, dark, and narrow that it has been named the Lane of Hell. Every step gives you a new pattern of pastel walls, grilled balconies spilling flowers, massive carved doors approached by tall stoops or curling stairways, tall double windows with glimpses of beamed ceilings, tiled floors, garden patios. At night the lanes are lit by ornate coach lamps.

Jardín de la Unión. A wedge-shaped little plaza in the heart of the city. Here the band plays on Tuesday, Thursday, and Sunday, while all of Guanajuato promenades on the tiled walks or watches the show from the benches. On Sunday, when the concert is attended by country folk as well as urbanites, the gay throng is so thick that when one promenader stops to greet a friend the entire circle piles up behind him to create a pedestrian traffic jam.

Commanding the plaza is the Teatro Juárez, a pile of *cantera* stone and marble, typical of nineteenth-century romanticism with its columns and balustrades, its friezes, the statues of the Muses looking down from above the portico, and its brocade and velvet-draped interior. It speaks of still another day, the lavish display of the gay nineties, and of the Porfirio Díaz epoch in Mexico.

Beside it is the Churrigueresque carved façade of the small Franciscan church of San Diego, built in 1663.

On another side of the plaza is the Hotel Luna, a Spanish colonial building that was formerly the mansion of a governor.

Calle Hidalgo, the main street, is rich in historical monuments. Just below the Jardín de la Unión is the busy Plaza de la Paz. Above, and dwarfing everything around it, stands the magnificent church of La Parroquia, dating from 1671. Within, at a side altar, is the celebrated image of the Virgin of Guanajuato, which was brought from Granada, Spain, in 1557, as a gift from King Philip II, in appreciation of the flow of silver from the Guanajuato mines. The image, which stands on a pedestal of solid silver, is said to date from the seventh century A.D.

Adjoining the church is El Curato, once the home of the curate Antonio de Labarrieta, a friend of Hidalgo. The baptistry was a gift of the Spanish marquises of San Clemente, and in the Chapel of St. Faustina is the tomb of the valiant rebel-priest Celedonio Domeco de Jarauto, who was shot in 1848.

Los Arcos. This little lane of arches was once the entrance to the old Casas Reales, from which the Spanish governors ruled. Benito Juárez lived there in 1858; it was here that he proclaimed Guanajuato the provisional capital of Mexico and formed his first cabinet.

No. 14, Plaza de la Paz. Once the home of Bernardo Chico, friend of Hidalgo, and recently in use as a normal school. Hidalgo stayed here in 1810, and in it chose the first short-lived independence government of Mexico.

No. 48, Plaza de la Paz. This severe eighteenth-century house was the birthplace of the Mexican historian Lucas Alamán, in 1792.

Home of Conde Rul y Valenciana. The noble house of Rul was the richest in Guanajuato and one of the wealthiest in all Spanish America, for it owned the fabulous Valenciana mine. It was the Count of Rul who built the glorious Valenciana church, mixing the mortar with powdered gold and rare Spanish wines. The house was designed by the famed Mexican leader of the neoclassical renaissance, Francisco Eduardo Tresguerras, in the eighteenth century. Baron von Humboldt was a guest in this mansion in 1803 (identified by a plaque in the wall).

Government Palace. Site of the old house of the Marqués of San Clemente. The original building was destroyed by flood; the present structure was begun in 1897 and completed in 1903.

Hidalgo Market. This enclosed market, with its pink stone portal, occupies the site of the old bull ring of Gavira. The sloping cobblestone street opposite the main entrance is piled high with Guanajuato pottery. The colorful display calls for cameras. Guanajuato pottery is of two types—one of red earthenware, the other highly glazed. A specialty are the glazed ash trays made in the humorous grotesque shapes of bats, frogs, elephants, and iguanas. The gleaming, gracefully shaped tea sets in soft creamy colors are irresistible. To see the potters at work or to give a special order, you merely take a taxi or climb up to San Luisito Street and walk into any house. This is the street of the potters and you can buy here from the artisans themselves.

Alhóndiga de Granaditas. This massive structure, begun in 1798 and completed in 1809, was originally intended as a seed and grain warehouse. Hardly had it been completed than Hidalgo stormed Guanajuato with his strangely assorted army. It was in the fortlike Alhóndiga that the royalists made their last stand. Hidalgo and his men attacked in vain. At last the warrior-priest called for volunteers to set fire to the wooden door. A sturdy young mine worker stepped forward. Using a flat heavy flagstone for a shield and brandishing a flaming torch, he ran through the hail of bullets to set fire to the Alhóndiga. The last of the defenders were trapped on the roof and fought to the last man.

In the turn of events a few months later, Hidalgo and his brave lieutenants, Aldama, Allende, and Jiménez, faced a firing squad in Chihuahua. Their heads were brought to Guanajuato and hung in iron cages from the four corners of the Alhóndiga as a lesson to all rebels, but they only served to inflame the patriotic fervor of a Mexico in arms against tyranny.

The Alhóndiga has been a state prison since September 1864, when Maximilian ordered the transfer to it of prisoners in the old jail of Los Arcos. Today the obliging guards will conduct you through the patios and historic vaulted stairways, while the prisoners crowd around to sell you the little objects that they carve cleverly from bone.

Templo de la Compañía. On the Plaza de la Compañía. This great Jesuit temple was begun in 1747, finished in 1765. Through some structural weakness the original dome fell in 1808, and the new dome of colonnades, built in 1884, is worked in a distinctive style. The church is magnificently proportioned within and without and is a masterpiece of colonial architecture.

State College. Built in 1732 by the Jesuits through a contribution by the sister of the Marqués of San Clemente. It was at first a modest little school and dormitory. Later it was enlarged and improved through the generosity of a local mineowner, Lascurain de Retana, after whom a street is named. In 1744 Philip V of Spain gave it the title of College. The meteorological observatory was added in 1827. It has been the State College since 1828. Visitors are welcome.

Casa Smith. A beautiful colonial house in an excellent state of preservation. It takes its name from its present owner, an American who has made Guanajuato his home and who sometimes rents one or two of his rooms to visitors. A plaque on the wall tells you that Maximilian stayed here in 1864.

ENVIRONS

Church of Valenciana. A short drive into the mountains along the Río Bravo brings one to the Church of Valenciana, which in itself is worth a visit to Guanajuato. It was dedicated in 1788. Its rosy stone façade is a mass of delicate carving. Three gold-carved altars and the relief work of piers and arches and columns are exquisite. The church is still in use, and on December 8, the Fiesta of La Purísima, forty men carry its images through the streets of Guanajuato. The once thriving village at the foot of the church contains the remains of many noble façades, now the homes of peasants.

The Catacombs. Above the railroad station are the extraordinary catacombs of the Panteón. Rocky Guanajuato has had difficulty in burying its dead. Those who can afford it are entombed in the heavy walls of the cemetery. Others rent space in the wall for five years, after which the bodies are disinterred and placed in the vaulted corridors of the catacombs. Something in the air or the clay of Guanajuato preserves the bodies as if they had been carefully embalmed, and to look through the glass doors at the foot of the spiral stone stairway at a seemingly endless line of mummies is the experience of a lifetime. You will be interested in having your guide translate for you some of the obituaries on the tombs in the wall. One of them reads: "José Y. Freyre . . . I was born innocent, I die ignorant. . . ."

In the rainy season the mountain streams become swollen and several times Guanajuato has suffered severe floods, the last one as recently as 1905. Today a series of giant dams above the city controls the rivers, and the huge tunnel of Coajin, built after the costly lesson of 1905, carries off the floodwaters. Guanajuato has made playgrounds, promenades, and parks around its dams, and the most popular is the Presa (Dam) de la Olla, a few minutes from the center by taxi or by the busses that leave at frequent intervals from the Jardín de la Unión. You can walk it in half an hour along the meandering boulevard called Paseo de la Presa de la Olla, where the wealthy families of postindependence days built their villas. Below the dam itself, with its pretty little walks, spreads the lovely garden Antillón, and above it is another garden with playground, dance pavilion, and a little lake for rowboats. This is Guanajuato's favorite picnic spot.

Pipila Monument. Pipila is the affectionate nickname given to José Barajas, the hero who volunteered to fire the door of the Alhóndiga. A huge statue of the young miner leaning on a flagstone and holding a torch stands behind the village. One sees it from the Jardín de la Unión towering high above on the hill called Hormiguera, a giant in rose cantera stone, guarding his beloved Guanajuato. An hour's scenic drive takes one high into the mountains, skirts the wild bluffs of La Bufa, from which the cantera stone is hewn, and gives one a magnificent view of the city. The road brings you finally to the foot of the monument, where you can better appreciate its work-manship. Set into a stone temple of deeper purple hue and over-looking broad steps, terraces, and balustrades, this impressive statue bears the fiery inscription in Spanish of which the hero would no doubt be proud: "There are still other Alhóndigas to burn." If you climb the steep stairs within the monument, you will emerge on the roof, near Pipila's shoulder, and enjoy a still broader view of the city, mountains, and valleys.

San Miguel de Allende. The first settlement in the state of Gua-najuato, it was founded in 1542 by the Franciscan monk Juan de San Miguel; "Allende" was added after the revolutionary hero of 1810. The little village that once nestled at the foot of Moctezuma Hill, above the gentle valley of La Laja, now climbs the hill itself in a series of stone steps and terraces lined with pastel adobe houses and sumptuous villas.

It was originally created as a rest station on the road north, and to bring the Otomí Indians into the Spanish orbit. The fields were planted in wheat, and Spanish weavers taught the Indians the art of fashioning the serape, the first made in Mexico. Soon colonial palaces, homes, and churches crowded the terraced plazas, and many of them still stand.

The Parochial Church in the central plaza, dominating the en-tire city, is remarkable for its originality of design. It was con-structed by an anonymous Indian architect and is a strange blend of crude boldness and soaring gracefulness. Different, too, are the eighteenth-century Oratorio of San Felipe Neri and the adjoining chapel of the Santa Casa de Loreto with its domes and lanterns. This chapel was the gift in 1733 of one of the great families of San Miguel—Manuel Tomás de la Canal and his wife. Their palace at the corner of the central plaza still stands as a symbol of the aristo-cratic elegance of the old days.

One of the most paintable cities in Mexico, San Miguel today is a favorite American-Mexican art center. It was "discovered" some years ago by the famous Metropolitan tenor and actor José Mojica, who came to visit and ended by building three houses and a studio. It was Mojica who designed the colonial *faroles*, or lanterns, that light the streets at night.

The Chicagoans Stirling Dickinson and Heath Bowman, one an artist, the other a writer, came to San Miguel looking for material for new works. Stirling Dickinson, along with Cossio de Pomar, the Peruvian artist, founded the now famous art school in the patio of a former convent.

Celaya. Indian, Spanish, and modern, this thriving agricultural town, under whose old colonial *portales* is sold everything from American tractors and refrigerators to local candies and serapes, sprawls over a rich plain called the Bajío. It was founded in 1571 and was the capital of the state before Guanajuato came into eminence. It is famed as the birthplace of the colonial architect and artist Tresguerras, whose house still stands opposite the modernistic Hotel Isabel. Celayans say the house itself is about three hundred years old, and it is still used as a private dwelling. Tresguerras gave his birthplace the beautiful Carmen Church and the green stone bridge over the Laja River. Celaya's milk-and-sugar candy is prized throughout Mexico.

Silao. Junction of the local railroad to Guanajuato City, Silao is a sleepy little Spanish town that in spite of its passion for fluorescent lights seems to be living in the past. It makes the distinctive serapes of brilliant colors and tufted wool geometric designs sold all over Guanajuato and Querétaro and prized by collectors because they are not to be found anywhere but in this region.

Irapuato. Founded in 1547, Irapuato has been a center of many historic battles from the colonial period to independence. A busy city, it is renowned for its excellent strawberries.

León de los Aldamas, in the gentle Valle de Nuestra Señora, was founded in 1576 and is the largest city of Guanajuato state, a flourishing industrial metropolis with numerous flowering plazas and fine old *portales* around the central plaza. It has a colorful market. The Municipal Palace has a richly carved exterior.

Dolores Hidalgo. This colonial city, founded in 1590, was the home of the heroic priest Miguel Hidalgo and abounds in interesting monuments, legend, and history. It is a favorite pilgrimage for people from all over Mexico every sixteenth of September in celebration of the national fiesta of independence. It was here that Father Hidalgo tried to lift his Indians from slavery by establishing a pottery, tannery, and textile works, introducing bee culture and the silkworm, and setting out vineyards. But the soldiers of the Spanish king wrecked his work, since all industry was forbidden in the colonies because of the mother country's monopoly. As he looked at the ruined fields and factories, the fire of rebellion against injustice was born in Hidalgo's heart, and the priest became a soldier.

Hidalgo's church is on the north side of the central plaza. His house, built in 1779, is on the corner of Hidalgo and Morelos Streets; President Juárez issued a decree that it be preserved as a national monument. From the same window from which the priest issued the famous Cry of Independence, the Emperor Maximilian exorted the people to be faithful to his rule.

The old colonial Presidencia Municipal, with its graceful arcades and balconies, was the property of Hidalgo, who bought it in 1803 from his brother and presented it as a gift to the government for public offices.

On the east side of the Jardín Independencia stands the Casa del Subdelegado (now Hotel Hidalgo), built in 1786. In 1810 the rebels surged up the stairway, capturing the Spanish governors. Its carved doors and windows and its ornate cornices and balconies are a tribute to the architectural genius of colonial Spain.

La Alfarería (pottery works), on the corner of Tabasco and Puebla Streets, was built by Hidalgo in his efforts to redeem the Indians through industry. It is in ruins today, but the pottery making that Hidalgo taught his people is now an important industry of Dolores.

TRANSPORTATION

A network of railroads links the towns and cities of Guanajuato state and provides easy, comfortable travel. Suggested round trip from Mexico City:

Pullman to San Miguel Allende. After exploring this lovely little city, you can take the train on a short trip to Dolores Hidalgo, and from there hire a car for the three-hour scenic ride to Guanajuato. With Guanajuato as your headquarters, you can take a side trip to León. On your rail return to Mexico City, stops can be made at Silao, Irapuato, and Celaya, which are but a few hours apart.

If you choose to visit Guanajuato on your way to Mexico City from the United States, you can change trains at Silao if you come by way of Ciudad Juárez, or at Querétaro if you are traveling on the Laredo route.

By automobile, turn off the Pan American Highway at Kilometer 167 near Ixmiquilpan.

Additional information covering routes and itineraries will be found in Chapter III, page 36, and Chapter IV, page 74.

Morelia

Morelia, capital of the state of Michoacán, was founded in 1541 under the name of Valladolid by Viceroy Don Antonio de Mendoza. Located 195 miles from Mexico City, Morelia has long been an artistic and intellectual center. The Morelians, like the French, are experts in the fine art of living well. But there is more to Morelia than its food, fine wines, and good talk. When Spanish nobility selected Morelia as the site to build their homes in the New World, they had the choice of the land. And Morelians say they chose the best.

The climate is dry, the sun mildly warm, and the atmosphere unvaryingly temperate. Blue skies and balmy days are the general rule.

Historic Shrines. The clean, sunny streets of this tranquil old town are studded with historic houses where independence war plans were laid and carried out. The most notable historic site is located near the San Agustín church, where, according to an inscription on the wall, "The immortal José María Morelos was born, September 30, 1765." According to local tradition, his mother was surprised in the street by the pangs of childbirth and darted into the nearest house, where she bore the child that was to be Mexico's great liberator.

The main plaza, known as the Garden of the Martyrs, is adjacent to the cathedral. A statue of Morelos occupies a commanding position in the plaza. On a scroll in the hand of the figure is inscribed: "Liberty to the Slaves, October 5, 1813."

The Cathedral. Begun in 1640 and completed in 1744, the cathedral is a good example of Spanish plateresque. Its magnificent proportions are characterized by a striking delicacy of line. The low-relief ornament is concentrated in customary Spanish fashion between the broad, massive tower bases, about the transept portals, and on the towers.

Government Palace. This example of early Spanish colonial architecture with its quaint turrets is typically Morelian. Formerly the Colegio Seminario, it now houses the state library, government archives, and various government offices.

Palace of Justice, Municipal Palace, and School of Arts. These buildings enclose charming patios in the old style that breathe an atmosphere of antique and slightly decadent elegance.

San Nicolás College. San Nicolás College (state university), founded in Pátzcuaro in 1540 by Bishop Vasco de Quiroga, is the oldest university in Mexico and the second of its kind on the continent. When Fray Juan Medina Rincón moved the episcopal diocese from Pátzcuaro, he also removed the old college, which was transferred to Valladolid, now Morelia, in 1580. The patriot priest Hidalgo studied and taught philosophy and theology within its cloistered walls, and Morelos was one of his pupils.

Church of San Francisco. This early Franciscan relic, founded in 1531, is one of the oldest churches in Mexico. Local tradition refers to a secret passageway from the crypt to the outskirts of the city, presumably dug by the Spaniards, who used the church as a fortress.

The Aqueduct. The highway entrance to Morelia is past a fine old aqueduct, sturdy relic of the Spanish dominion. It was completed in the eighteenth century at a cost of $100,000 and still brings water to the city from a source four miles distant. Brilliant bougainvillias splash their blossoms against the mellowed stones of its many arches.

A raised stone causeway, a continuation of the aqueduct called the Calzada de Guadalupe, is a favorite local promenade. It leads into the Garden of the Aztecs, where several Indian monoliths and fragments of stone idols stand. Passing beneath the aqueduct is a road that leads to the Woods of San Pedro, where there are shaded avenues, a music stand, and a miniature lake.

The Museum. The Morelia Museum contains a small but interesting collection of Tarascan sculpture and pottery. It serves as a preliminary introduction to the indigenous people of the region.

Market. The market place of Morelia is a conglomeration of flowers, fruits, vegetables, and meat produced in the fertile lands of the surrounding valleys. There are piles of shining black, highly glazed pottery, pots of burnished copper, serapes, and basketry in many colors. Visit the market and its open-air restaurant at night. The glimpses of exotic Mexican dishes and the strong pungent odor of highly spiced foods is an unusual experience.

Pátzcuaro

Pátzcuaro and its famous lake are about two hours by car or train from Morelia or a day's trip from Mexico City. The road passes the quaint Indian town of Quiroga, noted for its highly glazed pottery and lacquered wooden plates, boxes, and trays, and Tzintzuntzan, ancient home of the Tarascans.

The town is spread out on a sloping hillside a short distance above Lake Pátzcuaro. The 6,300-foot altitude gives the village nights that are brisk and days that are invigoratingly warm.

The Indians of this region are direct descendants of the once powerful Tarascans. Their dress is a simple white cotton blouse and pants and heavy dark blue serapes. The women wear voluminous accordion-pleated red flannel skirts that unfurl like enormous fans as they hurry through the streets. Dugout canoes ply the lake carrying passengers and produce, or the strange "butterfly" nets with which the Indians fish for *pez blanca,* small white fish that they sell in the local markets or consume in large quantities in their own homes. They are defiantly proud of their Indian inheritance and they have to this day remained aloof from the world, preserving intact their ancient rituals, customs, language, dances, and music.

Museum of Popular Arts. The Pátzcuaro Museum is housed in an old colonial mansion. Its spacious, flower-filled patio and surrounding rooms contain a collection of Tarascan relics, sculpture, and pottery as well as a display of modern crafts. There is a choice selection of local lacquerware, copperwork, textiles, pottery, silver jewelry, and costumes.

El Humilladero. A few minutes' walk beyond the edge of the village is the primitive chapel of El Humilladero. Lovers are advised not to kiss beneath the heavy foliage of the surrounding trees, for, according to local superstition, those who embrace beneath their shadows will disappear into the night and nevermore be seen. Nevertheless, it is a popular retreat for local lovers.

El Estribo. The lake is seen in its full beauty from the height of El Estribo (Stirrup Peak), a ten-minute drive from the center of town. Within view are all the little islands of the lake, particularly Jaracuaro, barely rising above the water's edge, and, dominating the lake, the rock of Janitzio, surmounted by the gigantic statue of Morelos.

The Islands. The Tarascan fishermen of this region love their lake and seldom leave it. The island of Yunuen was the home of the deaf Indian poet Vicente Hernández, whose simple lyrics celebrating the life of the island fishermen are recited by neighbors who cannot read his published works. Yunuen, one of the smallest and most charming of the islands, is inhabited by some fifty Indian families.

A sandy beach, green meadows where island cattle graze, a few ancient houses, and a fine old church comprise the island of Jaracuaro, famous for its native music and basketry made of the reeds that line the water's edge.

The foundations of ancient houses are cut into the mound of rock called Janitzio, which rises out of the lake a few miles from Pátzcuaro. The livelihood of the Indians who dwell in the crooked, precipitous streets of the village occupying one side of the island depends entirely on the lake. The young men fish while their elders and the women of the village repair old nets or weave new ones. The whole town glitters with fish nets spread out to dry across slanting rooftops or hung on poles along the narrow beach.

November 1 and 2 (All Saints' and All Souls' Days) are annually celebrated in the graveyard of the little town. Tombstones and wooden crosses are decorated with fruits and flowers; then a procession of villagers, singing in native Tarascan dialect, weaves through the cemetery, presenting each of the departed spirits with bread and wine. Hundreds of candles glimmer in the darkness and Janitzio takes on a fiesta air while lively "ghosts" emerge from the gaily decked tombstones to perform a *danse macabre* with joyous relatives and friends.

Flat, polished stones slope gradually into the water around the island of Chupicuaor, making it a superlative swimming beach and an ideal spot for a day's outing. It is an hour's distance from Pátzcuaro and accessible by boat or by car.

Tzintzuntzan. The old capital of the Tarascan Empire, now a sleepy Indian village, is a twenty-minute drive from Pátzcuaro on the road to Morelia. Centuries before the Conquest, the first Tarascans appeared on the shores of Lake Pátzcuaro, where they were greeted by clouds of golden, copper, and crimson-tinted hummingbirds. The wise men of the tribe took counsel among themselves and announced to their followers that the birds, which were really tutelary spirits, had spoken in the ancient tongue commanding that a great Tarascan city be erected on the spot so that the region might forever be the homeland of the Tarascan people. Thus Tzintzuntzan (from the Tarascan *huitzitzilin,* meaning "hummingbird") was founded.

One of the principal attractions of Tzintzuntzan today is the old parish church, in which is hung a celebrated "Descent from the Cross" ascribed to Titian. Ancient church bells are suspended from the branches of heavy, gnarled olive trees planted in the atrium by early Spanish settlers. They are said to be the oldest olive trees in America. A passion play is enacted here annually on Good Friday, combining the pomp and pageantry of medieval drama with native Indian masks and symbolism.

Fiesta in Pátzcuaro. From December 5 to 8 each year is celebrated the regional fiesta of Pátzcuaro. Down from the sierra, on burro and on foot, move files of silent Indians with their families and produce. From across the lake come huge canoes sunk deep in the water with their heavy loads. There is movement day and night in the cobbled streets of the town, where generally only an occasional figure is seen after ten at night. Once it arrives in town, each family sets up house. All that is needed is a portable peat stove. The earth, with or without a blanket, is their bed. The goods the Indians bring to sell are piled in the plaza. The more ambitious arrange their wares in improvised stalls covered with white, unbleached muslin.

The ancient church is adorned for the fiesta with a canopy of fish net leading from its entrance to the courtyard gateway. Calla lilies and little red field flowers are woven into the mesh. At night red and blue cylindrical paper lanterns containing candles are hung from the old trees in the church grounds. They are lit at twilight and then the music begins. There is the deep throb of a drum and the thin wail of the *chirimía,* a native reed flute. Then the dancers, fantastically dressed and wearing lacquered masks, gather beneath the fish-net canopy. There they perform the "Dance of the Fishermen," in which the central figure, wearing a huge mask, attempts to elude the nets spread for him by a group of encircling dancers. During the struggle that precedes his capture, they taunt their prey with bouquets of shining fish and flowers, shouting at him in Tarascan dialect.

Wearing spectacular turbans and regal costumes adorned with silver belts and necklaces, another group of dancers performs the "Moors and Christians," in which clashing swords flash in a rhythmic dance, one of the most impressive rituals of the country.

Finally, to the lilting music of violins, the *viejitos,* the bizarre "little old men," appear. Leaning on carved wooden sticks, they perform the intricate patterns of the characteristic dance of Pátzcuaro.

The dances are done for hours on end with hypnotic repetition. When they are over, everyone turns toward the plaza, where the rest of the evening's fiesta takes place. This usually consists of fireworks, merry-go-rounds, and peep shows.

Market. Not every day is fiesta time but every Friday is market day, a sort of minor weekly fiesta with the dances and carrousels omitted. The Pátzcuaro market is one of the most colorful in Mexico. Visitors should try to be at the water's edge when the boats come in at sunup loaded with Tarascans dressed in their finest and carrying chickens, vegetables, fish, lacquerware, copper pots, and new baskets to market.

PUEBLA

Puebla has no Indian history. Its streets were laid out by farsighted Spaniards in the sixteenth century. Since its foundation, Puebla has been a center of learning, culture, and Spanish tradition.

Historical Background. To know Puebla is to know the epic tale of Spanish conquest and domination, the furious struggle in which independence was achieved, and the most recent clashing of antagonistic forces that have formed modern Mexico. The streets have more than once been wet with blood. Behind the shuttered windows conspirators whispered, and bitter wars were waged in the city's plazas. Here Porfirio Díaz fled imprisonment when as a youth he fought for Mexican freedom against the French armies of Maximilian. The whole history of Mexico's turbulent emergence as a free nation is written with blood and heroism on Puebla's decorous streets and plazas. Historically and spiritually, Puebla is the Rome of Mexico.

Puebla's location was selected by sixteenth-century Spanish Franciscan friars with the aid of two guardian angels and shrewd common sense. The conquistadors needed an intermediate strategic base between Mexico City and their source of supplies at Veracruz that would also protect farmers of the region from hostile Indians. Puebla was the answer. Two angels, bearing a line and rod and pacing a beautiful volcano-flanked plain, appeared in a dream to Fray Julián Garces. It may be that the good Father invented this divine corroboration of a decision based on the practical secular judgment of Fray Toribio Motolinía, but the result was that a Spanish city, Puebla of the Angels, was founded on Mexico's central plateau. And on the sixteenth of April 1532, as recorded by Fray Toribio in his chronicles, "Eight thousand Tlaxcalan allies and many other Indians erected the first huts of the workmen. These allies came singing and dancing and playing upon their musical instruments. On this day also came forty Spanish families to settle in the new city."

Today the site selected by the two angels is a thriving commercial center. It is located 7,054 feet above sea level, eighty-four miles southeast of Mexico City, with which it is connected by a branch of the Pan American Highway.

The rail trip is slightly longer than the two-and-a-half-hour journey by car but equally interesting. The train first passes through desert country devoted to maguey and later descends into valleys planted to maize and wheat.

Handicrafts and Market. Many of Puebla's typical crafts are of native origin, while others, like the highly glazed Talavera pottery and tiles for which the town is famous, were introduced by the first Spanish settlers. The pottery factories afford glimpses of a highly skilled technique.

The Victoria Market is a huge sprawling affair crammed with food, drinks, and native crafts. Here the coarse white blouses embroidered with bird and animal motifs woven and worn by the Indians of the surrounding region may be purchased at a fraction of their worth. Here also one may purchase the terra-cotta pottery made for local consumption and the more elaborate Talavera ware that is shipped throughout the republic.

The Cathedral. The seventeenth-century Puebla Cathedral, severe and austere, dominates the city in its height and proportions.

A green-gold half-moon dome rises over the drab exterior. The interior is more lavish with its marble floors, gilded pillars, and green onyx and marble statuary.

Church of San Francisco. This seventeenth-century church, built by early Franciscans, has graceful towers and a unique red brick façade decorated with chiseled stone and glazed tile.

Santo Domingo Church and Rosary Chapel. A contrast in architecture is afforded by the contiguous Santo Domingo Church and its famous Rosary Chapel. The former, part of an old Dominican monastery, is a sturdy substantial building of gray stone. An opening to the left of the main altar discloses a gold chapel of intimate proportions. A profusion of gold-leaf and polychrome gargoyles, animals, and voluptuous angels adorns the interior.

Convent of Santa Rosa. Puebla is famous for its old kitchens. The *poblanos,* who take their eating seriously, make of their kitchens shining, immaculate little temples to the patron saint of the culinary art, San Pascual Bailón. A typical example may be seen in the arched, majolica-tiled kitchen of the former Santa Rosa Convent, now a miniature museum. The entire wall behind the large, gaily tiled peat stove is covered with three sets of pots: one for daily use, one for festive occasions, and one a miniature set that is purely decorative. In a corner of the room a Jacob's-ladder nest of pots rises from floor to ceiling.

Secret Convent of Santa Mónica. Some years ago government officials accidentally discovered that a narrow passageway behind the façade of an ordinary residence communicated with a spacious, hidden convent that, unknown to the inhabitants of Puebla, had persisted through the period of religious prohibition. The seventeenth-century building, which is now a museum of religious relics, consists of a labyrinthine series of passageways.

Church of El Carmen. The Puebla style of Moorish-Spanish decoration achieves its most striking expressions in the glittering El Carmen Church, whose façade is fantastic and colorful.

Casa del Alfeñique. Although this former signorial home, now a state museum, appears to consist of nothing more substantial than rose water and whipped cream, it is actually three centuries old. Its rose lava and majolica walls decorated with white stone are sturdy stuff. The interior is decorated with period furniture. There is a red silk brocaded living room, dressing room, bedroom, chapel, and typical Mexican kitchen.

Casa de los Muñecos. The mosaic walls of this ancient mansion bear glittering picture panels of snake charmers, dancers, saints, and devils in festive garments and gala mood.

State College and Church of La Compañía. The Puebla State College, formerly a Jesuit monastery, is distinguished by its large inner patio, pyramidal columns, and simple classic fountain. The huge adjoining Church of La Compañía is noteworthy for its blue and white tiled dome flanked by quaint flying buttresses.

Forts of Guadalupe and Loreto. Crowning the summits of two hills overlooking the east end of the town rise the famous forts of Guadalupe and Loreto, which have served the besieged city many times in its historic past.

Agua Azul. The Agua Azul is an outdoor swimming pool fed by natural warm sulphur springs. At the end of a day's sight-seeing the visitor may find unique refreshment in its invigorating waters.

ENVIRONS

The immediate vicinity of Puebla is dotted with pre-Hispanic villages where indigenous customs and a native way of life still prevail.

Huejotzingo. Eighteen miles before Puebla on the road from Mexico City. Hand-woven serapes from neighboring regions usually are suspended like banners in the market place beside the highway.

On the other side of the road is an old seventeenth-century Franciscan church and monastery. Its rows of monk cells are so arranged that on October fourth, the day of San Francisco, a beam of sunlight passes, like a blessing, down the entire length of the central corridor through the windows at either end. In its patio enormous geraniums climb to the height of the second-story arched balcony.

At carnival time, in February, several hundred inhabitants of the town participate in a three-day drama depicting the elopement of a bandit chieftain with a native maiden. The protagonists, wearing masks or stenciling their faces with black and gold paint, use the whole village as a setting for their medieval drama.

Atlixco. Twenty minutes from Puebla in the midst of maize and wheat country, it originally was an Indian village, later became a Spanish colonial settlement, and is now a thriving textile center.

Chipilo. A few minutes' drive from Atlixco is Chipilo, a unique and colorful hillside colony founded some years ago by Italian emigrants. The inhabitants still maintain the customs of their home-land, and although the men have adopted the Mexican *charro* costume, the women still wear the wooden shoes and bright bandannas of their native Italy.

Teziutlán. Teziutlán is in the heart of Puebla's gold, silver, and copper mining zone near the border between the states of Puebla and Veracruz. Easily reached by both highway and railway, it is a picturesque and very ancient town.

Tlaxcala. In 1519, in a letter to the Spanish emperor, Cortés compared Tlaxcala to Granada, saying that Tlaxcala was ". . . larger, stronger, and more populous than the Moorish city at the time of the Conquest and quite as well built." The Spaniards were amazed to find barbershops and steam and hot-water baths when they entered the Indian town. On that September morning in 1519, when the white men marched into the Tlaxcalan capital, the "flat terraced roofs of the buildings were covered with spectators eager to catch a glimpse of the strangers. Arches of verdant boughs, intertwined with roses and honeysuckle, were thrown across the streets. The whole population abandoned itself to rejoicing; and the air with songs and shouts of triumph mingled with the wild music of national instruments. . . ."

Tlaxcala, once the powerful capital of an independent oligarchy whose leaders aided Cortés in his capture of Tenochtitlán, is now a small state capital. It is located some thirty-five miles from Puebla, which was not even the substance of a friar's dream when Tlaxcala was at its height.

The weather-beaten, historic Church of San Francisco, built by the Spaniards in 1521, is one of the first monuments of their domination of the country. On its ancient pulpit the following words may still be read: "Here the Holy Evangel had its beginning in this new world."

The hillside Shrine of Ocotlán marks the spot where, in the first century of the Conquest, a miraculous spring gushed forth in answer to the urgent prayers of pious Indian converts seeking divine intervention against a drought then afflicting the community.

Santa Ana. Santa Ana is a tiny weavers' village fifteen minutes' drive from Tlaxcala. The factories are really enlarged private homes with charming patios where bluebirds and canaries sing to the shuttling of the looms. In these surroundings the complete process of textile making may be observed, from the carding, dyeing, and spinning of the wool to the weaving of the final product.

Cholula. Six miles north of Puebla rise the tiled domes, green cypresses, and adobe huts of Cholula, the ancient capital of the pre-Aztec Cholulan republic. Once a center of pagan worship, a veritable Jerusalem of Anáhuac, it is now a sleepy forgotten Indian town whose population has dwindled from 20,000 in the sixteenth century to a mere 6,000 at the present time. Before the Conquest Cholula was the great commercial center of the plateau and its inhabitants were noted for their mechanical arts, fine pottery, and excellent cotton and agave cloths. But the special fame of the capital derived from its venerable religious tradition, for it was here that the god Quetzalcoatl paused in his passage to the coast to instruct the Toltec inhabitants in the arts of civilization. He taught them better forms of government and a more spiritualized religion in which the only sacrifices were the fruits and flowers of the season.

It was in honor of the benevolent Quetzalcoatl that the great Cholula mound was erected. The date of the Cholula Pyramid is conjectural, but it is known that when the Aztecs entered the plateau they, even as the modern traveler today, gazed with wonder at this extraordinary monument. In those days the summit of the temple was occupied by a dazzling image of Quetzalcoatl adorned with heavy gold and gleaming jewels, but the earlier, spiritual religion had already given way to the practice of human sacrifice. From the farthest corners of Anáhuac, pilgrims came to worship at Quetzalcoatl's shrine.

Since the Spaniards could neither destroy nor erase the memory of Quetzalcoatl, they built a church above the Aztec temple that had in turn been superimposed on the old Toltec pyramid. Today the Church of Our Lady of Los Remedios dominates the landscape for miles around, a symbol of the rise of Catholicism on the Aztec foundation. It stands above the other Catholic churches of Cholula, nearly all of which are said to be built on the sites of pagan temples.

Querétaro

Long before Columbus discovered the New World the Otomí Indians founded a city under the sheltering slopes of Sangremal. It must have been rich and prosperous, for Moctezuma eyed it from the capital of his Aztec empire in the Valley of Mexico and forced it to become a part of his vast domain. That was in the fifteenth century, 174 years before the *Mayflower* touched the mainland of North America.

Then the Spaniards came. The Aztec-Otomí stronghold was captured in 1531 by a Hispanicized Indian chief named Fernando de Tapia. There is a legend about that conquest. The Otomís insisted they would fight to the last man unless the Spaniards laid aside their arms and engaged them in hand-to-hand battle to decide the issue. The Spanish forces agreed to this fair-play challenge, and Sangremal was the battleground of a gigantic mass combat. For twelve hours they fought, and then at sundown a vision appeared in the sky—St. James (Santiago) riding a white horse and carrying a flaming sword.

The enemy armies embraced, hailed Charles V of Spain as their emperor, and erected a stone cross on Sangremal to commemorate the strange battle and the miracle. Today, as witness to the legend the old Spanish Church of La Cruz stands on the spot, and above the door of the Church of San Francisco in Plaza Obregón, in the village now called Querétaro, is the image of Santiago on his horse carved in stone.

It was in Querétaro that the Franciscan monks of the Propaganda of the Faith founded their headquarters. From here they set out to carry their religion south through Central America and north to California, where they gave the city of San Francisco its name. Querétaro holds many relics and vestiges of the historic missions.

BIRTHPLACE OF THE REVOLUTION

In 1808 Napoleon crossed the Pyrenees and Ferdinand VII toppled from the throne of Spain. In Mexico it was the signal for rising against the choking ties of the crumbling empire. The Spaniards born in Mexico (*criollos*) were restless under the oppressive rule of the Spaniards sent from the mother country, and the enslaved Indians were ready to revolt. Secret groups of plotters formed all over the country. One of the most important met in Querétaro under the innocuous name of the Society for the Study of Fine Arts.

The *corregidor* (governor) of Querétaro, Miguel Domínguez, and his wife, María Josefa Ortiz de Domínguez, were among the plotters who were making plans for an uprising. But the conspiracy was discovered. In September 1810 the *Corregidora* was imprisoned in her apartments in the palace (today the Palacio Municipal) while the royalists debated what to do.

Late at night the imprisoned Corregidora stamped three times on the floor of her jail, a signal to her faithful guard Pérez, in the room below. Perez crept up the stairs and received the instructions whispered through the keyhole. The next moment he was riding like the wind to warn Captain Ignacio Allende in San Miguel and Padre Miguel Hidalgo in Dolores that all was discovered. It was the Paul Revere ride of Mexican history. The moment he received the news, Hidalgo called his Indians together, raised the Cry of Independence, and began the march on Guanajuato that was to end in his death and in the independence of Mexico.

The Corregidora is one of the most famous women in Mexican history. Mexico celebrates its Independence Day in September, commemorating in every city the great events of 1810 set off by the lady of Querétaro.

Querétaro figured in history again a few years later when the ill-fated Hapsburg emperor Maximilian fled to Querétaro to make his last stand. For seventy-eight days his forces withstood the siege, but at last the republican forces broke the wall of the Templo de la Cruz, which was being used as a fort by the imperialists, and the long struggle was over. Maximilian surrendered his sword on the Cerro de las Campanas (Hill of Bells), and there a month later he and his generals fell before a firing squad.

Plaza Obregón. This plaza is the heart of Querétaro. The classical fountain to Hebe at its center was a gift of the old Spanish family of Rubio. Here the band gives its Sunday concerts. On one side stands the Gran Hotel.

The plaza is dominated by the Church of San Francisco, formerly the cathedral, with the figure of Santiago above the door. One of the first churches of Querétaro, it dates back to 1545 and was a Franciscan center. The colored tiles of its dome were brought from Spain in 1540.

Its adjoining monastery, which was the Colegio Pío Mariano from 1850 to 1932, is now the Museo Pío Mariano, second only to the museum in Mexico City in importance. The museum is alone worth a visit to Querétaro. A beautiful colonial building, it has been excellently preserved. Its massive carved doors, splendid stone arches and stairways and *faroles,* the lovely old fountain in the patio, the cedar beams that are more than two hundred years old, the fluted tapering pillars formed originally of a single block of stone—all take one back to the glory that was colonial Spain.

Among the items on display are eighteenth-century cupboards, exquisitely carved, of cedar and mahogany; huge parchment choir books drawn by hand and bound in iron; paintings by Miguel Cabrera, one of the foremost of the neoclassic artists; and paintings by the monks themselves, crude in technique but shining with vitality. In the library are eight thousand books, most of them parchment tomes of the seventeenth and eighteenth centuries.

A monument to the Corregidora is in a tiny garden near the Plaza Obregón. Bronze and granite, with circular steps and guardian eagles, it was unveiled in September 1910. The streets surrounding the plaza have a quaint European air.

Plaza de la Independencia. A little park surrounded by old colonial buildings. On one side is the Palacio Municipal, the original *Casas Reales* of the Spanish governors. This was the home of the Corregidor and his rebel wife. One can visit the apartments on the second floor where the Corregidora was jailed when the plot was discovered. A marble plaque in the floor marks the spot where she stamped her foot to signal her jailer.

From the balcony of her apartments, every year near midnight on the fifteenth of September, the governor of Querétaro sends forth anew the Cry of Independence, as Hidalgo gave it in 1810, over a plaza crowded with people. Fireworks, dances, and general festivities follow the historic ritual.

Although still in use as a city hall, the palace is badly in need of repairs, and much of its original beauty has been lost. Its graceful center stairway, however, is noteworthy.

Standing before the Palacio, on one's right, is a handsome colonial house, the finely wrought railings of its balconies worked into coats of arms. This was the mansion of López de Ecala, of a noble

Spanish family, who was governor of the state from 1830 to 1832. Today it is a private house.

In the center of the plaza is a monument to Don Juan Antonio de Urrutia y Arana, the Marqués de la Villa del Villar del Águila. The Marqués, Querétaro's greatest benefactor, was instrumental in the construction of the great aqueduct that still furnishes Querétaro with its water, and spent on it more than eighty thousand dollars from his own pocket.

Maximilian loved this little plaza and used to linger here. Somehow the besiegers discovered the fact and one day a cannon ball screamed through the trees. It did not find Maximilian but it did destroy the monument, which was reconstructed in 1892.

Madero Avenue. This main artery, which stems from Plaza Obregón, is rich in historical and architectural treasures.

The huge Church of Santa Clara, on the plaza of the same name, was founded in 1633 and reconstructed in the eighteenth century by Mexico's most famous artist-architect, Eduardo de Tresguerras. Its interior is richly carved and the delicate tracery of the ironwork is an artistic triumph. The Convento de Santa Clara was in its day one of the largest in Mexico, and the land for many blocks around belonged to it, including what is now the Parque Madero, whose long lanes are roofed by the entwining branches of ahuehuete trees.

In front of the church is the Fountain of Neptune, in European Renaissance style, dating from 1797. The oldest fountain in Querétaro, it is a symbol of the European elegance of the past.

Along Madero Avenue are many buildings and houses whose age one can almost guess by the thickness of the doors and frames, the carved designs, the massive knockers, and the pillars and arches in the patios beyond. The handsomest and best preserved is the Escobar house, so called after the family that now owns it. The housekeeper will let you into the patio, where you can admire the fine ironwork of the grilled balconies, the pillars and arches, and the stairway whose walls are inlaid with blue and white tiles of delicate design.

Continuing down Madero Avenue, one comes to the old Government Palace, today the Casa del Agrarista, a colonial structure on which time has set its mark. The state government offices were housed in it in 1861. Benito Juárez stayed here in 1865 and again in

1867. And in postconstitution days, when Querétaro was declared
the capital of Mexico, it was the home of the government of the
republic.

At the head of the central stairway the agricultural workers have
painted a small but colorful satiric mural. The most interesting feature of the building is the wooden spiral stairway, or *caracol*, at the
back. It is composed of 172 steps, and not a single iron nail was
used in its construction. Its handsome ceiling still shows the fine
work of the colonial artists. Ascend it to the stone roof for a good
view over the city.

Across the street from the Casa del Agrarista rise the carved red
walls of the Church of San Felipe, built in the light plateresque
style. The altar is simple, but the gold sunburst above it surrounding the figure of the patron saint is striking. Set into the wall near
the door are the tombs of Querétaro's bishops.

Palacio Federal. Formerly the cloister of the Augustines and
nicknamed the Querétaro Alhambra. The work of the colonial architect Ignacio Mariano de las Casas, its portico bears some fine relief work and filigree. Time has destroyed much of its splendor, and
the plumed angels that once were at the base of the dome are no
more. But the eighteenth-century fountain, the Moorish-Spanish pillars carved with rosebuds, and the odd caryatids with flat uplifted
hands that surround the arcades of the patio tell the story of its ancient magnificence. The adjoining building, once the monastery, is
now the post office.

Church of Santa Rosa de Viterbo. One of the earliest reconstruction works of Tresguerras, this church, which dates from 1752,
is opulent almost to a fault. The exterior, with the curious inverted
arches of the curved buttresses, is as impressive as it is unusual.
Within, the church is of gilt carved wood with inlaid marble and
fine filigree work and Churrigueresque altars among the best in
Mexico. Maximilian's soldiers burned the main altar and it is said
they derived much gold from it. The odd confessionals with their
gilt and wood carved doors are delicately painted. Doors and window shutters are magnificently carved. Santa Rosa used to be an important musical center; its blue and gold organ, useless now, is still
a work of art. The huge adjoining monastery is now a hospital.

Teresitas. Adding to the variety of Querétaro's religious architecture is this early nineteenth-century church, built in classic style and more like a Greek temple than a Spanish house of worship.

Church of La Cruz. This temple with its large monastery was constructed shortly after the Conquest on the slope of Sangremal, the site where Indians and Spaniards erected the stone cross commemorating the miracle of Santiago.

It became the home of the Propaganda Fide in 1683. From this headquarters of the Faith the Franciscan monks started on the historic missions that took them to Central America and California, and here they wrote many of the valuable documents to which historians today go for information on the colonization of Mexico.

Because of their strategic position and fortlike construction, Maximilian's men used the church and monastery for their headquarters. The breach made by the republican forces in the monastery wall in 1867 is protected by an iron fence. Before it in a cactus and rock garden is a monument to the Corregidora. Beyond is the Panteón, the first cemetery of Querétaro, now closed. From the bell tower one can get a view over the entire city and see the extent of the great aqueduct.

Across the street is a tiny stone church with the curious date of 1421 over the door. No one knows when it was actually built, but it is known to be the first church constructed in Querétaro and one of the first in Mexico. It is still in use.

Capuchines Church. This fortlike colonial church, on a side street near the Parque Madero, served as a prison for Maximilian and his generals. It is now a barracks and the adjoining monastery holds government offices.

Kindergarten. No. 10, Allende Sur. This colonial building, once a religious college, is now a kindergarten. Its noteworthy feature is the two-sided tortuous spiral stone stairway to the gallery and roof. The window of the alcove frames the towers of San Agustín. At the foot of one side of the staircase is the dark punishment chamber with a small shuttered peephole set into the wall. The water spouts around the patio are carved into fantastic shapes.

Academy of San Fernando. Located opposite the Escobedo Market. In its broad salon the statesmen of Mexico gathered for the sessions of the National Congress during the North American intervention to discuss the peace treaties signed in 1848 by which the

United States won the Mexican territory that today forms its South-west. The first sessions of the Constitutional Congress of 1916–17 were celebrated in this colonial building.

Santiago Church. Located on Sixteenth of September Street. The convent of this old church holds a tiny garden surrounded by stone pillars delicately carved with cupids. At its heart is a colonial fountain shaded by tall trees. Seen through the fine ironwork of its gates, the park with its fountain, arches, and pillars is a picture out of an old print. A noble vaulted stairway leads to the apartments above.

Teatro de la República. Theater of the Republic, formerly known as the Teatro de Iturbide, where the Emperor Maximilian and his generals Miramón and Mejía were tried and condemned to death. In this same historic spot the congress met that drafted the Constitution of 1917, under which Mexico is governed.

Cerro de las Campanas. Hill of Bells. Maximilian and his staff fled to this hill from the Templo de la Cruz on the entrance of the republican forces. Here he surrendered his sword, and here, on June 19, 1868, he and his generals met their death before a firing squad. A few years later Mexico granted permission to the Austrian government to build the brown stone Expiatory Chapel on the slope. It was inaugurated in 1901.

ENVIRONS

Aqueduct, Hercules, and La Cañada. The road to the village of La Cañada (Place of Orchards) leads past the Church of la Cruz and follows the aqueduct. This monumental line of arches was begun in 1726 and completed in 1735. The principal part consists of seventy-four arches fifty feet high resting on pillars forty-six feet thick. The aqueduct is five miles long. Ornamental *faroles* or coach lanterns hang from two of the central arches.

As one rides on toward Cerro Colorado (Red Hill) the landscape becomes more picturesque, the foliage greener and denser, with orchards and gardens crowding hills and ravines. On Cerro Colorado is a curious pair of carved red pillars, the remains of an old toll gate erected by the Spaniards.

Hercules is a factory town of model adobe houses, its center the textile factory founded in 1844. The local statue of Hercules was brought from Italy.

La Cañada, the village of orchards and gardens, shows little evidence of its more prosperous past. Its dirt and cobblestone streets are picturesque.

The Alameda and El Pueblito. The road to the village of El Pueblito passes the Alameda Park, which, with its tennis courts and stadium, is a favorite sports and picnic spot. Old haciendas mark the road, some in ruins, some still thriving.

El Pueblito contains a colonial church, famous throughout Mexico for its miraculous Virgin. Adjoining it are the ruins of a monastery. The country folk store alfalfa in it. Little is known of the history of this architectural gem, but from its size and beauty there can be no doubt that it was once a rich and powerful religious center.

On the outskirts of El Pueblito are the ruins of an Indian city that the Mexican government is excavating.

TRANSPORTATION

For the traveler coming by rail from the United States, Querétaro lies on the Laredo, El Paso, and Guadalajara-Nogales routes, so that it can be visited either coming or going by a convenient stopover. From Mexico City to Querétaro, one can go by rail in six hours or by car over a paved road in four hours (see page 71).

Taxco

Few of the momentous events of Mexico's political history took place in Taxco. Its influence on the economic history of the country, however, has been important. Before the Conquest it was a poor Indian town with none of the established popularity that existed around the religious and political centers; it came into existence because of the proximity of the precious metals in the region, and doubtless the first inhabitants were crude miners. Aztec records indicate that the community paid an annual tax of gold to Moctezuma, the Aztec emperor, and Cortés was not long in discovering the source of some of the treasures he took in Tenochtitlán.

But the village did not come into prominence until about the middle of the colonial period, when a French miner, Josephe le Borde, known to Mexicans today as José de la Borda, stumbled on a rich silver vein. According to legend, Borda was returning to Mexico City after having given up his search for precious metals. If you are told the story by one of the *taxqueños*, you will be asked to imagine him plodding along on his diminutive burro, discouraged and nearly

penniless, when suddenly his burro stumbles and sinks into soft
ground. Borda, dismounting, discovers the soft earth hides a rich
silver deposit. In gratitude, he later builds one of the most ornate
churches in Mexico, at a cost, one is told, of ten million pesos. The
church, today the outstanding architectural feature of the village,
was dedicated to San Sebastián and Santa Prisca. It was completed
in 1757. A small bribe to the attendant will enable you to climb to
the top of one of the towers for a fine view of the village and a
close-up of the huge dome. The latter is decorated with glazed tiles
in vivid colors—ultramarine, orange, green, and white. The façade
of the church is baroque; the altarpieces within are the most elaborate Churrigueresque. The best of the paintings are by Miguel Cabrera, one of the most prolific painters of the eighteenth century.

There are several other smaller churches scattered about the town,
and some of these are worth visiting. The Santa Veracruz, for instance, is the scene of the most important annual fiesta, which takes
place on the fourth Friday of Lent.

Perhaps the most interesting features of the old town are its streets,
narrow cobblestone little alleyways, some quite steep and all of
them lined with picturesque old colonial houses. Among the most
handsome of these and easily visited is the Casa Humboldt, once
owned by Borda but named after Baron Alexander von Humboldt,
famous explorer, who stayed there when he visited Mexico. Casa
Figueroa, overlooking the plaza, just above the Borda fountain, is
a restored palace, now the studio and home of Fidel Figueroa, a
native Taxco artist. The palace was constructed in the best colonial
style about the middle of the eighteenth century by a Spanish count.
For a long time it was known as La Casa de Lágrimas (The House
of Tears) because the man who built it was a judge who cruelly
imposed unjust fines on the Indians. The Casa Sáenz is a reconstruction by the American artist William B. Spratling for the late Dr.
Moisés Sáenz, educator and diplomat.

Spratling is also responsible for making Taxco the center of the
silversmith's art, and his large factory and sales shops are visited by
thousands each year. Several newcomers have opened small factories, and some of these are turning out exquisite pieces of silver
jewelry and silver tableware. Some excellent hand-blocked textiles
are being made in Taxco now, and several shops are turning out
costume dresses, shirts, and hair bandannas.

The government and the residents of Taxco have attempted to preserve the place as a typical colonial town. Its jewel-like setting, surrounded by towering granite mountains, its perfect climate, and its quiet atmosphere give it a rare charm. It is an ideal spot for rest and relaxation.

There are several excellent hotels in Taxco and its environs and their rates compare favorably with similar establishments elsewhere in Mexico. For further information regarding the hotels in Taxco and other details, see page 201.

CHAPTER VII

THE YUCATÁN

THE Yucatán peninsula, so different from the rest of Mexico as to be almost a separate land, is one of the most fascinating parts of the whole country. This is where the Mayan civilization flourished in the centuries preceding the Spanish invasion. Today the silent abandoned cities of this, perhaps the highest indigenous culture on the American continent, stand like haunting enigmas, holding secrets that may never be divulged, while offering tantalizing glimpses into a lost civilization.

THE LAND

The peninsula juts eastward toward Cuba to outline the southeastern curve of the Gulf of Mexico and forms the northwestern edge of the Caribbean Sea. It is a low-lying, flat limestone shelf, without rivers or streams. Rain water passes quickly through the porous limestone and collects in caverns below the harder surface rock. At places the surface has eroded through to the caverns below, forming *cenotes*, or natural wells, from twenty to seventy feet deep. These, plus man-made wells, are the land's only source of fresh water. The entire peninsula is covered with jungle growth. In the northwest, where the annual rainfall is light, the bush is low and scrubby; toward the southeast the rainfall grows progressively heavier and the vegetation correspondingly taller and more dense.

The single cash crop of Yucatán is henequen, or sisal, as it is called commercially—a century-plant fiber used in making rope and coarse bags. The area around Mérida has been largely cleared of the bush and planted with henequen. Farther inland, where the rainfall is heavier, the henequen plantations give way to cornfields, and these in turn to the uncleared jungle. In this wild interior

157

jungle another product of commercial importance is exploited—
chicle, from which chewing gum is made, obtained by tapping the
sapodilla tree.

CLIMATE

It is a hot land, with a mean maximum temperature of around
90 degrees Fahrenheit and a mean minimum of 64 degrees. The
daily variation can be as much as thirty or forty, especially in the
winter months, and winter nights are often cool enough to make
blankets feel comfortable. The rainy season comes in the summer-
time (May to November) in the form of thunderstorms and showers, hard but brief. The rest of the year has only very occasional
showers and from time to time cold storms from the north. In general, winter days are warm and balmy and summer days surprisingly
fresh because of the constant breezes.

CLOTHING

Summer-weight clothing is worn in Yucatán the year around. On
winter evenings a sweater or light coat may prove useful, and for
a summer visit take a light raincoat or an umbrella. Comfortable
walking shoes are necessary when visiting the ruins.

ROUTES TO YUCATÁN

The port of Progreso may be reached by boat from the United
States or from Veracruz, Mexico. Pan American Airways planes fly
to Mérida from New Orleans in two hours and forty minutes, and
from Miami via Havana in just under three hours. From Mexico
City the Compañía Mexicana de Aviación (CMA), a subsidiary of
Pan American Airways, and Aerovias Braniff have regular service
to Mérida and other Yucatecan cities. As yet neither railroad nor
highway connects Yucatán with the rest of Mexico.

LOCAL TRAVEL

From Mérida there are roads leading to Chichén Itzá and to
Uxmal, two of the largest and most beautiful of the Maya cities, as
well as an excellent paved road to the port of Progreso. Several
narrow-gauge railroad lines radiate out from Mérida, the three most
important going north to Progreso, south to Campeche, and east to
Valladolid.

There are several hotels in Mérida (see page 189), of which the Montejo, Itzá, and Casa Camara are the most popular; and at Chichén Itzá there are the Mayaland Lodge and Casa Victoria. Progreso and Campeche (see page 172) have hotels, but accommodations are simple.

YUCATÁN HISTORY

The Mayas of today apparently know little of the vanished culture of their ancestors, and most of our knowledge comes from the studies of archaeologists. They have been able to piece together much of the story, but there are still unsolved mysteries that may never be explained.

In its broad outlines this is the story as figured out by archaeologists: An Indian tribe living in the Petén area of what is now northern Guatemala learned, probably between one thousand and two thousand years before the birth of Christ, to cultivate maize. Thus converted from hunters and fishermen into sedentary farmers, this tribe—the Maya—began to develop a distinctive civilization. By the second century A.D. they had already developed not only an advanced stone architecture but also an accurate calendar and a system of hieroglyphic writing. The astronomical knowledge required to work out this calendar, correct to the day in a period of 374,400 years (as accurate as our present-day Gregorian calendar), is astonishing when compared with the level of scientific knowledge in the Old World at that time. Perhaps even more astonishing is the fact that the Mayas in their mathematics had already worked out positional writing and the abstract quantity of zero, at least five centuries before the zero was known in the Old World.

The stage was thus set for a golden age of art, science, and religion. Through the next five centuries the Mayas built monumental cities throughout an ever increasing area. By the seventh century the culture of the Old Empire, as this period is called, extended as far south as present-day Honduras, as far east as the state of Chiapas, and north into the Yucatán peninsula. The great centers of this period were all in the southern and eastern section; Yucatán at that time was only a marginal province.

Then in the seventh century came a general collapse. This is one of the great unsolved mysteries of archaeology. What happened? No one knows for sure. Perhaps, as Dr. Morley suggests, the wasteful agricultural methods of the Mayas depleted the land until it would no longer support the population. Perhaps, as Dr. Spinden suggests, the centuries of sustained artistic effort were followed by a moral and cultural degeneration. Spinden also mentions the possibility of epidemics of disease, like yellow fever and malaria. Others suggest that civil war broke out, that earthquakes frightened the people into moving, and a variety of other possibilities. But whatever the reason, these splendid cities, into which had gone the highest artistic genius of the race, were abandoned and in time were covered by the jungle.

The people moved north into the Yucatán peninsula and set up their civilization anew in this land that they called Mayab—Land of the Chosen. Early in the eleventh century the three dominant cities of the area, Chichén Itzá, Uxmal, and Mayapán, formed a confederation known as the League of Mayapán. Thus began the great era of the New Empire, two centuries of peace, prosperity, and a brilliant art renaissance. Then civil war disrupted this happy existence. Chichén Itzá and Mayapán went to war. The rulers of Mayapán called in warriors from a Mexican tribe to the west, with their aid defeated the Chichén Itzá army, and then apparently handed over the vanquished city to these Mexican allies. Mayapán thus became the overlord of the whole peninsula for the next two and a half centuries. Finally, in the middle of the fifteenth century, the Maya nobles of Chichén Itzá and Uxmal rose up against their oppressors. Marching to Mayapán, they razed the city and killed every member of the ruling family except one son who happened to be away.

After this violent upheaval both victors and vanquished abandoned their cities. The people of Mayapán set up a new capital at Tibolón, several miles to the east; those of Uxmal founded Mani, about thirty miles away; those of Chichén Itzá went far south into the Petén area, the original home of the Mayas, and established the city of Tayasal on Lake Petén Itzá.

Thus when the Spaniards arrived in the New World in the early sixteenth century, they found a civilization already broken up and dispersed.

Yucatán was not conquered by Cortés, conqueror of Mexico, though his ships touched the peninsula en route to Veracruz in

1519. It was not until 1527 that a Spanish expedition went to Yucatán, led by Francisco de Montejo, who had accompanied Cortés to Mexico in 1519. But the invaders were forced to retire in the face of furious opposition by the Indians. Again in 1531 Montejo attempted to subjugate the Mayas, and again he failed. Then in 1540 yet another expedition, this one commanded by his son, Francisco de Montejo the younger, was able to push victoriously into the peninsula from a landing on the west coast. A decisive defeat inflicted on a coalition of Maya chieftains in 1541 ended all further resistance, and the Spaniards were undisputed masters of the area. From that time on, Yucatán was a part of Mexico, both in the colonial period and after independence was declared from Spain. Today the peninsula is divided into three units: the state of Yucatán, the state of Campeche, and the territory of Quintana Roo.

WHAT TO SEE

Mérida. Mérida, capital of the state of Yucatán, is the point of departure for the Maya ruins, and an interesting sight-seeing goal in itself. It was founded as a Spanish city by Francisco de Montejo the younger, in 1541, on the site of a Maya city named Ichcansiho, or Ti-Ho, as it was also called.

It is a city of spacious limestone houses whitewashed or pastel tinted, wide avenues, narrow streets, and green parks shaded by large trees. The population is 115,244. A unique feature is the quantity of windmills, probably fifteen thousand or more of them, which draw the city's water supply from the limestone caverns below the surface. Another distinctive feature is the city's cleanliness, on which visitors invariably comment.

Visit the sixteenth-century cathedral and the Montejo House (both on the main plaza or Zócalo). The latter is still used as a residence, as it has been since Francisco de Montejo built it in 1550. Other colonial remnants are to be found along the streets leading off the Zócalo. The Archaeological Museum is second only to the National Museum in Mexico City. Handmade pottery and Yucatecan hammocks are the best purchases to be made in the huge market. Gold and silver filigree jewelry, articles of tortoise shell and mother-of-pearl, and alligator and snakeskin bags are available in the shops.

Chichén Itzá. It is about seventy-five miles from Mérida to Chichén Itzá. The road for the first forty miles passes through henequen plantations, and then enters the uncleared Yucatecan jungle.

Chichén Itzá is perhaps the most interesting of all the ancient cities of Yucatán because of the fusion of two cultures, the Mayan and the Mexican; and for this reason it has been most intensively studied by archaeologists. In 1924 the Carnegie Institution of Washington sent an expedition under Dr. Sylvanus G. Morley, and ever since that time excavation, clearing, and reconstruction of the fascinating city have been carried on by Carnegie and the Mexican government. Consequently today's visitors are able to see and understand much more than could those of even two decades ago, when many of the buildings were hidden beneath the jungle.

The city was founded probably sometime between the years 471 and 530 A.D. by the Itzás, one of the early groups of Mayas migrating north from the Old Empire cities to the south. The site was undoubtedly chosen because of the two *cenotes*, or large natural wells, not more than a half mile from each other. The name Chichén Itzá means "The Mouths of the Wells of the Itzá." The city appears to have been abandoned in the middle of the seventh century and to have stood unoccupied until, two centuries later (the date is recorded as 964 A.D.), the descendants of the original settlers returned to it. From this time on, it was one of the leading cities of the Mayan empire, being one of the three members of the League of Mayapán.

Then came the disruption of the league and the subjection of Chichén Itzá to Mexican rulers. These were possibly Toltecs, but there are differences of opinion as to which of the western tribes it was that took over the city. It was in this period of foreign domination that Chichén Itzá became the outstanding religious center of the country, and most of the monumental buildings were erected at this time, all showing the dominant influence of the foreign culture. The Mexicans brought with them their god Quetzalcoatl, the "Feathered Serpent," who as Kukulcan (the Maya translation of the name) became the principal deity. It was in this period that the northern of the two *cenotes* of the city became a "Well of Sacrifice." Probably it had always been regarded with veneration; but under the new rulers it was used for a sacrificial pit into which maidens were thrown to appease the gods. Besides the living sacrifices, treasured articles of gold, jade, pottery, and the like were thrown into the well. It is from these articles, recovered from the bottom, that it is learned how widespread was the fame of the sacred well of Chichén Itzá. Articles from as far away as northwestern Mexico and Costa Rica were cast into the well, probably by pilgrims who had made the long journey through the jungles in order to offer these tributes to the gods.

The northern section of the ruins is the newest and the most pronouncedly Mexican. Surmounting the highest pyramid (generally called El Castillo) is the Temple of Kukulcan, the Feathered Serpent. The pyramid is especially interesting, for it encloses an earlier, purely Maya one, and even the early temple that crowned it, all of which lay undiscovered until only a few years ago. Through tunnels cut through the exterior walls one can enter this more ancient sanctuary and see the remarkable carved red jaguar found there.

From the Temple of Kukulcan one can survey the rest of the city. To the east is the extensive Group of the Thousand Columns, where columns form colonnades enclosing a plaza of five acres dotted with temples and courts. The magnificent Temple of the Warriors rises on the north of this group. It is really two temples, an ancient Maya one covered over and superimposed by a Mexican-Maya one. The Temple of the Tigers is west of El Castillo, and beyond it the largest and most beautiful of the several ball courts of the city, where the Maya game of *tlachtli*, somewhat like modern soccer and basketball, was played.

To the south is an older section that shows less of the Mexican influence. The round tower of the Observatory (called El Caracol), where probably astrologer-priests observed the passage of the sun and the planets through the specially aligned windows; the magnificent House of the Nuns, one of the most massively beautiful Maya buildings in all of Yucatán; and the several smaller temples and palaces make up this interesting group.

A short distance to the south of this area is the group of ruins known as Old Chichén. These are the oldest structures of the region and are believed to have belonged to the original city, before its abandonment in the eighth century.

Uxmal. Uxmal may be visited in one day from Mérida. Return to Mérida for the night, as there is no lodging at the ruins. It is a drive of about an hour and a half over a good road. Much of the site remains to be cleared and excavated, but the cleared parts are enough to indicate the past glory and grandeur of this ancient capital.

Uxmal is more purely Mayan than Chichén Itzá, having been subjected only slightly to the Mexican influence. Ruined though it is, it is still majestic, with great heavy buildings adorned with stone carvings unrivaled in the Mayan New Empire. The history of the city has not been so well established as that of Chichén Itzá. It probably was founded at the time of the abandonment of the Old Empire cities. By the eleventh century, when the League of Mayapán was formed, Uxmal was a populous and powerful center. Like Chichén Itzá, it came under the domination of Mayapán during the thirteenth and fourteenth centuries, and with Chichén Itzá it overthrew the hated Mayapán rulers in the middle of the fifteenth century. Then the inhabitants of Uxmal, like those of the other two cities, abandoned their beautiful capital. The new city they founded at Maní, thirty miles or so to the east, never attained the splendor of the old city.

The Governor's Palace of Uxmal is one of the most impressive examples of Mayan architecture, and indeed is considered by some the most magnificent single building of pre-Columbian America. Long, low, and massive, standing upon the topmost of three broad terraces, superbly decorated with carved stone blocks, some twenty thousand in all, fitted together to form an endless variety of masks, serpents, and geometric designs, it has astonished and puzzled visitors since the days of the Spanish Conquest. Not far away is the Nunnery Quadrangle, with its several buildings displaying elaborately carved façades. The House of the Pigeons, so called from the delicate fretwork design of the decoration, the House of the Dwarf on its high pyramid, the ball court, and others of the ruined monuments strain the imagination with their mystery.

Other Trips. Chichén Itzá and Uxmal are the only large ruins as yet easily accessible in the Yucatán. However, others can be visited, even by car, if you are willing to put up with the discomfort of driving over rough trails scratched into the limestone. Still others can be reached only on horseback. Others, along the east coast, can be explored by getting a small boat and sailing along the coast.

Besides these monuments of the past, the modern cities and villages of Yucatán are picturesque and interesting. Campeche is the oldest Spanish settlement in Yucatán. Overlooking the blue waters of the Gulf of Campeche, surrounded by heavy walls built to protect it from pirate attacks, it is a quiet and charming Spanish colonial city. It was near here that the Spanish conquerors landed in 1540 to subdue the Mayas, and Montejo himself founded the city in that year (see page 172).

If you hear of fiestas in any of the villages, you should make every effort to attend. You will find the village buzzing with activity— booths set up around the square to provide refreshment and diversion; often an improvised bull ring where bullfights are conducted in an unorthodox and far less grim manner than the classical Spanish fight; and at night the *jarana,* a graceful Yucatecan dance, which enthusiastic couples dance until dawn.

CHAPTER VIII

ENCYCLOPEDIA OF PLACES

MEXICAN towns follow no distinct pattern that any writer has been able to define and delineate as typically Mexican, and yet Mexican towns do have an atmosphere, a style, or a character that is not Guatemalan or Cuban or Colombian. Certainly it is not like anything in the United States. One writer says, ". . . a typical Mexican town of adobe houses and red tile roofs." Arizona, New Mexico, and Texas have hundreds of towns that would fit this description, and yet they lack that "certain something" that makes a Mexican town a "typical Mexican town." It is not entirely the result of coloring that these towns get from their picturesque inhabitants either, or the primitive transportation—oxcarts and burros—seen in nearly every village. These features are common to towns in other Latin-American countries. And though most of the places the average traveler sees have this indefinable characteristic, no two towns are alike. Our best service, therefore, is to provide the information about these places that will help you to see for yourself and thus be your own delineator. It is more pleasure that way—for both of us.

Some novice traveler may say that this is not the place for an index of towns and villages in Mexico and such catalogued information, but on our first trip and on our hundredth we said there ought to be a handy guide to all the towns of tourist interest, and experience has taught us what information would be most appreciated. And this is as good a place as any to put it.

Until recently nearly all sources of information in Mexico were notoriously unreliable. The accuracy of the data one collected at the Ministry of the Interior became questionable when one got figures covering the same information from the Ministry of Agriculture. And this was doubly true of municipal government offices. Further, if one had to depend on our own United States foreign service for any of this information, one soon discovered that originally inaccurate data had been garbled in bureaucratic transit. Obviously, no writer of guides could go around counting noses in every town and village, or personally check the altitude of every place with his own altimeter, or measure off the miles between them. Be tolerant, therefore, if you are still using an old copy of Terry's *Guide to Mexico*. But with us—we have no such excuse. Mexico's statistical bureaus are as streamlined and efficient and (more important!) accurate today as any government data-dispensing offices anywhere. Furthermore, several agencies in the United States have had occasion to double-check the Mexican data recently, and we have kept one eye cocked on their findings as we compiled the following information. These, principally, were the Pan American Union and the American Automobile Association. But in any case where all sources disagreed (and this happened quite frequently in spite of our new-found faith), we took our own guess from what we knew of the place. In the final analysis, therefore, only we are responsible for these figures, and any dissenters will be told, "Well, you must admit that we hit it pretty close."

The dollar sign ($) wherever used in this chapter represents Mexican pesos.

ACAPULCO, state of Guerrero (ah-kah-POOL-koh—from the Nahuatl "place of the reeds or bamboos"). Altitude: 13 feet. Population: 9,915. Climate: Tropical and generally sultry.

Transportation: Paved road and daily bus service to Mexico City via Cuernavaca and Taxco; airways (Aeronaves) to Mexico City, Oaxaca, and Uruapan. By highway it is 282 miles from Mexico City.

Importance: Considered the most famous resort on the Pacific coast of Mexico. Tourists and sports activities are the principal industries.

History: It is believed that the Spaniards first visited Acapulco in 1521. Diego Hurtado de Mendoza sailed from this harbor June 30, 1522, to explore the South Seas. In 1555 vessels from the Orient began to bring silk, spices, and paper to Acapulco in exchange for silver (read Bret Harte's poem "Lost Galleon"). The ships' cargoes were carried overland between Acapulco and Mexico City by muleback. Watch for traces of the old cobblestone road as you descend the mountain approaching Cuernavaca. Except for the excitement caused by the arrival of a ship, throughout the seventeenth and eighteenth centuries Acapulco was just another sleepy little village. The paved highway connecting it to Mexico City was completed in 1927 and tourists found it soon after.

Visit: Caleta Beach, mornings only; Hornos Beach, afternoons only. Fortress of San Diego, constructed in 1616, to protect the town and the galleons in the harbor.

Environs: Pie de la Cuesta, a picturesque beach unfit for bathing but interesting for its high surf: a narrow strip of sandy beach separates the pounding surf from the Laguna de Coyuca, a quiet freshwater lagoon surrounded by luxuriant tropical vegetation. Puerto Marqués, a remote old seaport now little used except by adventurous picnickers who love jungle scenery and isolated beaches.

Sports: Swimming in crystal-blue sea water with or without strong surf (moonlight bathing is especially popular); sailing and motorboating; water skiing and fishing. Glass-bottom-boat rides are popular, as a most interesting variety of fish in many magnificent colors can be seen near the shores. Golf and tennis are available at various clubs. Fishing, however, is the most important sport. Acapulco holds the world's record for sailfish, the season for which is November to April. Several strange fish are common in local waters: the sunfish, which, when born, is only a tenth of an inch long and grows to ten feet, increasing its weight sixty million times; the *cornuda* or hammerfish, a combination of shark and whale; giant stingrays; turtles five feet long; marlin, and many others. Hunting in the surrounding jungles: deer, jaguars, alligators, parrots, and wildcats.

Dishes: Seviche, raw fish softened in lemon juice. *Callos de Hacha,* a delicious shellfish.

Handicrafts: Seashell novelties, snakeskin belts and purses, and tortoise-shell work.

Fiestas: Holy Week and the preceding carnival.

Hotels: The wide range in quality and price of accommodations in Acapulco is almost equal to that found in Mexico City, except that prices generally are higher in Acapulco. If you plan a long stay and must live inexpensively, then take a room at one of these hotels for the first day or two while you shop around; taxi drivers will help you find comfortable pensions or rooming houses. The following are minimum daily rates, American plan (rooms with meals), and quoted in Mexican pesos.

Name	Single	Double	Remarks
De las Américas	$50	$85	New, cottage-type, de luxe.
Las Anclas	35	60	Good, small.
Bahía	45	70	Newest; near Caleta Beach.
Los Flamingos	50	80	Clean, comfortable; 30 rooms.
Las Hamacas	40	70	Native family style; 100 rooms.
Manzanillo	22	40	Second-class but fair.
La Marina	30	55	Near the fishing wharf.
Mirador	30	55	Good, older hotel; 50 rooms.
Del Monte	35	60	Very good; 20 rooms.
Mozimba	30	45	Good; middle-class.
Las Palmas Courts	27	44	At Playa Langosta Beach.
Papagayo	45	70	Attractive, modern; 200 rooms.
Los Pingüinos	27	50	Facing Hornos Beach.
Quinta María	18	30	For rugged travelers.
Reforma Casa Blanca	65	100	De luxe accommodations.
Rincón del Mar	20	36	Beautifully located.
La Riviera	35	70	Elegantly French.

ACTOPAN, state of Hidalgo (ak-TOH-pahn). Altitude: 6,529 feet. Population: 2,839. Climate: temperate.

A picturesque little village seventy-three miles north of Mexico City on the Pan American Highway. The road turns off here for Tula, supposed ancient capital of the Toltecs.

Most interesting on Wednesday, market day. The old convent of St. Augustine, constructed in 1546, is now a rural normal school.

AGUASCALIENTES, state of Aguascalientes (Spanish for "hot waters" or "hot springs"). Altitude: 6,165 feet. Population: 82,234. Climate: mild and usually delightful.

Transportation: Highway and daily bus service to Guadalajara and San Luís Potosí; airways (PANINI) to Mexico City and Durango; railway to El Paso, Texas, Mexico City, and San Luís Potosí. By rail it is 585 kilometers (365 miles) to Mexico City.

Importance: State capital and center of an agricultural region. Many hot springs in vicinity.

Visit: Governor's Palace, constructed by Tolsá for the Marqués of Guadalupe. Cieneguilla Hacienda. Cathedral, built in 1738, and San Diego Church. Institute of Sciences and the ancient house of the

Conde de Rul. A column in the principal plaza, designed by Tolsá, locates the geographic center of the republic.

Environs: Ojo Caliente and La Cantera hot springs. San Miguelito River and the Calles and Rodríguez dams. Barrio Cavillo, an orchard-surrounded suburb.

Dishes: Try the local *charamuscas,* a kind of taffy.

Handicrafts: Colorful but mediocre serapes and drawn embroidery.

Fiestas: Fiesta de San Marcos, usually end of April or first of May; official date is April 25.

Hotels: The Hotel Paris is the only one we can recommend; forty rooms, all with bath; food, fair. Minimum daily single rate with meals, $10.

AMECAMECA, state of Mexico (ah-may-kah-MAY-kah). Altitude: 8,103 feet. Population: 7,422. Climate: mild and generally delightful during the day but chilly at night.

Transportation: Paved highway and daily bus service to Mexico City (thirty-seven miles).

Importance: Trading center for a large agricultural and lumber area. Town is located at the foot of the volcanoes Ixtaccíhuatl and Popocatépetl, and their ascent usually begins here. Site of historic religious shrine.

History: Amecameca was an Indian metropolis centuries before the arrival of the Spaniards. On the summit of a high hill near the village is a small church built around a cave that was once the home of a very holy man, Fray Martín de Valencia, who came to Mexico in 1523. He was greatly revered by the simple Indians and after his death was buried in the cave. In time he was made a saint, and his grave is the mecca of thousands of Indians who come here during Holy Week.

Visit: Santuario de Sacramonte; climb to the top of the hill for an excellent view of the valley with Ixtaccíhuatl and Popocatépetl rising sharply in the background. Market, best on Sunday, is generally interesting. The cathedral dates from the sixteenth century.

Environs: Tlalmanalco, a village on the road to Mexico City, contains an old Franciscan convent with frescoed cloisters and an open-air chapel. Ozumba, the nearest town to Popocatépetl, has an old Franciscan church with some unusual paintings; near the village are the picturesque gardens of Chimalhuacán and the Cascada de Chimal (waterfall).

Sports: See "Mountain Climbing," page 233.

Fiestas: Carnival and Holy Week.

Hotels: Make this town a day's excursion from Mexico City or Cuernavaca.

CAMPECHE, state of Campeche (kahm-PAY-chay—from the Maya *kim,* "serpent," and *pech,* "tick"). Altitude: 25 feet. Population: 23,166. Climate: sultry, tropical.

Transportation: Plane (CMA) to Veracruz or Mérida; boat to Veracruz (Compañía Mexicana de Navigación); railway to Mérida, 180 kilometers or five hours (United Railways of Yucatán); highway to Mérida, 108 miles.

Importance: Capital of the state. Production center of precious woods (logwood, dyewood, mahogany, and others), chicle, sugar cane, rice, tobacco, sisal, cotton, and indigo.

History: Region first explored in 1517 by Hernández de Córdoba; city founded in 1540 by Francisco Montejo. Taken many times by pirates, among them William Park in 1597, Diego el Mulato in 1631, the Englishman Jacob Jackson in 1644, and Laurent Graff, the infamous Lorencillo, in 1685. Because of the pirates and to avoid new attacks by them, the city was walled.

Visit: The city walls, twenty feet in height and eight feet thick, and the castles within them: San Miguel, Puerta de Tierra, San Pedro, and Santa Rosa. The cathedral, Temple of Carmen, Government Palace, Alameda, Museum of Natural History and Archaeology, and Botanical Gardens.

Environs: San Francisco. Many Maya archaeological ruins. *Cenotes,* or natural wells.

Dishes: Sea food, especially oysters.

Handicrafts: Tortoise-shell and mother-of-pearl work, and "Panama" hats.

Fiestas: Annual religious fiesta, October 22.

Hotels: Castlemar, on the sea; thirty-five rooms with baths; $6 to $10 single. Campeche, on the Plaza de Armas, forty-three rooms, mostly with baths; $6 to $8 single. Cuauhtémoc, on the Plaza de Armas; sixteen rooms with baths; $8 single. Villa, in town; nineteen rooms with baths; $6 to $9 single. All rates are European plan.

CELAYA, state of Guanajuato (say-LAH-yah—from the Basque word *zalaya,* meaning "level land"). Altitude: 5,850 feet. Population: 22,766. Climate: mild, dry.

Transportation: Rail to Mexico City, about seven hours (Ferrocarriles Nacionales); paved highway via Querétaro, turn off Pan American Highway at Kilometer 167 near Ixmiquilpan; busses to Querétaro, Acámbaro, and Irapuato.

Importance: Trading center for cattle and grain-producing region.

History: Town founded by Basque immigrants in 1570.

Visit: El Carmen Church and its paintings made by the colonial architect and painter Francisco Eduardo Tresguerras, born in Celaya in 1765 and buried in the Church of San Francisco.

Environs: A picturesque central highland rural region.

Fiestas: Holy Week; Virgin of Guadalupe, December 12; and January 11 to 20, annual dances *El Plumero, La Sonaja,* and *Pastorelas.*

Hotels: Isabel, at Avenida Hidalgo 15; a few rooms with bath and telephone; restaurant, bar, and roof garden; minimum, $7 single, $14 double. Hotel Juárez, twenty-six rooms, $3 minimum single. Hotel Mexico, thirty-two rooms, $3 minimum single.

CHALCO, state of Mexico (CHAHL-koh). Population: 3,028. An ancient Axtec town on the Mexico City–Amecameca highway, twenty-two miles from Mexico City. Has an old Franciscan church.

CHAPALA, state of Jalisco (cha-PAH-lah—from the Nahuatl *chapalal* meaning "the sound of waves on a sandy beach"). Altitude: 5,159 feet (altitude of lake). Population: 1,000. Climate: mild and usually delightful, a sort of perpetual Indian summer.

Transportation: Paved road and daily bus service to Guadalajara (thirty-two miles).

Importance: Famous principally for Lake Chapala, largest lake in Mexico. The village is becoming a favorite with artists and writers. Radioactive sulphur springs in the vicinity.

Environs: Picturesque village of Ajijic.

Sports: Swimming, fishing, sailing, hunting, and horseback riding.

Hotels: Hotel Nido, about a block from the beach; hot water and baths; minimum rates, American plan, single, $10; double, $18. Hotel

Villa Montecarlo, with private beach; minimum rate, American plan, $25 per day per person.

CHIHUAHUA, state of Chihuahua (chee-WAH-wah—from the Tarahumara meaning "place of the workshop"). Altitude: 4,634 feet. Population: 56,805. Climate: like autumn during the winter; hottest during May, June, and July.

Transportation: Paved road and daily bus service to Ciudad Juárez; railway to Ciudad Juárez and Mexico City; airways (LAMSA) to Nogales, Ciudad Juárez, and Mexico City. Chihuahua is 1,613 kilometers by rail from Mexico City; 360 kilometers from Ciudad Juárez; and 237 kilometers by highway from Ciudad Juárez.

Importance: Capital of the state; mining and manufacturing center; and important distribution point for northern Mexico. One of the world's largest smelters is located here. Home of the Chihuahueños, tiny Chihuahua dogs.

History: Founded in 1707 by Friar Francisco Múñoz and known as San Francisco de Cuellar until 1718, when the name was changed to San Miguel el Real de Chihuahua. Don Miguel Hidalgo y Costilla, father of Mexican independence, was imprisoned and finally executed here in 1811. The region's rich silver mines played an important part in the financial rehabilitation of Spain (and the Vatican) in viceregal days. In more recent years the town was the seat of operations of many revolutionary bandits. Today it is as American as southern Texas towns are Mexican.

Visit: San Francisco Cathedral, founded 1717, and the Palacio de Gobierno, built around an older tower in which Hidalgo was imprisoned. Pancho Villa's home. Silver mines.

Environs: Near the town of Casas Grandes are prehistoric ruins resembling the Zuñi ruins of New Mexico. Curative baths at San Diego; the Picos de Majalca is a summer resort; and El Toronto is a large artificial lake.

Sports: Jaguar hunting from February to June.

Fiestas: Santa Rita, May 22.

Hotels: Hotel Palacio Hilton, of the American Hilton hotel chain; minimum, single, $8; double, $14, European plan.

CHILPANCINGO, state of Guerrero (cheel-pahn-SEEN-goh—from the Aztec, meaning "place of the wasps"; also known as Ciudad

Bravo). Altitude: 4,500 feet. Population: 8,330. Climate: temperate to warm, but generally dry.

Transportation: Paved highway and daily bus service to Mexico City, Cuernavaca (144 miles), and Acapulco (92 miles).

Importance: Center of a large irrigated agricultural area and cattle-raising district.

History: The first Mexican congress met here in 1813.

Visit: The Palacio de Gobierno, the sixteenth-century bridge, and the old cemetery.

Fiestas: New Year's Fair, December 24 to January 6, with many native dances.

Hotels: Hotel Kilometer 300 is small (eleven rooms and baths) but comfortable; rate, $15 double.

CHOLULA, state of Puebla (cho-LOO-lah—the "Holy City of Aná-huac"). Altitude: 7,042 feet. Population: 2,100. Climate: mild and pleasant.

Transportation: Frequent bus service to Puebla (nine miles) and Mexico City (seventy-six miles).

Now considered a suburb of Puebla, Cholula had a population of over 100,000 with four hundred shrines and temples when it was destroyed by Cortés. In the center was the largest pyramid in the Western Hemisphere, supporting on its top the Temple of Quetzalcoatl. The pyramid is now overgrown and surmounted by a colonial church, the Santuario Los Remedios, built in 1666. Another interesting church is the famous Capilla Real (Royal Chapel), notable for its strong Moorish influence and sixty-three domes. The Cholula market is worth a visit.

Fiestas: Fiesta de Los Remedios, September 8.

Hotels: Stay in Puebla.

CIUDAD JUÁREZ, state of Chihuahua (see-oo-DAHD WHA-rayz—named for President Benito Juárez). Altitude: 3,752 feet. Population: 48,881. Climate: temperate, dry.

Transportation: Located across the international bridge over the Rio Grande from El Paso, Texas; airways (LAMSA) to central Mexico; and railways (Ferrocarriles Nacionales) to Mexico and (Southern Pacific) to the United States.

Importance: Principal border town in northern Mexico, port of entry, and trading center for large area. Products: cotton oil, whisky, cheap cotton clothing.

History: First revolutionary congress of Mexico held here in 1810. During the reform period President Benito Juárez established his headquarters here.

Visit: Market and central plaza; curio shops; Zaragoza Gardens near town.

Environs: Casa Grande ruins (similar to Pueblo and Zuñi Indian ruins north of the border). Mormon colonies near by, such as Dublán, Juárez, Díaz, and Fernández Leal. Pichachic, ancient town founded in 1665, has an interesting church. Canyon in Barranca del Cobre at La Mesa is worth a visit. Thermal baths of Aguacaliente de Baca.

Dishes: Chili con carne, or *chile con frijoles,* if you can stand it hot.

Handicrafts: Silver, leather goods, souvenir postcards.

Fiestas: San Lorenzo, August 10, with a dance called *Matachines;* Virgin of Guadalupe, December 12.

Hotels: Stay in El Paso.

CIUDAD MANTE, state of Tamaulipas. See El Mante, state of Tamaulipas.

CIUDAD VALLES, state of San Luís Potosí (VAH-yehs). Altitude: 312 feet. Population: 7,240. Climate: subtropical.

Located on the Pan American Highway 145 miles south of Ciudad Victoria.

Important distributing point for surrounding region, which produces coffee and cattle. Railway and bus connections to Tampico, Monterrey, and Mexico City.

Hotels: Hotel Casa Grande, fifty rooms with baths; good; $10 single and $15 double. Hotel Valles, forty-five rooms with baths; good, slightly cheaper. Colonial Courts, just north of town, has nineteen units with baths; nice; minimum $15 double.

CIUDAD VICTORIA, state of Tamaulipas (see-oo-DAHD veek-TOH-ree-ah). Altitude: 1,470 feet. Population: 25,825. Climate: mild to subtropical.

Transportation: Plane (CMA) to Nuevo Laredo or Mexico City;

railway and bus service to Nuevo Laredo or Mexico City; and Pan American Highway. By highway it is 326 miles from Laredo, Texas; 180 miles from Monterrey; and 438 miles from Mexico City.

Importance: Capital of the state. Center of a rich agricultural region and vacation spot. Good overnight stop on Pan American Highway.

History: First named City of Our Lady of Refuge of Aguayo upon its founding, October 6, 1750. Later changed on April 21, 1825, to Victoria in honor of the Mexican hero and first president of Mexico, General Guadalupe Victoria.

Visit: Juárez Park; main plaza; cathedral.

Environs: Good deer and tiger hunting; mountain climbing; horseback riding; fishing. Hotel Sierra Gorda will provide useful information on these sports as well as guides and directions to reach an excellent sea-fishing place on the Gulf of Mexico called La Pesca. See La Peñita, a spot of rustic beauty, and the Falls of Juan Capitán.

Dishes: Try *machacado* (eggs with dried beef and choice pork sausage); *pansaje* or *pancita* (pastries); and *nogada* (a candy made of milk and nuts).

Fiestas: Annual religious fiesta, May 19, with street fair and *matachines* dances.

Hotels: Sierra Gorda, located in town; eighty rooms with bath, some air-conditioned; minimum single, $12. Campo Victoria, a tourist camp on the Pan American Highway one kilometer north of town; thirty rooms with bath; minimum single, $10. Palacio, in town; forty rooms with bath; minimum single, $10. Hacienda San Engracia, a modern and comfortable guest ranch at foot of Sierra Madre Mountains, thirty-five miles southwest of town; colonial atmosphere, swimming pool; twelve rooms with bath; single with meals, $40 daily.

COATZACOALCOS, state of Veracruz (or Puerto Mexico).

A drab and sultry coastal town on the Gulf of Mexico at the mouth of the Coatzacoalcos River.

Transportation: Railway to Veracruz (Tehuantepec Nacional); and airways (Aeronaves) to Mexico City, Puebla, and Veracruz, and (Golfo y Pacífico) to Veracruz, Ixtepec, and Salina Cruz.

Importance: Rail and river terminal and commercial center serving large tropical area.

Visit: The market is interesting, and river trips are thrilling for the adventurous.

Hotels: Ask the local airways agent to recommend the best available.

COLIMA, state of Colima (koh-LEE-mah—originally an Aztec town called Cajitlan, or "place where pottery is made"). Altitude: 1,538 feet. Population: 30,000. Climate: subtropical.

Transportation: Airways (PANINI) to Mexico City, Uruapan, Manzanillo, and Guadalajara; and railways to Manzanillo and Guadalajara.

Importance: Capital of the state of Colima and trading center for large agricultural area.

There is little to see from a tourist standpoint. The Colima volcano, looming to a height of 12,278 feet back of the city, and its twin, El Nevado (14,370 feet), add some extraordinary scenery to the setting.

Fiestas: Annual agricultural fair, October 30.

Hotels: Try to avoid staying overnight in Colima, but if you must, then take your pick: Carabanchel, Fenix, and Occidental, all on or near the plaza. Rates from $15 up per day, single, with meals.

CÓRDOBA, state of Veracruz (KOHR-doh-bah—after the Spanish city). Altitude: 2,697 feet. Population: 17,865. Climate: semitropical, warm, and generally moist.

Transportation: Highway and daily bus service to Mexico City and Puebla; railway to Mexico City and Veracruz; plane (Aeronaves) to Mexico City, Veracruz, and Coatzacoalcos.

Importance: Trading center of a large semitropical agricultural region producing sugar, vanilla, bananas, mangoes, and coffee. Railway division point for connections to the Isthmus of Tehuantepec for those who want to avoid going by way of Veracruz.

History: Settled in 1618 as a way-station stop on the route from Veracruz to Mexico City in the early days of the Spanish Conquest, it has changed little in succeeding years. The climatic conditions are not conducive to much history-making activity.

Visit: Little of tourist interest exists in Córdoba. To enjoy the place one should spend time visiting some of the plantations in the region.

Environs: Tropical forests, sugar-cane plantations, pineapple and banana plantations are easily accessible. Most interesting is a primitive Indian village, Amatlán, where original indigenous mores and customs still prevail. Metlac Barranca, Fortín, the town of Orizaba (see page 193), and the snow-capped Pico de Orizaba are near.

Fiestas: Patriotic fiesta, May 21.

Hotels: If you get stuck, try the Hotel Zevallos in an historic old building constructed in 1681; European plan, minimum daily single, $7; double, $12. A new hotel is under construction. Until it is completed don't get stuck, go on to Fortín (de las Flores), thirty-four miles, where there are several good hotels: Hotel Ruiz Galindo, American plan, single $40, double $75; Posada Loma, American plan, single, $30; double, $55.

CUAUTLA, state of Morelos (KWOW-tlah). Altitude: 4,254 feet. Population: 6,431. Climate: mild to subtropical.

Transportation: Paved highway and daily bus service to Mexico City (sixty-five miles).

Importance: Old resort town generally patronized by natives; trading center for large agricultural and cattle-raising area.

Visit: The hot springs called Agua Hedionda with swimming pool and bathhouses about two miles south of the village. Near the springs is the village of Oaxtepec, once the favorite garden retreat of Moctezuma.

Hotels: San Diego, twenty rooms, some with bath; American plan, minimum daily, single, $15; double, $20. Hotel Vasco, thirty rooms, thirty baths; American plan, minimum, single, $20; double, $35; bungalows, $60 for one or two persons.

CUERNAVACA, state of Morelos (queer-nah-VAH-cah—literally "cow's horn," a Hispanicized twist given by the Spaniards to the Nahuatl Indian Cuauhnahuac, meaning "near the woods"). Altitude: 5,043 feet. Population: 14,500. Climate: warm, semitropical, ideal most of the year.

Transportation: Paved highway to Mexico City, forty-six miles; also railway, though bus and taxi service are better.

Importance: Capital of the state and trading center for large agricultural district. Famous as a comfortable resort for centuries.

History: Aztec emperors had their summer homes here. Later,

Cortés followed their example, as did Maximilian and Carlota, many other rulers of Mexico, and José de la Borda, the "silver king." It is today the favorite resort of Mexican and foreign celebrities.

Visit: The Palacio de Cortés, begun in 1530, has undergone many alterations, is now the seat of state government, and contains many interesting paintings and sculptures, including murals by Diego Rivera; the latter were a gift to Mexico by the late ambassador Dwight Morrow; good view from the roof. The cathedral, founded by Cortés in 1529, is one of the oldest churches in the republic. It is of early Franciscan fortress-like construction. The Capilla del Tercer Orden (Chapel of the Third Order), at the southwest corner of the cathedral, built at the same time as the cathedral, shows some interesting Indian sculptures on both sides of the atrium. The Jardín de la Borda (Borda Garden) opposite the cathedral was once the chief show place of Cuernavaca; it was the home of José de la Borda, a Frenchman who came to Mexico in 1716, made millions in mining, and built his home here; it served as the summer home of Maximilian and Carlota in 1864 and is now a small hotel. The Church of Nuestra Señora de Guadalupe, erected by Borda's son, was used by the Borda family as a chapel; it adjoins the gardens on the north. The Pyramid of Teopanzolco, near the railroad station, was probably built by the Aztecs, though it may date from the earlier Tlahuicas. San Antonio, a suburb village, is the home of the famous Cuernavaca pottery; the Salto San Antón (waterfall) near by is scenic. Chapultepec, east of town off the Cuautla highway, has a bathing pool, bathhouses, and a pavilion surrounded by cypresses.

Environs: The sugar mill at Atlacomulco, erected by Cortés in 1535, is the oldest *ingenio de azúcar* (sugar mill) on the continent. Emperor Maximilian's shooting lodge at Acapacingo (near the sugar mill) is falling into decay. The cave of Cacahuamilpa, largest known cave in Mexico, is forty-six miles southwest. The Empress Carlota inspected the cave in 1866 and on one of the walls wrote: "María Carlota reached this point." Sebastián Lerdo de Tejada, an opponent of monarchies and one-time president of Mexico, visited the cave in 1874 and beneath the above inscription significantly wrote: "Sebastián Lerdo de Tejada went beyond." Xochicalco (House of Flowers) is an old Aztec ruin about eighteen miles west of town. Tepoztlán is a mountain town, occupied almost entirely by direct descendants of the Aztecs, beautifully located, with a background of awe-inspiring cliffs. The Pyramid of Tepozteco, the native deity who is credited with the discovery of pulque, stands on a cliff overlooking the town. Tepoztlán is thirteen miles northeast of Cuernavaca. Yautepec is a picturesque little village (population, 4,316) on the Río Yautepec in a region of orange trees and sugar cane on the Cuautla road east of Cuernavaca. The Zempoala Lakes are about twenty-three miles northeast; good fishing and superb mountain scenery.

Handicrafts: Various types of huaraches (sandals); Indian pottery; hand-woven belts, blouses, and baskets; silver jewelry; leather belts and bags.

Fiestas: Covadonga, September 8; Candelaria, February 2; and San Antón, June 13.

Hotels: There are several excellent hotels in Cuernavaca and some inexpensive pensions or boardinghouses. To select one of the latter for a long stay, one should stop a day or two at one of the hotels and inspect and select the pension with care. The local and Mexico City publications carry their advertisements, and notices are frequently posted in the post office and plazas of Cuernavaca. Rates shown below are minimum daily for rooms with bath and meals.

Name	Single	Double	Remarks
Bella Vista	$15	$30	Nice and comfortable, 50 rooms.
Chula Vista	25	45	Very good, 100 rooms.
Gran Hotel Casino	30	55	100 rooms, first-class.
Hernando Cortés	35	40	Small, family type.
Mandel's Inn (AAA)	15	20	One mile north of town.
Marik (AAA)	15	25	Modern, excellent, 70 rooms.
Palacio	30	50	Small, family hotel.

There are several good second-class hotels, centrally located, with rates from $10 single and $15 double, American plan. The best of these are the Colón, the Florida, and the Miraval.

DURANGO, state of Durango (doo-RAHN-goh—named for the old Basque city). Altitude: 6,209 feet. Population: 33,412. Climate: temperate.

Transportation: Railway to Torreón and Felipe Pescador; airways

(LAMSA) to Mexico City, Mazatlán, Nuevo Laredo, and Torreón, and (PANINI) to Culiacan and Mexico City; road and regular bus service to Torreón.

Importance: Capital of the state and one of the most important silver- and iron-mining centers in the republic. Cotton mills.

History: Region was generally inhabited by nomad Indians until its settlement in 1563 by the Spanish.

Visit: The cathedral, begun in 1695 and completed in 1750. Palacio de Gobierno; Plaza Principal; Mercado; and iron mines in vicinity.

Environs: Lerdo, and the important mining center of Tepehuanes.

Sports: Durango is the starting point for big-game hunting: jaguars, bears, deer.

Hotels: Hotel Roma is about the only choice; rooms with bath, single, $6 up; double, $9 up.

EL BAÑITO, state of San Luís Potosí (bahn-YEE-toh—"little bath"). A resort stop on the Pan American Highway at Kilometer 463 (478 miles from Laredo and 7 south of Ciudad Valles).

Importance: Thermal springs and swimming pools. Starting point for hunting trips—wild turkey, deer, jaguar, and quail. Horseback riding and hiking.

Environs: Mico waterfall; El Salto waterfall; and Jilitla, a typical village. Tancanhuitz, a village especially interesting on market days.

Hotels: The Hotel Balneario el Bañito is the center of this spot. Owned and operated by an American couple; southern fried chicken, steaks, and coffee are the specialties; minimum daily rates, European plan, are $7 single and $14 double.

EL MANTE, state of Tamaulipas (el MAHN-tay—formerly Villa Juárez and sometimes called Ciudad Mante). Altitude: 295 feet. Population: 7,000. Climate: generally sultry.

Importance: Trading center for a large agricultural (sugar-cane) district. Largest sugar mill in the republic located here. Junction of Tampico road and Pan American Highway.

Visit: Sugar mill, in operation from November to April.

Environs: Good hunting region: mountain lion, jaguar, ocelot, wild turkey, deer, wild boar, javelina, and quail.

Hotels: Hotel Mante is the best choice until a new one under con-

struction is completed; forty rooms with bath; rates, $10 single and
$15 double.

FORTÍN, state of Veracruz (frequently Fortín de las Flores or El
Fortín). See under Córdoba, above.

GARCI-CRESPO, state of Puebla. See under Tehuacán, below.

GUADALAJARA, state of Jalisco (gwah-dah-lah-HAH-rah—after the
city in Spain; Guadalajara people are usually called *tapatios* and
tapatias). Altitude: 5,199 feet. Population: 255,000 (second largest
city) in the republic. Climate: semitropical, springlike, and agreeable the year round.

Transportation: Highways and daily bus service to Mexico City
(428 miles) and El Mante; railway to Mexico City, Manzanillo,
Nogales, and Irapuato; and airways (CMA) to Los Angeles and
Mexico City. Hourly bus service operates to various towns and villages in the vicinity.

Importance: Capital and largest city of the state, second city of
the republic, and commercial and transportation center of western
Mexico. Local industries include glass (hand-blown blue is famous),
pottery (made at the near-by village of Tlaquepaque), tequila, and
a wide range of heavy manufactures.

History: The city was founded in 1530 by Captain Cristóbal de
Oñate, who named it after the city of Guadalajara in Spain, birthplace of Nuño de Guzmán, original conqueror of the region.

Visit: Seventeenth-century baroque-style Palacio de Gobierno,
facing the city's largest square. The cathedral, in Byzantine and
Gothic, Tuscan, Arabic, Mudejar, Corinthian, Doric, and other styles,
begun in 1571 and completed in 1618, contains a famous Murillo
painting, "The Assumption of the Virgin." Museo del Estado (State
Museum), archaeological relics and some valuable paintings. The
orphan asylum, where Clemente Orozco painted some of his most
famous murals. Santa Mónica Church (seventeenth century) and
San Francisco Church (sixteenth century). Penitentiary, where in-
mates work at different crafts and sell products to visitors.

Environs: Zapopan Church (about an hour from city) of the
seventeenth century, base of California missionaries. About six
miles east is Tlaquepaque, a charming village where pottery is made.

Lake Chapala, thirty-two miles southeast. Juanacatlán Falls and Oblatos ravine. Los Altos is a picturesque village, typical of Jalisco state, and subject of many *mariachi* songs. Tequila, reached by paved road, is the home of the famous Mexican drink.

Sports: Horseback riding, hiking in Oblatos, swimming (many pools), golf, fishing and boating on Lake Chapala.

Dishes: Pozole, corn and meat with chili sauce. *Almendrado,* a tequila drink; "Devil's Blood," another one, prepared with orange and chili.

Handicrafts: Leather chairs and tables, hats, baskets, pottery, glassware, bags, various Indian textiles, silver and gold work.

Fiestas: Principal one is June 29 in San Pedro Tlaquepaque in honor of the patron saint.

Hotels: Most Guadalajara hotels are quiet, modern, and comfortable, reflecting the atmosphere of the local way of life. Rates are slightly under those charged in Mexico City for equal accommodations. Several good pensions or rooming houses are available and may be located through advertisements in the local press. The following hotels are recommended; your choice can be determined by price. The rates shown are for rooms with bath, and without meals.

Name and Address	Single	Double	Rooms
Fenix y Anexos, López Cotilla 285	$15	$20	70
Gran Hotel, Morelos 2450	20	30	42
Guadalajara, Colón 180	15	25	30
Del Parque, Juárez 845	15	25	70
Roma, Pedro Moreno 219	19	36	65
Virreinal, Corona 209	20	25	25

GUANAJUATO, state of Guanajuato (gwah-nah-WHAH-toh—from the Tarascan *guanaxhuato,* "hill of frogs"). Altitude: 6,835 feet. Population: 23,521. Climate: agreeable all year.

Transportation: Highway through Irapuato and Querétaro connecting with Pan American Highway at Kilometer 167 near Ixmiquilpan; railway to Silao, connecting with El Paso–Mexico City line. Local busses operate to surrounding villages.

Importance: Capital of the state; center of rich silver- and gold-mining region; exceptionally picturesque old colonial town.

History: Guanajuato's history is in evidence in countless shrines and ancient landmarks along its twisting, narrow streets. Its mines, discovered in 1550, kept the Spanish treasury solvent for centuries, and some of them still produce.

Visit: Guanajuato's main street, Calle Hidalgo, a winding lane, broad and narrow by turns, from which stem the twisting, climbing *callejones* or alley-like streets. One is so narrow it is called Callejón del Beso (Lane of the Kiss). Jardín de la Unión, a small plaza surrounded by Teatro Juárez, the Hotel Luna, and the Churrigueresque Franciscan church of San Diego, built in 1663. La Parroquia Church dates from 1671 and contains the Virgin of Guanajuato, brought from Spain in 1557 as a gift from King Philip II in appreciation for the flow of silver from the Guanajuato mines. Los Arcos was the entrance to the old Casas Reales, from which the Spanish governors ruled and where Benito Juárez lived in 1858 and proclaimed Guanajuato the provisional capital of Mexico. Among several old homes, see the Casa del Conde Rul y Valenciana, home of the owner of the richest mine and donor of the Valenciana Church. Mortar used in the construction of the latter was mixed with powdered gold and rare Spanish wines; architecture by the famous Francisco Eduardo Tresguerras. Hidalgo market. Alhóndiga de Granaditas, as its name implies, was originally intended as a grain storehouse, but it was used by the royalists as a fort when the town was stormed by Hidalgo. Later Hidalgo himself was beheaded and his head hung from one of the corners of the Alhóndiga.

Environs: Church of Valenciana. The catacombs (a chiller thriller). Pipila Monument.

Handicrafts: Colored pottery, textiles, and tooled leather.

Fiestas: San Ignacio, July 31.

Hotels: Hotel Luna, old but pleasant; American plan, single, $15. Hotel Posada Santa Fe, newer and more expensive.

GUAYMAS, state of Sonora (GWY-mahs—from a Cahita word meaning "shoot arrows at the head"). Altitude: 9 feet. Population: 20,360. Climate: warm and dry in winter, slightly sultry in summer.

Transportation: A motor road runs to Nogales (268 miles); also the Sud Pacífico de México (Southern Pacific of Mexico) railway; or airways (Aeronaves) to Mexico City, Mazatlán, Hermosillo, and Nogales.

Importance: The best sport and commercial fishing port on the Gulf of California.

Sports: Deep-sea fishing facilities at Guaymas or across the peninsula at Hotel Playa de Cortés. Deer and jaguar hunting in surrounding region.

Dishes: Fresh shrimp, oysters.

Hotels: Playa de Cortés, on the beach and away from the village, operated by the Southern Pacific; rates begin at $50 per day, single, American plan. Less expensive is the Hotel Miramar in Guaymas. Rates for fishing boats depend on your ability with Spanish, the season, and the home life of the boat owner. Prices are stable and fixed at Playa de Cortés.

HERMOSILLO, state of Sonora (air-moh-SEE-yoh—"Little Beauty"). Altitude: 693 feet. Population: 30,000. Climate: mild and dry during most of the year.

Transportation: Railway and highway to Nogales (180 miles); airways (CMA) to Los Angeles, Guadalajara, and Mexico City, and (Aeronaves) to Nogales and Mexico City.

Importance: Capital of the state and center of large agricultural area.

Visit: Pueblo Seri, across the river.

Sports: Big-game hunting in the rugged country east of town.

Hotels: Moderno and Ramos, about the same in price and accommodations; single from $10 per day, American plan.

IGUALA, state of Guerrero (ee-GWAH-lah). Altitude: 2,398 feet. Population: 12,008. Climate: semitropical, arid.

Located on the Acapulco highway, 77 miles south of Cuernavaca and 159 miles from Acapulco.

Famous as the seat of Mexican independence. Note the large tamarind trees in the plaza. Friday is market day, and an interesting annual fair is held during the early part of December.

JACALA, state of Hidalgo (hah-CAH-lah). Altitude: 4,593 feet. Population: 2,000. Climate: temperate to cool.

Located on the Pan American Highway, 168 miles north of Mexico City and 59 miles south of Tamazunchale. Bus service to Mexico City. A ranching center.

Hotels: If you get stuck, try Simpson's Court and Restaurant on the north edge of town; $12 double.

JALAPA, state of Veracruz (hah-LAH-pah—from the Indian word *xalliapan,* meaning "sands of the river." Frequently called Flower Garden of Mexico). Altitude: 4,541 feet. Population: 46,825. Climate: subtropical.

Transportation: Paved highway, daily bus service and railway to Veracruz and Mexico City. By highway it is 77 miles from Veracruz and 205 miles from Mexico City.

Importance: Capital of the state; center of a coffee- and tobacco-producing region.

History: Situated on the site of an old Indian village and for centuries a way stop on the Veracruz–Mexico City road.

Visit: Hilly and picturesque streets and flower-filled gardens.

Environs: Hacienda Pasquel (coffee); Coatepec, a colorful Indian village; and Teocelo, a power plant. Waterfalls, subtropical vegetation, and quaint old houses abound in the region. Hardy souls should take the excursion from Jalapa into the magnificent tropical country to Apazapam by train and thence to Jacomulco on horseback. The ancient Totonac ruins of Cempoala may be reached by train (National Railways) from Mexico City to Jalapa to Cardel, thence by bus to Angostadero; or by car by branching off the Jalapa–Veracruz Highway at Puente Nacional.

Handicrafts: Some of the (perishable) flower creations are nice.

Hotels: Hotel Salmones, ninety rooms, ninety baths; single, $10; double, $20; pleasant and about the only choice.

LINARES, state of Nuevo León (lee-NAH-rays). Altitude: 1,265 feet. Population: 9,918. Climate: temperate to subtropical.

Located on the Pan American Highway eighty-two miles south of Monterrey in the center of extensive farming and ranching district. Railway and bus service to Monterrey and Mexico City. Leading industries are the manufacture of brick, tile, brooms, and furniture.

The Parochial Church and the Church of Señor de la Misericordia are worth a visit.

Hotels: Chester Courts, on the highway at the north edge of town, have several units with baths; plain but comfortable; rate, $10 double. Hardwicke's Canada Courts, off the highway, nice; double, $15.

MANZANILLO, state of Colima (mahn-zah-NEE-yoh—local name for the "poison tree"). Altitude: 6 feet. Population: 6,800. Climate: tropical.

Transportation: Railway to Guadalajara (356 kilometers) connecting with lines to Nogales and Mexico City; airways (PANINI) to Guadalajara, Colima, Uruapan, Morelia, and Mexico City. Local busses ply between Manzanillo and outlying villages and to Colima.

Importance: Fishing town and seaport; growing as a shore resort. Products are bananas and coconuts.

Visit: Cuyutlán Beach on the road to Colima, one of Mexico's best.

Hotels: Miramar, $10 single, European. Hotel Colonial, best, with air-conditioned rooms, free bus service to beaches; rates, European plan, from $10.

MAZATLÁN, state of Sinaloa (mah-zaht-LAHN—from the Nahuatl, meaning "place of the deer"). Altitude: 12 feet. Population: 31,000. Climate: mildly tropical.

Transportation: Railways (Sud Pacífico de México) to Guadalajara and Nogales; airways (CMA) to Los Angeles, Guadalajara, and Mexico City, (Aeronaves) to Nogales and Mexico City and intermediate towns, (LAMSA) to Nuevo Laredo and intermediate towns, and (PANINI) to Mexico City and intermediate towns.

Importance: Harbor. Principal products are coconuts, marjoram, limes, and canned fish.

Visit: Villa Unión, which until the latter part of the last century was used by pirates; Paseo Olas Altas; Crestón del Faro.

Environs: Islands, De Soto, De la Piedra, and Lobos, famous for large variety of birds, particularly parrots.

Hotels: Belmar, minimum, single, European plan, $5; double, $10.

MÉRIDA, state of Yucatán (MAY-ree-dah). Altitude: 25 feet. Population: 115,244. Climate: tropical, sultry February to May, but generally agreeable for the rest of the year. For a detailed description of Mérida and the Yucatán, see page 157.

Transportation: Airways (CMA) to Veracruz and Mexico City; Pan American World Airways operates daily service north to New Orleans and south to Central America and Panamá; RAMSA operates a freight and passenger service to Tuxtla Gutiérrez. Railways carrying passengers and freight operate daily service to Progreso, the principal port of Yucatán, and south to Campeche, besides shorter connecting lines in other parts of the peninsula. By highway it is 108 miles to Campeche and 75 miles to the Maya ruins at Chichén Itzá. There is a daily bus service to the latter place and to the ruins at Uxmal. Steamship service (the Yucatán Line) operates to New Orleans and (Compañía Mexicana de Navigación) to Veracruz.

Importance: Capital of the state, principal trading center of the Yucatán peninsula, and capital of the world's largest henequen-producing area.

History: Founded in 1541 by Francisco Montejo, Jr., on the site of the old Mayan city of Ti-Ho and named after the old Spanish city.

Visit: Sixteenth-century cathedral; Montejo House (note façade with two Spaniards standing with their feet on the heads of Indians, symbol of the Spanish dominion); and museum.

Environs: Ruins of Chichén Itzá, accessible by bus or taxi (seventy-five miles); include the Temple of Kukulkan (Quetzalcoatl), Thousand Columns, Temple of the Tigers, Ball Court, Temple of the Warriors, House of Nuns, the Caracol, Sacrificial Well, and the Chichanchob; one of the most imposing groups of Maya ruins in the hemisphere. Another large group, the ruins of Uxmal, are south of Mérida and also reached by bus or taxi. There is a good hotel at Chichén Itzá but none at Uxmal.

Sports: Good hunting in the jungles half a day's ride from Mérida; swimming in pools, or at Progreso (thirty-five kilometers).

Dishes: Panuchos (tortillas with black beans and chicken); *puchero* (prepared with vegetables and rice); *muepibpollo* (barbecued chicken in a pie); *relleno negro* (a spiced dish served with black sauce); and *papatzul,* a native concoction too hard to describe.

Handicrafts: Gold filigree jewelry, hand-woven hammocks, sandals, native costumes, and "Panama" hats.

Fiestas: Carnival week is the gayest festival of the year in Mérida.

Hotels: Mérida, small and definitely second-class; rates, European plan, $20 single and $30 double. Itzá, once the best in town and still fair; minimum rates, European plan, $10 single and $15 double. Montejo, the newest and best; rates, minimum, American plan, $30 single and $55 double; European, $15 single and $25 double. The

Mayaland Lodge at Chichén Itzá, seventy-five miles from Mérida, is exceptionally nice; rates, minimum, American plan, $40 single and $75 double per day. The Casa Victoria near it is an old hacienda; room and board may occasionally be had there for about one third the prices at the Lodge.

MONTEMORELOS, state of Nuevo León (mohn-teh-moh-RAY-loss). Altitude: 1,608 feet. Population: 5,544. Climate: temperate to subtropical.

Located in the center of Mexico's orange and lemon belt on the Pan American Highway forty-nine miles south of Monterrey. Railway and bus service to Monterrey and Mexico City.

Fiestas: Annual fair and fiesta, July 15 to 25.

Hotels: Florida Courts, on the highway, has twelve units with baths at about $12 double.

MONTERREY, state of Nuevo León (mohn-tehr-RAY—"King's Mountain"). Altitude: 1,752 feet. Population: 220,000. Climate: variable, but generally pleasant.

Transportation: Paved highway and daily bus service to Nuevo Laredo (146 miles), Torreón, Reynosa, and Mexico City (618 miles). Railway to Nuevo Laredo, Mexico City, Torreón, Matamoros, and Tampico. Airways (CMA and American) to Nuevo Laredo and Mexico City and intermediate points. Busses operate to numerous outlying villages in the region.

Importance: Capital of the state and principal industrial city of the republic. Industries include steel, glass, beer, cement, textiles, and meat packing.

History: Founded by Diego de Montemayor in 1596.

Visit: Palacio de Gobierno; cathedral, begun in 1630; the Plazas Zaragoza and Hidalgo; El Obispado Viejo (Old Bishop's Palace), on a hill with a good view of the valley.

Environs: Horsetail Falls; Chipinque on the mountain with good view; Saddle Mountain; Topo Chico; El Diente; and the Cañón de Santa Catarina.

Dishes: Roast kid; *abuelos* (brown-sugar candy containing nuts).

Handicrafts: Mostly from distant towns in the region; the best are leather objects (kidskin especially).

Fiestas: Monterrey Fair, held through May; picturesque events, bullfights, parades, fireworks.

Hotels: Monterrey has several good hotels, and the motorist who crosses the border late in the day finds it a good overnight stop. Rates and service are comparable to southern Texas hotels. All rates are European plan, minimum, daily.

Name	Single	Double	Rooms with Bath
Hotel Colonial (fair)	$12.00	$15.00	85
Hotel Genova (good)	7.50	10.00	69
Gran Hotel Ancira (very good)	10.00	15.00	150
Hotel Monterrey (families)	10.00	15.00	150
California Courts (motel)	8.00	10.00	48
El Paso Autel (motel)		13.00	24
Regina Courts (motel)		10.00	56

MORELIA, state of Michoacán (moh-RAIL-ee-ah—for the hero of independence, José María Morelos y Pavón). Altitude: 6,234 feet. Population: 47,600. Climate: mild and generally pleasant throughout the year.

Transportation: Paved highway and daily bus service to Mexico City (195 miles) and Guadalajara (233 miles); railway to Mexico City and connections to all points north; airways (PANINI) to Manzanillo, Uruapan, and Mexico City.

Importance: Capital of the state, cultural and business center for the central western section of Mexico. Morelia is a beautiful old city with a delightful Old World atmosphere, reminiscent of the eighteenth century.

History: Founded in 1541. The original name was Valladolid, but this was changed in 1828 in honor of the hero of Mexican independence, General José María Morelos y Pavón, who was born here. It was also the birthplace of the Emperor Agustín de Iturbide.

Visit: The cathedral, one of the handsomest in Mexico, was a century in building (1640–1744), and is an outstanding example of the best in plateresque ornamentation. Palacio de Gobierno, Museo del Estado, and Colegio San Nicolás are worth a visit. The latter is the oldest college in the Western Hemisphere. Church of San Francisco (1531) is one of the three oldest in Mexico. Casa de Morelos, birthplace of the hero.

Environs: Old aqueduct, built about 1789; Tiripetio and its collection of books; and Cointzio thermal baths.

Dishes: Ates (fruit sweets) and chili-hot meat dishes.

Hotels: Hotel Alameda, modern, thirty rooms with bath; minimum, single, $10; double, $18. Hotel Roma, good, thirty rooms with bath; minimum, single, $7; double, $12. Hotel Virrey de Mendoza, good, fifty-three rooms with bath; minimum, single, $10; double, $15. There are several second-class hotels and pensions. Taxi drivers are the best help in finding one of the latter.

OAXACA, state of Oaxaca (wah-HAH-kah—a Spanish corruption of the Indian *huaxyacac,* meaning "place of the gourds"). Altitude: 5,128 feet. Population: 33,867. Climate: semitropical and generally mild and pleasant.

Transportation: Paved highway and daily bus service to Puebla (257 miles) and Mexico City (342 miles); railway to Mexico City; and airways (Aeronaves) to Ometepec, Acapulco, and Veracruz, (CMA) to Tapachula and Mexico City, and (RAMSA) freight to Ixtepec, Tuxtla Gutiérrez, and Mexico City.

Importance: Capital of the state and commercial center of a large agricultural area; birthplace and home of two outstanding revolutionists, Benito Juárez and Porfirio Díaz; chief products, cochineal, jungle products, ceramics, and textiles.

History: The Valley of Oaxaca was thickly populated and contained several large cities centuries before the coming of the Spaniards. Ruins of these cities make the region around Oaxaca today one of considerable tourist attraction.

Visit: Museum, containing Monte Albán jewels; Santo Domingo Church, La Soledad Church, and the cathedral; pottery factories and serape weavers; market on Saturday.

Environs: Archaeological ruins of Mitla, twenty-six miles to the southeast; Cuilapan Convent, ten miles southwest; Zaachila, capital of the Zapotecs, where the "feather dance" is held each year; and Monte Albán, the Mixtec and Zapotec ruins, about twenty minutes from Oaxaca. Santa María del Tule has the largest and oldest tree in the world; it was a thousand years old when Columbus discovered America. These villages are in the region: Tlacochahuaya, known for its municipal palace with beautiful carvings; Tlacolula, with its gay Sunday market; Teotitlán del Valle, a weaving center; Ocatlán, unglazed pottery and toys; Coyotepec, black pottery; and Santo Tomás, weaving.

Dishes: Oaxaca is famous for a cheese rolled up like a ribbon; tamales with a distinctive flavor and wrapped in banana leaves; and a wide variety of *mole* sauces—green, yellow, red, and black. Mezcal, a strong drink, usually sold in potbellied black earthenware jugs.

Handicrafts: Pottery, serapes, steel knives, fiber baskets and bags, hand-woven tablecloths, and silver and gold filigree.

Fiestas: Folkloric fiestas generally take place on the two Mondays following July 16. Others are Carnival Week; Noche de Rábanos, December 23; Nochebuena, December 24; regional fair, December 8. The famous plume dances are performed in the July fiestas.

Hotels: Hotel Monte Albán, fifty rooms with bath; American plan, single, $14 to $25; double, $22 to $40; fair and frequented by native families. Hotel Marqués del Valle has one hundred rooms with bath; American plan, minimum, $15 single and $30 double; the best.

ORIZABA, state of Veracruz (oh-ree-SAH-bah—originally an Aztec city called Ahuaializapan, "Joyful Waters"). Altitude: 4,211 feet. Population: 47,910. Climate: mild and usually pleasant with occasional fogs.

Transportation: Paved highway and daily bus service to Mexico City (197 miles), and railway to Veracruz and Mexico City.

Importance: Cotton mills and commercial center; popular as a winter resort.

History: The Aztecs conquered the town long before the arrival of the Spaniards, who as early as 1553 were utilizing the power in many gushing streams in the neighborhood.

Visit: José Clemente Orozco paintings in the Federal School; market place.

Environs: Plantations of coffee, sugar cane, and bananas. The region is famous for its orchids, camellias, and gardenias. Citlaltepetl or Orizaba Peak (18,320 feet) is visible from nearly any street. Metlac ravine. Tuxpango, to which a descent can be made by cable car through beautiful tropical scenery. Jalapilla, old country residence of Maximilian and Carlota. Other interesting places are San Andrés Tenejapan, Ixtazoquitlan, and Barrio Nuevo.

Hotels: The best is Grand Hotel de France; seventy rooms and fifty-five baths; American plan, single, $18 to $20; double, $30 to $36. The Ruiz Galindo Hotel at El Fortín (famous for its swimming pool of gardenias) has 165 rooms with bath; minimum rate, American plan, $40 single and $70 double. The Posada Loma, east of El Fortín at Kilometer 333, has five neat units with bath; American plan, single, $30; double, $50.

PACHUCA, state of Hidalgo (pah-CHOO-kah). Altitude: 8,023 feet. Population: 53,354. Climate: generally cool, dry.

Transportation: Highway and daily bus service to Mexico City (fifty-five miles); railway to Mexico City.

Importance: Capital of the state, and largest silver-producing center in the world. About 15 per cent of the world's supply comes from mines in this vicinity.

History: Aztec mining villages were located in this region centuries before the arrival of the Spaniards, who founded Pachuca in 1534. The mines have been successively worked by the Indians, Spaniards, English, Mexicans, and Americans.

PÁTZCUARO, state of Michoacán (PAHTZ-kwah-roh—from the Tarascan, meaning "place of delights"). Altitude: 6,934 feet. Population: 9,557. Climate: mild and pleasant throughout the year.

Transportation: Paved highway and daily bus service to Morelia (forty-one miles), Guadalajara, and Mexico City; railway to Morelia and Mexico City.

Importance: Largest of the villages on Lake Pátzcuaro and center of the Tarascan Indian country.

History: Founded in 1540 on the site of the summer home of the Tarascan monarchs, by Vasco de Quiroga, a priest sent by Charles V to help the Indians of the region. He looked after their interests, taught them many new crafts, and fulfilled his mission so well that he was made the first bishop of Michoacán.

Visit: La Colegiata Church; state museum (good); markets around the plazas; and El Estribo, overlooking the town and lake.

Environs: Take a trip on the lake to Janitzio on a small island and climb to the top, then to the top of the huge Morelos monument. The sculpture is by Ruiz and the interior murals by Alva de la Canal. Other charming villages are Cucu Chuchu, Iguatzio, Jarácuaro,

Erongarícuaro, and Tzintzuntzan. The latter was the ancient capital of the Tarascan empire. Primitive Indian fishermen around the lake with their strange butterfly nets, dugout canoes, and round paddles are picturesque.

Dishes: Broiled whitefish in lemon sauce.

Handicrafts: The best Tarascan *bateas* (wooden trays) are made in Pátzcuaro and are available in several good shops. Masks used in native dances and finely embroidered blouses are also interesting buys.

Fiestas: One of the most famous in Mexico is held here December 8, when Indians from miles around attend and the plazas are filled with their handicrafts and agricultural products.

Hotels: The best is the Posada de Don Vasco, modern and attractive, $10 single and $18 double, European plan. El Lago is a small hotel near the railway, $7 to $10. There are several pensions—ask any taxi driver.

PUEBLA, state of Puebla (PWEH-blah—from *carta de puebla,* or "letter of authorization" permitting its settlement). Altitude: 7,091 feet. Population: 150,000. Climate: temperate and generally excellent throughout the year.

Transportation: Paved highway and daily bus service to Mexico City (eighty-five miles) and to Jalapa and Veracruz; railway to Mexico City, Orizaba, Córdoba, Jalapa, and Veracruz; and airways (Aeronaves) to Mexico City and Veracruz.

Importance: State capital; commercial and religious center; tile, pottery, and onyx manufacturing.

History: Founded by the Spaniards (Franciscan fathers) in 1532, it remains today one of the most Spanish cities of the republic. Its architecture is typically colonial and the atmosphere of its streets reminiscent of old Spain. It was here, on May 5, 1862, that two thousand Mexicans won a great victory over six thousand French, during the latter's attempt to establish the empire of Maximilian. This battle is commemorated by a national holiday and is the origin of the many streets named Cinco de Mayo in Mexico City, Puebla, and elsewhere in Mexico.

The Chinese princess who was brought as a slave to Acapulco and thence to Puebla for a rich *pueblano* lived here and wore the costumes of the Indians, to which she added embroideries and spangles brought from China. When the costume was later copied by natives it became the national costume now familiarly called *china poblana*.

Visit: The seventeenth-century cathedral with valuable paintings and tapestries; Church of Santo Domingo with its artistic and elaborately decorated Rosary Chapel; and the Santa Mónica Convent of flagellant nuns. House of Alfeñique, archaeological and historical museum. The José Luís Bello y González Museum at Avenida Tres Poniente 302; open ten A.M. to one P.M. Tuesday to Saturday; contains some valuable objects of colonial times. Museum at Fortress of Loreto. The Balneario de Agua Azul, a swimming pool and sulphur baths.

Environs: Amozoc, a small village east of Puebla, noted for silver spurs and earthenware toys. At Tepeaca are the ruins of one of the first fortified convents built in Mexico, dating from about 1530. Cholula, the "Holy City of Anáhuac," once the center of the Toltec kingdom, is a suburb west of Puebla. Tlaxcala, Texmelucan, and Huejotzingo are also west of the town and easily reached.

Dishes: There is a beautiful tile kitchen at the Santa Rosa Convent where it is said one of the nuns invented the national dish called *mole poblano*. When preparing to receive the visit of the archbishop she threw together a great many ingredients and made a delicious sauce or *mole* for the turkey. No Mexican today feels that turkey is properly served unless it is accompanied by this sauce. Try also stuffed peppers served with nut sauce; *muegano,* a sort of cake; and *camotes,* candied sweet potatoes.

Handicrafts: Talavera tile, pottery, and onyx handicrafts are famous. This is a good place to buy the varicolored straw mats and shopping bags also.

Fiestas: The principal fiesta is held in the suburb of Cholula (see above) on September 8.

Hotels: Hotel Colonial, a good family-type hotel; seventy rooms with bath; rates from $15 single and $20 double. Hotel Italia, old-fashioned; sixty rooms with forty baths; rates, $10 single and $20 double. Hotel Royalty, very good; forty rooms with bath; minimum rates, $15 single and $30 double. Pan American Courts, on the highway on the west edge of town; fairly new and comfortable; minimum rate, $15. The Café Cristal at Reforma 105 serves American and Mexican dishes.

QUERÉTARO, state of Querétaro (kay-RAY-tah-roh—in Indian times known as Taxco). Altitude: 5,948 feet. Population: 33,563. Climate: temperate and generally pleasant throughout the year.

Transportation: Highway and bus service connecting with the Pan American Highway at Ixmiquilpan (ninety-five miles); railway to Laredo, El Paso, Guadalajara, and Mexico City (269 kilometers).

Importance: State capital, railway center, and commercial town serving a large fertile valley region.

History: Founded in 1440 by the Otomí Indians, conquered by the Aztecs under Moctezuma, and then by the Spaniards in 1531. It was made a *ciudad* in 1655 by a royal order signed by Felipe IV. The town figured prominently in early revolutionary days.

Visit: Churches of Santa Rosa and Santa Clara; museum with some excellent paintings; St. Augustine Convent; House of Escobar; Children's Home; Aqueduct; and Federal Palace. The Maximilian Chapel on the Hill of Las Campanas is historically interesting. Convent of La Cruz, where Maximilian was imprisoned; note the peculiar tree growing in the yard that has thorns in the shape of a cross.

Environs: Opal mines.

Fiestas: Principal ones occur around Christmas, when there are bullfights, cockfights, and other sports events, and dances.

Hotels: Gran Hotel, facing main plaza; rooms with bath, meals, minimum, single, $15; double, $25.

SABINAS HIDALGO, state of Nuevo León (sah-BEE-nahs ee-DAHL-goh). Altitude: 951 feet. Population: 5,828. Climate: temperate.

An old mining town on the Pan American Highway sixty-five miles north of Monterrey. Power's Café and Curio Store used to be a good place to stop for meals and coffee, but it has run down in recent years.

SALTILLO, state of Coahuila (sahl-TEE-yoh—Spanish for "little falls"). Altitude: 5,212 feet. Population: 49,700. Climate: Usually cool, sometimes cold.

Transportation: Paved highway and daily bus service to Monterrey, Matamoros, and Torreón; railway to Monterrey, Mexico City, and Texas points.

Importance: Capital and chief commercial and industrial city of the state, and a favorite health resort.

History: First settled in 1555. The town is known legally as Leona Vicario, because this famous Mexican Jeanne d'Arc was born here. Saltillo was once the capital of a vast territory that included Texas and part of Colorado.

Visit: The Alameda; Cathedral of Santiago; Palacio de Gobierno; statue of Manuel de Acuña, Mexican poet who was born in Saltillo; and Calzada de los Héroes.

Environs: Diamante Pass, eleven miles south and 2,200 feet above the city, affords some good views. Buena Vista Battlefield, scene of a bloody battle in 1847 between American forces under General Zachary Taylor and a Mexican army under General Antonio López de Santa Ana.

Dishes: Machacado, meat fried with chili sauce. Try it with some of the Madero wines from Parras de la Fuente (sixteen miles south).

Handicrafts: Woolens and kidskin articles.

Hotels: Hotel Arizpe-Sainz is good; sixty rooms with bath at $15 single and $25 double. Hotel Casa Colonial is a pleasant place but not pretentious; twenty-four rooms with bath; $12 single and $14 double. There is a nice tourist court, Huizache Courts, on the east edge of the town; twenty units with bath; about $15 double.

SAN JOSÉ PURUA, state of Michoacán (see also under Zitácuaro).

A famous mineral spa. The hotel and baths are among the finest in Mexico; 125 rooms with bath and several private bungalows; rates, American plan, minimum daily, $40 single and $70 double. For reservations and information one should apply to the hotel's Mexico City office at Reforma 146.

SAN LUÍS POTOSÍ, state of San Luís Potosí (san-loo-EES poh-toh-SEE). Altitude: 6,156 feet. Population: 77,161. Climate: temperate to cool.

Transportation: Highway and daily bus service to Guadalajara and to Antiguo Morelos on the Pan American Highway; railway to Mexico City (527 kilometers) and Texas points; airways (LAMSA) to Chihuahua, Ciudad Juárez, Nogales, and Mexico City.

Importance: State capital and large mining (silver) center.

Visit: Municipal and executive buildings; the Presa (dam); La Paz Theater; churches, San Francisco and El Carmen.

Environs: Ojo Caliente, thermal waters; Santa María del Río, noted for its woven silk *rebozos*. Hunting (jaguar and deer) in the surrounding hills.

Handicrafts: Wooden inlaid boxes.

Hotels: Hotel Colonial, eighty rooms with bath, newest and best; rates, $10 single and $15 double. Hotel Progreso, fifty rooms with bath, fair; rates about the same as the Colonial. The Plaza is smaller, noisier, and cheaper.

TAMAZUNCHALE, state of San Luís Potosí (tah-mah-soon-CHAH-lay—most Americans call it "Thomas and Charlie"). Altitude: 394 feet. Population: 2,487. Climate: subtropical.

Located on the Río Moctezuma, at the north foot of the Sierra Madre Oriental; it is the last town of importance on the Pan American Highway before the long climb over the mountains toward Mexico City (227 miles). Bus service to Monterrey and Mexico City.

Hotels: Hotel Cadilac, a small pleasant hotel; minimum rates, $10 single and $15 double. Texas Hotel, new, under construction in 1947. D. Z. Courts, fair; $25 double. Pemex Camp and Restaurant has twelve units with bath; $15 double. Quinta Chilla Courts, south of town, $15 double.

TAMPICO, state of Tamaulipas (tahm-PEE-coh). Altitude: 11 feet. Population: 82,895. Climate: warm in winter, sultry in summer.

Transportation: Highway and daily bus service connecting with Pan American Highway at El Mante; railway to Monterrey and San Luís Potosí; airways (CMA and Pan American) to Brownsville, Monterrey, Veracruz, and Mexico City.

Importance: Largest seaport in Mexico and principal oil center.

Visit: Cathedral; Casa Mata; fish market.

Environs: The Quintero grottoes with an underground river containing eyeless fish; archaeological sites of Los Esteros and Tancasnequi; Santa Juana, where bones of prehistoric mammoths were found; Tanilul thermal baths; Dos Bocas oil fields.

Sports: Sea bathing (at Miramar Beach), golf, riding, tennis, boating. Fishing in the Pánuco River, salt-water lagoons, and offshore. Hunting is generally good and game plentiful.

Dishes: A wide variety of fish food is served in the better hotels and restaurants.

Hotels: Hotel Imperial, about the best; one hundred rooms with bath; rates, $8 single and $12 double. Hotel Inglaterra, same rates but smaller. Hotel Rivera, fair; one hundred rooms with bath; average rates, $10 single, $15 double. Tampico Tourist Hotel is about the same in price and quality as the Rivera.

TAPACHULA, state of Chiapas (tah-pah-CHEW-lah). Altitude: 493 feet. Population: 19,400. Climate: tropical and usually quite sultry.

Transportation: Paved highway to the Guatemala border (eleven miles); railway to Veracruz and Suchiate; airways (CMA and Pan American) to Oaxaca, Mexico City, and Guatemala City, and (RAMSA) to Tuxtla Gutiérrez, Ixtepec, Oaxaca, and Mexico City.

Importance: Railway and agricultural center and largest town in southeastern Mexico; coffee, bananas, and border trade with Guatemala are important.

Visit: Market contains wide variety of local products, Mame Indians, orchids.

Environs: Banana, sugar-cane, rubber, tobacco, cacao, and sisal plantations; Izalco ruins, archaeological monuments; San Benito bathing beach at Puerto Madero, seventeen miles southwest by car.

Hotels: Internacional, newest, and our only recommendation; fifty-two rooms, most with bath; rates from $15 American plan.

TAXCO, state of Guerrero (TAHS-coh—from the Nahuatl word *tlachco,* meaning "ball court"). Altitude: 5,609 feet. Population: 4,963. Climate: semiarid, temperate, and generally delightful the year round.

Transportation: Paved road and daily bus service to Mexico City (101 miles), Cuernavaca (55 miles), and Acapulco (182 miles).

Importance: Artists' colony and silversmiths' center of Mexico; preserved by the government as a typical colonial town; mecca for tourists.

History: The original Indian town was founded near here about 1445 and for years paid tribute to Moctezuma in the form of gold bricks. It was conquered by Cortés in 1531, and silver was discovered soon after. It attained its greatest prosperity (before American tourists discovered it!) during colonial days when the French mining engineer Josephe le Borde, known to Mexicans as José de la

Borda, discovered a very rich silver vein and amassed an immense fortune. In gratitude he erected in 1757 the ornate twin-towered church to San Sebastián and Santa Prisca that occupies one side of the tiny main plaza. The production of silver jewelry and trinkets has been the principal industry ever since.

Visit: Silversmith shops and see craftsmen at work. Casa Humboldt, Casa Figueroa, and Casa Sáenz are good examples of colonial architecture and interesting historically. The market is not unusual but sometimes picturesque on Sunday.

Environs: See under Cuernavaca.

Handicrafts: Silver jewelry and trinkets, hand-woven and hand-blocked textiles, tinware and leatherwork.

Hotels: There is a wide range in hotel rates and quality of accommodations in Taxco and, for the size of the place, a proportionately large number of establishments. However, it is difficult to secure rooms without advance notice nearly any time of the year. The following rates are minimum daily and shown in Mexican pesos:

Name	*Plan*	*Single*	*Double*
Casa Humboldt	American	$20.00	$40.00
De La Borda	American	35.00	60.00
Los Arcos	American	30.00	50.00
Melendez	European	6.00	12.00
Posada de la Misión	American	40.00	70.00
Rancho Telva	American	30.00	50.00
Taxqueño	American	20.00	40.00
Victoria	American	25.00	50.00

TEHUACÁN, state of Puebla (tay-oo-ah-KAHN). Altitude: 5,497 feet. Population: 16,278. Climate: mild.

Transportation: Paved highway and daily bus service to Puebla, Orizaba, Córdoba, and Mexico City (158 miles). Railway to Puebla, Mexico City, and Oaxaca. Airways (Aeronaves) to Veracruz, Puebla, and Mexico City.

Importance: Noted for its mineral baths, especially recommended for the treatment of liver, kidney, and stomach disorders.

Environs: Garci-Crespo, a resort centering around the famous mineral springs and modern bottling works.

Hotels: Hotel Garci-Crespo, one of the best in Mexico; 150 rooms with bath; minimum rates, American plan, single, $35; double, $65. Hotel El Riego and Gran Hotel Mexico are in Tehuacán; rates,

American plan, $25 single and $40 double. The Reforma is a small hotel catering to middle-class native families; rates, American plan, $12 single and $24 double.

TLAXCALA, state of Tlaxcala (tlahs-KAH-lah—from the Aztec, meaning "land of corn"). Altitude: 7,386 feet. Population: 3,261. Climate: temperate to cool.

Transportation: Highway and bus service to Mexico City (seventy-two miles). Road to Tlaxcala turns off Mexico City–Puebla highway at Texmelucan, fifty-six miles from Mexico City.

Importance: Capital of the state and trading center for a remote Indian region.

History: The present town shows little of its grandeur when this was the seat of government for the powerful Tlascalan tribe. The Tlascalans were the first allies of Cortés, and their assistance was the deciding factor in Cortés' conquest of Mexico.

Visit: Church of San Francisco, where the first Christian services in North America were conducted in 1521. Shrine of Ocotlán.

Environs: Ancient ruins at San Esteban Tizatlán, about two miles north of Tlaxcala. By paved road from Tlaxcala are the villages Santa Ana (famed for weaving) and Apizaco (hand-carved canes).

Handicrafts: Serapes and woolen cloth are excellent.

Hotels: Stay in Puebla.

TOLUCA, state of Mexico (toh-LOO-cah—a corruption from Indian words meaning "place of reeds" or "trees"). Altitude: 8,793. Population: 43,429. Climate: temperate to cool with cold nights.

Transportation: Paved highway and daily bus and railway service to Mexico City (40 miles) and Morelia (155 miles).

Importance: Capital of the state and center of a large agricultural and cattle-raising region.

History: Founded in 1533 on the order of Cortés, though various Indian tribes had inhabited the valley for centuries.

Visit: Friday is the best day to visit Toluca, when the large native market is at its best. Indians bring their handicrafts and agricultural products from villages many miles distant. Prices, however, are about the same as those in Mexico City because of the large number of tourists who come here.

Environs: Volcano El Nevado de Toluca; drive to the top. The archaeological zone of Calixtlahuaca is five miles north and well worth a visit.

Handicrafts: This is the place to buy hand-woven blankets, serapes, baskets, needlework, toys, and pottery; some of Mexico's best of these are made in the villages roundabout.

Hotels: Travelers generally plan to visit Toluca en route to Morelia and Guadalajara, or as a day's round trip from Mexico City. If you must stay in Toluca, we suggest you try to find accommodations in a private home or one of the better pensions.

TORREÓN, state of Coahuila (tohr-ray-OWN—"watchtower"). Altitude: 3,741 feet. Population: 76,600. Climate: temperate.

Transportation: Highway and daily bus service to Monterrey (234 miles) and Saltillo; railway to Ciudad Juárez and Mexico City (1,136 kilometers); airways (LAMSA) to Ciudad Juárez, Nogales, Mazatlán, and Mexico City.

Importance: Wheat and cotton center. There is also a large smelter (iron) and cotton mills.

History: Founded in 1887 at the old El Coyote Rancho. It took its name from a watchtower erected on the ranch to guard against Indians. A comparatively new town, Torreón got its biggest growth when irrigation and mines were developed.

Dishes: Try the various preparations of kid, especially roasted. Grapes, dried figs, and wines are also good.

Hotels: Hotel Galicia, fifty rooms with bath; rates, $10 single and $25 double. Hotel Salvador, sixty-four rooms and fifty baths; rates from $5 up. Hotel Naves, thirty-nine rooms with bath; rates from $6 up. Hotel Río Nazas, under construction.

TUXTLA GUTIÉRREZ, state of Chiapas (TOOST-lah goo-tee-AIR-rays—from the Nahoa word *tuxtla,* meaning "the place of rabbits," and after the hero Joaquín Miguel Gutiérrez). Altitude: 1,776 feet. Population: 25,477. Climate: tropical, though not disagreeable.

Transportation: Highway and daily bus service to Arriaga, the nearest railway connection; airways (CMA) to Tapachula, Oaxaca, and Mexico City, and (RAMSA) to Mérida, Tapachula, Ixtepec, Oaxaca, and Mexico City.

Importance: Capital of the state; leading commercial center serving a large and fertile agricultural area; trading center for a large and varied Indian population. Coffee is the principal product.

Visit: The market contains an interesting variety of products and is generally attended by Indians in a number of different costumes, representing remote villages in the surrounding mountains. The state museum is worth a visit.

Environs: The Río Chiapa (or Mezcalapa) flows by the city and adds a picturesque touch. Busses and cars are available for trips to the isolated villages of San Cristóbal de las Casas (large Indian center and point of departure for expeditions into the jungle) and Comitán, near the Guatemalan border. Chamula, Tzotzil, Tzetzal, and Lacandon Indian tribes are in the region and may be seen in the towns of Tenejapa and Zinacatán. The ancient Maya ruins of Palenque, Yaxchilan, Chincultic, and Tonina are also accessible from Tuxtla Gutiérrez.

Hotels: Hotel Brindis is our only suggestion; fifty rooms with bath; rates, $9 single, $17 double. Several pensions are available but one should make inquiry after arrival.

URUAPAN, state of Michoacán (oo-roo-AH-pan—from Tarascan words meaning "where flowers are blooming"). Altitude: 5,285 feet. Population: 20,583. Climate: Early Spaniards enthusiastically referred to Uruapan as the "Paradise of Michoacán." Its climate is mild and slightly tropical.

Transportation: Paved highway and daily bus service to Guadalajara, Morelia, and Mexico City (312 miles); railway to Morelia and Mexico City; airways (Aeronaves) to Acapulco and (PANINI) to Manzanillo, Colima, Morelia, and Mexico City.

Importance: Departure point for excursions to the volcano Parícutin; commercial center for a large agricultural area.

Visit: Orchards of Quinta Ruiz and Quinta Hurtado; La Camelina; springs of Río Cupatitzio, called Rodilla del Diablo (Devil's Knee); La Guatapera; and sixteenth-century church. Market day is Sunday.

Environs: Parícutin, one of the world's most spectacular sights, is about twenty-four miles by auto. Overalls and hats (protection against falling ash) can be rented at the hotels in Uruapan. Rent a taxi for the trip or go by bus—don't attempt to drive your own car, as the road is treacherous and hard to follow. Arrange to stay at the volcano long enough to see it at night. Tzaráracua Falls, Lake Camécuaro, and Lake Zirahuén are half-day trips from Uruapan.

Dishes: Chicken, tamales, *atoles,* and *buñuelos* are local specialties. There is a liquor made of sugar cane—recommended for the adventurous only.

Handicrafts: Uruapan is famous for its green, black, and brown pottery; wooden curios such as guitars, boxes, and spoons; embroidered blouses and table linen; and especially large lacquered trays and boxes. Uruapan and Pátzcuaro artisans make the best trays in Mexico.

Hotels: Hotel Mirador, fifty rooms with bath, fronting on the Jardín de los Mártires; minimum rates, $10 single and $18 double. Hotel Progreso, fifty rooms, some with bath; rates from $8 up single.

VERACRUZ, state of Veracruz (veh-rah-CROOS—the "true cross," named by the Spanish conquistadors). Altitude: 23 feet. Population: 71,720. Climate: tropical, generally humid, with sultry *caniculares* (dog days) in August and September.

Transportation: Paved highway and daily bus service to Mexico City (282 miles) via Jalapa and Puebla; two railways to Mexico City, one via Jalapa and Puebla and the other via Córdoba, Orizaba, and Puebla; airways (Aeronaves) to Puebla, Córdoba, Coatzacoalcos, and Mexico City, (CMA) to Mérida, Campeche, and other Yucatán and Tehuantepec points, and (Golfo y Pacífico) to Ixtepec and Coatzacoalcos.

Importance: Principal port of entry from eastern and Gulf points and most important town on the Gulf of Mexico.

History: Hernán Cortés landed here April 27, 1519, and began his expedition of conquest of the Aztec kingdom.

Visit: Old fortress of San Juan de Ulua, on an island in the bay, for many years used as a fort for the defense of the port and later as a prison, dockyard, and arsenal. Good fishing is available at Boca del Río, at the mouth of a wide river.

Environs: Alvarado, a small typical coastal town on the Río Papaloapam, reached by rail. Tlacotalpan, a picturesque river town, is reached from Alvarado. The Totonaca ruins at Cempoala where

Cortés had the first public mass said in a small chapel regarded as the first erected in America. Near Cempoala is the excellent Chachalacas Beach.

Hotels: Hotels are not so numerous in Veracruz as they are in Acapulco on the other coast, but they are just as varied in quality and price. The Gulf coast, in our estimation, is more attractive because it offers more of the atmosphere one expects to find in a tropical seaport, better beaches, and more varied surroundings. If you are not interested in following celebrities, try this region of the Gulf coast. The rates shown below are minimum daily. They are all good hotels, so your choice should be determined by price and location.

Name	Plan	Single	Double
Hotel Imperial (old, in town)	European	$15	$25
Hotel Lux (old, near beach)	European	15	25
	American	30	50
Hotel Mocambo (new, resort type, on beach 5 miles south)	American	25	50
Hotel Victoria (overlooking the sea at the boardwalk)	European	20	40
Hotel Villa del Mar (nice and comfortable)	American	28	50
	European	15	25

ZIMAPÁN, state of Hidalgo (seem-ah-PAHN). Altitude: 6,410 feet. Population: 2,689. Climate: temperate, dry.

A four-hundred-year-old town on the Pan American Highway 127 miles north of Mexico City. Frequent bus service to Mexico City and Ixmilquilpan. Of interest are the cathedral with baroque entrance; a huge cypress tree; and the Hotel Fundición, built on the ruins of an old smelter.

Hotels: Hotel de la Fundición; excellent; sixty-five rooms with bath; $12 single and $15 double, European plan; meals are good and reasonable.

ZITÁCUARO, state of Michoacán (see-TAH-kwah-roh). Altitude: 6,398 feet. Population: 11,434. Climate: generally warm days with cool nights.

Located on the Mexico City–Morelia–Guadalajara highway and a railway to Maravatio.

An agricultural and lumbering center in a picturesque valley.

Road to the famous mineral spa San José Purua turns off five miles north of the village. The hotel and baths are among the finest in Mexico. For reservations and information one should apply to their Mexico City office at Reforma 146 (see also under San José Purua, above).

CHAPTER IX

MYSTERIOUS MEXICO

O F THE three principal architectural classifications that we mentioned in Chapter V—prehistoric, colonial, and modern—as divisions of the main scenic interests in Mexico, the most excitingly mysterious are the ancient temples and palaces built by the races inhabiting the region centuries before the Spanish Conquest. Time, the ravages of nature, and the neglect of man shroud in deep mystery civilizations that were old when Rome was a mud village. The hundreds of these archaic sites scattered from border to border in Mexico make it the richest archaeological region in the world—and the easiest for the layman to visit. A balanced tour for the average traveler should include at least one day of visiting some one of these ancient ruins. For the serious student of archaeology a lifetime of study only scratches the surface of the vast storehouse of enigmas. A summary of all the facts uncovered by four centuries of studious research is little more than an *apéritif* for the job yet to be done. However, here are the suppositions now generally accepted as facts.

ARCHAIC HISTORY

Mongol or Asiatic ancestry of the indigenous races of Mexico is no longer seriously doubted because the more reliable sciences, coming to the aid of an anthropological guess, have made it a fact. For instance, by taking into consideration the geologic conditions supposed to have existed in the Bering Strait about ten to fifteen thousand years ago, anthropologists believe that the ancestors of such peoples as the Eskimo, Sioux, Blackfeet, and Aztec crossed the strait and poured into the Americas during postglacial times. Modern anthropology, utilizing special features such as the cephalic index and blood groups, has also helped to trace down the origin of these migrants.

The Amerindian doesn't resemble the most typical of the Mongoloids, such as the Chinese and Mongols; but there are others in Asia, with its great spread in racial types, that are almost identical in lines of division with the indigenous races found in the Americas. If we were to make extensive trips throughout Siberia, Mongolia, Tibet, and Sinkiang we would find types like the American Eskimo and the North, Central, and South American Indian.

The Mongoloid migration is the only one that enjoys a scientific acceptance. Nevertheless, this lone explanation of the origin of the Amerindian has been somewhat modified by investigations made during the last few years. The hypothesis, as put forth by the French anthropologist Rivet, maintains that there is a possible Malay-Polynesian or perhaps even Australian migration. It is supposed that they were excellent sailors, in that they reached the Christmas Islands off Chile and left archaeological vestiges now attributed to them. This hypothesis rests upon the fact that identical Polynesian roots are to be found in some American dialects, even as far north as California; and native artifacts have been found that apparently have the same origin.

Thus a few facts and many hypotheses make up the most reliable information we have. The migration to the Americas occurred in diverse waves. It is possible that the oldest of these, formed by Australian peoples, moved to Tierra del Fuego in South America, using the antarctic as a bridge; nevertheless, this migration must have been small. A second wave was made up of Malay-Polynesian peoples whose linguistic influences have been found along the entire Pacific coast of the Americas; but this migration was also of little importance. The north Asiatics came next, superimposing their characteristics on the archaic peoples who had already arrived here. This movement is the only one proved scientifically. And finally, today's Eskimo population, descendants of a very late migration, are unmistakably Mongoloid.

These cultural links of the Americas with other continents or islands are also postulated by gentlemen known as epigraphers and stratigraphers, who glue a dozen pieces of terra cotta together to reconstruct a very old washbasin. These scholars then point out the very remote similarity of certain Mayan decorative compositions to the ornaments on jade talismans or signets of the pre-Han period in China two thousand years ago, an analogy that, in reality, is much too vague.

Modern methods of archaeological and anthropological investigation have their greatest chance for expression in Mexico, and these expressions are now of importance. But this was not always the case. Until recently "classical archaeologists," excavating in Europe and North Africa, considered the hypotheses and facts brought up in Mexican archaeology as wild fancies. They, among others, played down the advanced civilizations of Aztecs, Toltecs, and Mayans by referring to them and their activities with derogatory terminology.

These "classical archaeologists," although deriding archaeological activity in Mexico, did not particularly harm it. The pernicious effects came from the vain charlatans of archaeology, the publicity hounds, and the parasites usually found in this field of investigation. During the middle of the nineteenth century, when the remains of early Mexican civilizations had begun to interest the world, archaeologists like Waldeck, Norman, and Zavala amateurishly scratched about the ruins, published volumes of pompous misinformation, and then received the plaudits of all. Control by the Mexican government of these activities during the last century was so indifferent that many itchy-fingered "archaeologists" actually shipped veritable archaeological treasures of precious metals, whole chunks of pyramids, and monoliths weighing tons out of the country.

Fortunately, all investigators were not of that type. Charnay the Frenchman, Catherwood the Britisher, and Stephens the American, all serious-minded men of archaeology, if not of science, made valuable contributions to the knowledge we have of Mayan civilizations. Friederichsthal, another contributor of worth-while information, was the first to take into the jungles of southern Mexico a daguerreotype apparatus, the very best there was in those days, for taking pictures. (All his pictures were ruined by the humidity and heat of the jungles.) Much of the information gathered by these gentlemen is still of use to modern archaeologists, but almost all of their assumptions are, to a certain point, incorrect. However, the first steps in this field of investigation were the same in all parts of the world. They were based upon tradition and a superficial examination of the few facts known in those times. The leading authority today is unquestionably Dr. Sylvanus G. Morley, an American. His authoritative book *The Ancient Maya* we highly recommend.

PRE-CONQUEST HISTORY

Using the name of the Saviour and the Catholic Church of Spain as a pretext, the ravenous gentlemen in the clanking panoplies of Spanish imperial might moved insolently forward in a barefaced search for riches. Their pompous march from the coast toward the great metropolis of Tenochtitlán (later to become Mexico City) was hailed by the mystic Moctezuma II as a veritable miracle, a historical prophecy come true. Quetzalcoatl, the Omnipotent, had at last come to rule! But the brazen thirst for gold and the progressively uncouth manners of these conditional gentlemen from Spain first invited the dislike and later fomented the positive hatred of Tenochtitlán.

The inevitable victory by these Christian gentlemen over Tenochtitlán was followed by such a methodical destruction of pyramids, temples, palaces, institutions, and homes that archaeologists today can reconstruct but little of that architectural grandeur. These Iberian wreckers not only felled walls but utilized the blocks of red and black volcanic *tezontle* to build palaces for their own greedy selves.

Today there are only the obviously biased chronicles of the Spanish historians who accompanied Cortés, and we know almost nothing of Aztec historians, whose perfectly legible and readable manuscripts were foolishly destroyed. Yet, if we are to believe one of these Spaniards, Tenochtitlán was unique, for the chronicler writes that the Aztec capital was more beautiful than Venice—Venice, the jewel-like city of the European Renaissance.

This elegant city, Tenochtitlán, and its vast territories known as Anáhuac, represented two centuries of work and warfare. Well-planned political activities within the military theocratic system, however, were one of the most important reasons for the rapid development of this city-state. The Aztecs launched their formal political career sixty years after having humbly founded Tenochtitlán on islands shrouded in fog and surrounded by morasses.

It was in 1383 that Acamapichtli was elected and proclaimed the first king. This historical event as well as other historical events in Mexico seem isolated from the world and clouded by time, but they appear related and much clearer when we take note of simultaneous events in other parts of the world. In Europe, Petrarch and Boccaccio had just died; living were Donatello and Ghiberti; while soon to surge as geniuses were Botticelli and Michelangelo. The Hundred Years' War between England and France was well under way. An international ecclesiastical disgrace involving two rival popes was the scandal of the day: Urban VI of Rome and Clement VII of Avignon called each other "antichrist." In China the Ming dynasty had definitely thrown out the Mongol rule. India, after having advanced under the rule of Mohammedan sultans, was about to receive another invasion. And Acamapichtli ("bunch of cane stalks") ruled in Tenochtitlán.

Acamapichtli married a woman of royal birth (i.e., of Toltec blood) and became the father of two sons, but his third and greatest son, Itzcoatl ("serpent of obsidian") was the son by a mistress of plebeian birth. The first two, Huitzilihuitl ("hummingbird's plume") and Chimalpopoca ("escutcheon that unites") succeeded in their turn as kings, but both were killed for attempted revolts against their neighboring oppressors, the Tepanecas of Tacuba (now a suburb of Mexico City) and the mighty city-state of Atzcapotzcalco (also now a suburb).

(These odd-sounding names like "bunch of cane stalks" and "serpent of obsidian" were always pseudonyms, not real names. The assumed name was given at childbirth for reasons completely superstitious; it was the belief then, as it is today among certain peoples of the world, that one's real name in possession of a witch or sorcerer was dangerous. The real name, taken from the calendar name of the birthday, was kept secret forever.)

Itzcoatl, the bastard son who proved to be one of the most brilliant statesmen in the history of the world, was confronted, upon becoming king, with these formidable problems: first, two powerful, maltreating neighbors; second, the *pili* (nobility) occupied a most precarious position as rulers, a position barely sustained by a few drops of aristocratic Toltec blood. These *pili* were lacking in territory and wealth, and their dignity as princes was lowered by having to work alongside the *mazehual* (plebe).

The freedom-loving Itzcoatl convinced his hounded, overworked people to fight a war by compromising the nobility. He pledged his servitude as well as that of the other nobles to the workers if the war for independence should be lost. Itzcoatl joined with the people of Texcoco, the Acolhuas, and other factions in the Valley of Mexico, decisively to squash Atzcapotzalco, the great and strong. Tacuba, fearing the coalition, was easily convinced by a new plan as set forth by Itzcoatl. The fighting alliance was to include Tenochtitlán, Texcoco, and Tacuba; but in time the too clever Itzcoatl reduced Texcoco and Tacuba to insignificant powers and thus solved the two pressing problems of his kingdom: the *pili* became a landed aristocracy, and the workers enjoyed a well-earned freedom and prosperity.

Huitzilihitl's son, Moctezuma, was elected to succeed Itzcoatl, and was soon followed by Tezozomoc, son of Itzcoatl. (The king was elected from a group of qualified candidates. The king's son was the favorite, of course, but if he was incapable as a leader someone else was chosen.)

Tezozomoc did not accomplish anything more exceptional than marrying his cousin, the daughter of Moctezuma. This couple reared three amazing sons: Axayacatl ("face in the water") who began his reign in 1469; Tizoc ("withered legs"), the cripple whose distaste for warfare led to his liquidation in 1486 by a conclave of high priests; and Ahuitzotl ("imaginary animal"), who led the three combined armies to Mayan territory as far as Guatemala, and even received tributes from the Incas of Peru. He was the father of the great leader Cuauhtémoc.

But the history we are better acquainted with was made by the two sons of Axayacatl, Moctezuma II (sometimes spelled Montezuma in English-speaking countries) and Cuitlahuac.

Moctezuma II was king when Cortés, the European man of business, was approaching Tenochtitlán. Moctezuma II, who had degenerated into a sort of mystic and godlike king, was killed by the indignant public for his refusal to repulse Cortés when the Spaniards entered over the city's undefended causeways. Cuitlahuac, the bold and patriotic successor, threw Cortés and his horsemen out of the city in the most shameful manner for the Spaniards. But the smallpox of the Old World, bequeathed by the Spaniards, killed Cuitlahuac in eighty days, and an epidemic of terrifying proportions struck the naturally susceptible Aztec population at the moment Cortés returned with forty thousand indispensable Tlaxcaltecan allies. Cuauhtémoc ("eagle that falls"), the new king, son of the great Ahuitzotl, led the last defense of Tenochtitlán in the most fantastic, heroic, and tragic siege of history, which lasted three months. Stricken by smallpox and reduced to insects and roots for nourishment, the Aztec people's army finally collapsed from starvation and disease.

Spanish imperial might moved insolently into the ghastly, stinking city to cut the political evolution of Tenochtitlán forever.

Tenochtitlán. Tenochtitlán, undoubtedly one of the most populated cities in the Americas four hundred years ago, now lies nine feet under the Mexico City of today. To do a thorough archaeological investigation of Tenochtitlán (what was left of it by the Spaniards) would necessitate the destruction of the massive metropolitan cathedral, the digging up of the city's central square, the tearing down of the National Palace, the National University, the National Museum, etc. All these important structures of today are directly over the Teocalli, Cuauhtlinchan, and other temples, pyramids, palaces, and buildings of importance.

Since economic and other circumstances do not permit the thorough explorations of Mexico City's muddy foundations, very little is known of Tenochtitlán. It is known that Tenochtitlán was founded upon a few islands in the huge lake of Texcoco, a lake that still exists but that has receded considerably. In time these islands were artificially enlarged by the utilization of embankments; and from north, south, and west radiated three dikes from these islands to the edges of the lake. These dikes were cut in certain places by canals that passed under bridges to facilitate communication within the city. Four causeways, connecting the islands and the lake's edges, were the objects of much praise by the Spanish conquerors. Tlaltelolco, a section of Tenochtitlán, had a system of canals so intricate that almost every house was an island. (It is no wonder that Cortés not only attacked with infantry over the causeways, but with brigantines and barges as well!)

This Venice of Anáhuac culminated in the Templo Mayor. This was a gigantic pyramid larger than the Pyramid of the Sun in Teotihuacán, and the latter pyramid is larger than Cheops in Egypt!

The Templo Mayor was the last stronghold of the Aztecs against Cortés and his men, according to Sahagún, the Spanish historian.

Judging from literature on archaeology and archaeological ruins themselves, one would imagine that only pyramids were built in Tenochtitlán and no homes at all. There were houses in all Aztec cities, but it is natural that a family would hardly build a structure comparable to one built by the community; and these structures built by the community were constructed in the most grandiose and lasting way possible. But it is difficult to understand the type of architecture and the type of life in general of the Aztecs in Tenochtitlán if a knowledge, however scanty, of the all-important religious aspects is not had.

Religion to the citizens of Tenochtitlán meant everything. Almost nothing was done without religious significance; games, sports, architecture, politics, wars, women's hair styles, and all sorts of imaginable activities were related and devoted to religion. The very existence of the citizens of Tenochtitlán was dedicated to the satisfaction of the gods.

The intellectual classes, basing themselves upon an unusually developed philosophy, had a religion whose essence consisted of an idea, "the idea that could not be reproduced." Tloque Nahuaque, which means "that which is next to us," was their god. This god was so philosophical that it was never personified or represented in any way. But this god was hardly popular. It was necessary for the masses to have a deity or deities who would give, produce, and cure. Aztec philosophers got busy and produced an easily understandable and mystic religion very much like those of today. A god was invented for every activity of life; sometimes there was even a god for aspects of an activity. The people, with religion in their own hands, soon grafted on enough magic to suit everybody. Religion was made so acceptable by overloading it with mystifying, complicated legends and legendary characters that the Aztecs, in their theology, even had a queer sort of Dante, Quetzalcoatl, who traveled through several hells asking for the bones of men disappeared from the earth. From those bones he created man and woman. These impressive, countless gods, aided by the religious significance of the moon, the stars, and the sun, easily captured the minds of superstitious people. Since life depended upon the pleasure or displeasure of the gods, it is no wonder that the biggest structures, the most expensive and ornate temples, were dedicated to their mythology. The pyramid, in this case the Templo Mayor of Tenochtitlán, was their greatest architectural expression in honor of religion.

The sun was their main preoccupation. According to their ingenious and very charming mythology, the sun did not exist in the first creation of the world. A conference of gods held at Teotihuacán ended by having all of them pledge their lives in order to bring the sun. The sun did appear, but refused to move until all the gods had kept their promise; that is, until they had all killed themselves. The indignant gods shot an arrow at the insolent sun. The sun, however, caught that same arrow and turned it upon the gods, killing them all.

The sun was the warrior par excellence. Early every morning he had to fight the huge army of stars (representing the other gods), and to have strength for the monumental task he needed the "precious liquid"; he needed life itself.

Human sacrifice, then, was inevitable. It did not include cannibalistic activities, as has been thought for so many years, although during the ceremony it was necessary to taste the blood, by that manner partaking with the gods of the same food. Wars were necessary to capture prisoners for sacrifice at the Templo Mayor in Tenochtitlán; and the prisoners were considered "divine," because they were to feed the voracious sun.

Principal Archaeological Sites

Although many hundreds of archaeological discoveries have been catalogued and their approximate locations fixed on maps, most of them are virtually inaccessible to the average traveler. Fortunately, however, the most important and the most outstanding examples of these prehistoric ruins are easily reached by either highway, train, bus, or plane, and every visitor to Mexico should include at least one in his itinerary.

CHICHÉN ITZÁ

Chichén Itzá (chee-CHEN eet-SAH) is located near the center of the Yucatán peninsula, about seventy-five miles east of Mérida.

Route. There are no highway or railway connections between Yucatán and the rest of Mexico. The best approach is via airway (CMA) from Mexico City, Veracruz, and Campeche, and (Pan American) from New Orleans and Guatemala City; or by steamer (Yucatán Line) from New Orleans to Progreso and thence by rail or taxi to Mérida. Taxis and busses operate between Mérida and

Chichén Itzá; the latter make two runs daily. There are good hotels in Mérida and at the ruins (see page 188).

History. The history of the Mayas and a description of the ruins at Chichén Itzá are included in Chapter VII, "The Yucatán."

MITLA

Mitla (MEET-lah—Zapotec for "repository for souls"), located twenty-six miles east of Oaxaca, consists of four principal palaces with lesser ones surrounding them. They are among the most elaborately sculptured in Mexico.

Route. Go first to Oaxaca via the Pan American Highway (paved all the way if you go by way of Puebla); by rail from Mexico City or Puebla; or airways (Aeronaves, CMA, and RAMSA) from Mexico City and Tapachula. Taxis and busses are available in Oaxaca. Hotels in Oaxaca, see page 193.

Description. Each of the four principal structures in this archaeological zone is built around a central patio. Three of the palaces have rooms on all sides except the west. In a cruciform underground chamber beneath one building is a huge monolithic column called *la columna de la muerte* (the column of death) because of the local belief that one can tell his life expectancy by embracing the column and measuring the space remaining between the finger tips. The mosaic patterns, numbering some fifteen different designs, are unique among the pre-Conquest ruins of Mexico. The most elaborate is the Hall of Mosaics, a room in which all the walls form a continuous sculptured design.

MONTE ALBÁN

Monte Albán (MOAN-tay ahl-BAHN—Mixtec for "green hill") in the suburbs of Oaxaca, about four miles northwest of the central plaza.

Route. Go first to Oaxaca via the routes mentioned for Mitla, above. Hotels in Oaxaca, see page 193.

Description. This famous archaeological zone covers a considerable area, and includes many mounds. It is beautifully situated atop a hill overlooking the picturesque Valley of Oaxaca and its backdrop of majestic mountains. There are remains of several elaborate buildings, foundations, terraces, and patios belonging to several periods or civilizations dating from about 500 B.C. to the middle of the fifteenth century. Most of them are still covered by the debris of their own decomposition and plants. They have, in fact, been left practically untouched. In 1931 Professor Caso excavated several remarkable tombs and discovered the remains of Mixtec noblemen. They were surrounded by funeral urns containing precious jewels and gold, jade, and pearls. There were goblets and bowls carved of quartz and numerous interesting artifacts. The collection is now called the Monte Albán Jewels. They are on exhibit in the Museum of Oaxaca.

PALENQUE

Palenque (pah-LEHN-key—from the Spanish, meaning "stockade"), though difficult of access and nearly buried in the dense tropical forest of Chiapas, ranks among the finest ruins of ancient cities on the American continent.

Route. Via steamship (Mexican Navigation Co.) from Veracruz or Coatzacoalcos to the port of Frontera (Álvaro Obregón), state of Tabasco, thence up the Usumacinta (150 miles) by motor launch to Emiliano Zapata (Montecristo). The ruins are about thirty miles southwest of Emiliano Zapata and six miles from the Indian village of Palenque. Only the hardiest travelers should undertake this trip. An easier way is to fly (CMA and CAV) to Villahermosa, capital of Tabasco, and arrange for ground transportation or plane (to E. Zapata) from there. There are no hotel facilities near the ruins, and very poor ones at Villahermosa.

TEOTIHUACÁN

Teotihuacán (teh-oh-tee-wah-CAN—from the Aztec, meaning "place where gods reside") is the most popular archaeological zone in Mexico, largely because of its accessibility and its tremendous size.

Route. Follow the Mexico City–Laredo highway to Venta de Carpio, where the road forks northeast to Teotihuacán. The ruins are about thirty miles northeast of Mexico City. There is a bus service from the bus station at Soledad 50, Mexico City; the telephone number of the bus station is L-27-32. Hotels in Mexico City; take box lunches for a full day's trip.

History. Archaeologists, working assiduously for many years at Teotihuacán, now find that all the information gathered has been incorrectly applied. Teotihuacán, until a few years ago, had been considered Toltec. To a few curious investigators, Teotihuacán seemed too ancient compared to other Toltec ruins, so they cautiously labeled it "Classical Teotihuacán" or "Classical Toltec."

Modern scientists, through investigations at Tula, gave the clue to the mystery. Tula, they say, and not Teotihuacán, was the great capital of the highly cultured Toltec peoples. Tula is now definitely a major zone.

Archaeologists now also agree that there was an ancient independent Teotihuacán culture that had nothing to do with the so-called "Classical Toltec."

There are but two ways to calculate the dates of Teotihuacán's existence: first, the nonexistence of metals. This places Teotihuacán's life before the year 1000. Second, finding a relationship between ceramics of the Tzakol stage of the first Mayan empire and the ceramics of Teotihuacán further help finally to place the life of Teotihuacán from the fourth to the ninth century A.D.

At the present time, the most informed archaeologists on Teotihuacán are, strangely enough, those who are working with the Tula ruins. They are now in a position to discount all the misinformation gathered at Teotihuacán and definitely fix Toltec limits, and thus help to separate the once entangled histories of these two cities.

The first two historians who wrote about Teotihuacán, Ixtlilxochitl and the Spaniard Torquemada, called Teotihuacán the religious capital of the Toltecs, while Tula was the political capital.

The great pyramids in Teotihuacán, including the multicolored murals in temples that have been recently unearthed, attest to a great but little-known civilization.

Later Nahoa civilizations felt a religious respect, perhaps even fear, of Teotihuacán, according to the early Spanish chroniclers. The ordinary citizen of Tenochtitlán, Texcoco, or Tacuba would have nothing to do with the religious, magical, haunted, and very old Teotihuacán, where the mystic presence of the great god Quetzalcoatl was evident.

Description. The archaeological zone of San Juan Teotihuacán (full name) covers an area of eight square miles. The construction is of volcanic stone from the extinct volcano Cerro Gordo, standing to the north of the ruins. The group consists of a number of excavated and unexcavated large and impressive pyramids and structures, all connected by a wide avenue called the Camino de los Muertos (Highway of the Dead), so named from the tomblike mounds that flank it.

The Pyramid of the Sun is the largest of the group and it dominates the entire zone. It is 216 feet high and 721 by 761 feet at the base. It is composed of five pyramidal forms, one on top of another, with outer walls of volcanic rock. It was originally covered with a thin layer of stucco, and this in turn was painted in colorful designs. It was not used as a burial mound, since a tunnel bored in from the eastern side at ground level shows the interior filled with dirt and rubble. The pyramid is considerably larger than any in Egypt, but differs principally in that its top is truncated, like all others in Mexico, to provide a base for a superimposed temple. A wide and steep stairway on the western side leads to the top. Do not attempt the climb if you suffer from any heart ailment or lung difficulty. A temple to the sun god, Tonatiuh Itzcuatl, which stood on the top at the time of the Conquest, was destroyed by Zumarraga, first archbishop of Mexico.

The Pyramid of the Moon, like the larger Pyramid of the Sun, stands in a court surrounded by smaller unexcavated buildings. It faces the northern end of the Camino de los Muertos. It is 140 feet high and 426 by 511 feet at the base. The Goddess of Water, now the largest monolith in the National Museum in Mexico City, was discovered in a cave at the bottom of this pyramid.

The Temple of Quetzalcoatl at the southern end of the Camino is a large group of indeterminate buildings, stairways, carved jaguar heads, and amphitheaters. There are many other interesting structures and temples in the zone, and a large field museum.

The present inhabitants of the villages around the pyramids are Aztecs, who engage in agricultural and handicraft work.

TULA

Tula (TOO-lah—Place of the Reeds) was the legendary capital of the Toltecs.

Route. Via railway or the Mexico City–Laredo highway. By highway turn off at Actopan at Kilometer 118 (seventy-four miles from Mexico City). Tula is fifty-five kilometers (thirty-five miles) from the turnoff. One can make the trip by train (Buena Vista Station in

Mexico City) in two hours. Food of a sort can be had in this village, but hotel accommodations are limited.

History. The available sixteenth-century historical sources concerning the Toltecs (*Anales de Cuauhtitlán*, works by Motolinía, and others) are more or less in agreement that the Toltecs first appeared in the central plateau of Mexico in the eighth century. Archaeological, ethnological, and other sources give hints in a more or less scientific manner that the Toltecs were members of the great Nahoa nation, migrating from the north, notwithstanding a possible origin in the region known as Huasteca, and related to the Olmecs.

The *Anales de Cuauhtitlán*, the most reliable historical source we have on Tula, gives not only the date of the founding of Tula but that of its destruction and abandonment, and even the dynastic succession of ten sovereigns. Mixcohuatl-Mazatzin seems to have been the first king, in 804, and Huemac, the last, in 1116. Much of Tula's history is filled by the presence of a semilegendary man, Quetzalcoatl, who seems to be the first Toltec migrant and leader of the majority of these archaic Nahoa elements who followed him to southern Mexico. It is even possible that the mysterious end of the first Mayan empire in the ninth and tenth centuries was due to a rapid invasion, a sort of blitzkrieg, by these Toltecs led by Quetzalcoatl.

In 1116 what remained of the Toltec people in Tula were hurled southward. The followers of Xolotl, the southbound Chichimec leader, who was attracted by the stories that reached his ear of Toltec agricultural wealth and refinements of life, swarmed down upon Tula with a new weapon, the bow and arrow. The Toltecs, defending themselves with the *atlat* (arrow hurler, a simple instrument that gave more length and leverage to a man's arm), were no serious antagonists to this new weapon, a weapon that later defeated even the Mayas.

A few of the fleeing Toltecs settled in the Valley of Mexico; but faced with continual threats and a very real military failure, their last leader, the tragic Huemac, was forced by the weakened condition of the Toltecs to commit suicide in the forest of Chapultepec, a forest that today forms part of Mexico City's famous urban Chapultepec Park.

The Toltecs, at every new discovery by archaeologists, take a step upward on the Amerindian cultural ladder. They were easily one of the greatest and one of the most cultured peoples in the Americas—perhaps the greatest.

The Aztecs, much later, considered a person noble if he possessed Toltec blood. And the greatness of Maya civilizations seems to be traced to Toltec knowledge of architecture, mathematics, agriculture, and art.

Description. The modern village of Tula is built almost entirely of stones taken from the old Indian temples of this archaeological zone. Broken idols and sculptures of colossal proportions lie scattered about the town, and some of them bear a striking resemblance to the ruins of Chichén Itzá in Yucatán. The main structures of the ruins are within walking distance of the town's plaza, and although not so intricate or elaborate in design as Palenque or Mitla, still they are well worth a visit.

UXMAL

Uxmal (oosh-MAHL—from the old Maya, meaning "three times destroyed"), another sacred city and more Mayan in architecture than Chichén Itzá.

Route. Go first to Mérida (see Chichén Itzá, above). The site is fifty-eight miles south of Mérida on a good paved road. There is a daily bus service from Mérida, and taxis may be hired there. Take box lunches, for there are no accommodations for food or lodging at the ruins.

History. The history of the Mayas and a description of the ruins at Uxmal are included in Chapter VII, "The Yucatán."

MINOR ZONES

The Valley of Mexico is especially rich in minor archaeological sites, the least of which would be comparatively important had they been discovered in some region of the United States, where such treasures are scarce. And in recent years, through excavations and continued research, many of these former minor zones have turned out to be important major zones. Of the minor zones and archaeological sites not covered by the preceding information, those easiest to visit from Mexico City, and described in Chapter V, page 95, are: Tenayuca Pyramid, Santa Cecilia Pyramid, El Pedregal, and the Cuilcuilco Pyramid. Other sites well worth a visit are those near Toluca and Cuernavaca, *q.v.*

CHAPTER X

MEXICAN RECREATIONS

O NCE upon a time, within the memory of many travelers, the only attractions in Mexico besides colonial towns and picturesque citizens were the Sunday-afternoon bull-fights. Dinner marked the end of the day and night owls had to roam far and wide to find sufficient diversion to keep awake until midnight. The war, the influx of Europeans with a Continental attitude toward night clubs, and spree-seeking Americans with money and desire to ape the Europeans brought about a change that has left all of the larger towns in Mexico looking like any average town in the United States—at least at night. The sounds, too, are similar, and only a critical ear can detect the faint overtones of native contributions—cornets and saxophones make more noise than guitars and marimbas.

Daytime entertainment has been widened in variety and increased in sonorescence by the same influences. Any American spectator sport can be seen in Mexico today, in addition to many unusual native and European spectacles. Furthermore, these exhibitions are not staged for the benefit of the visiting firemen. The Mexicans didn't adopt baseball and football to please American tourists. You have only to see one game, either professional or amateur, to understand that these and other familiar American sports are as much a part of Mexican life today as the so-called native sports.

The range of entertainment and spectator sports, therefore, is obviously considerably greater than in the United States. If you want a full life and a merry one during your trip to Mexico, you have only to stay awake. And it has its unexpected compensations, for we know one man who solved his hotel problem by never registering at one—he used the men's washroom for his daily shave and change and just laughed when the clerk said, *"Siento mucho, pero no hay camas"* (Sorry, but there are no beds).

There are a number of social and sports clubs in the principal cities of Mexico that Americans may join. There are also motion-picture theaters in most of the cities, where both Mexican and United States films are shown. In the capital the average cost of admission in first-run theaters is four pesos (eighty cents). Mexico City is more cosmopolitan than the other cities of Mexico and offers the type of recreational and social activities that are offered by the larger cities of Europe and the United States. Each city or town has its *plaza* (park), and one of the chief forms of recreation is to gather in these parks for social conversation and promenades.

Mexico, and in particular the capital, offers numerous facilities for sports, such as horse racing, wrestling and boxing matches, baseball and football (soccer) games, *jai alai* (a Basque game), golf, tennis, horseback riding, and swimming. Fishing and hunting are popular sports at Lake Chapala and other interior parts of the republic, and deep-sea fishing is an important sport on both the Gulf and Pacific coasts.

Sporting supplies are available locally but are considerably more expensive than in the United States, and Americans going to Mexico would do well to take such equipment with them.

The Palacio de Bellas Artes (Palace of Fine Arts), a beautiful marble edifice in the heart of Mexico City, houses a large concert hall and two smaller halls for chamber music and lectures, as well as galleries for art exhibitions. The Mexican Symphony Orchestra has been established successfully for many years, and throughout the year visiting artists give recitals and concerts. There is an opera sea-son with members of the Metropolitan Opera Company of New York often taking leading roles.

The Benjamin Franklin Library, which is under the direction of a group of Americans, contains a good collection of books in English. There are also lending libraries operated by the Junior League Club and the American Book Store.

BASEBALL

American baseball fans should see a Mexican big-league game. Although a comparative newcomer in the field of sport, Mexican baseball is now attracting larger crowds than any other spectator sport. Since there are no equivalents in Spanish for most of the terms used in baseball, you will recognize many English words and phrases. In any case you will be able to enjoy the game, and when you hear someone shout, "*Sentados!*" just remember that it means "Down in front!"

BULLFIGHTS

Bullfights were originated by the Moors in Spain about the twelfth century. Originally they were intended to develop proficiency in the use of martial weapons and for the celebration of festal occasions. They were first known as *fiestas de toros*—bull celebrations. In the early years of the sport, accidents were common and frequent. Old accounts tell of Spanish fiestas in which no less than ten knights lost their lives in a single *fiesta de toros*. During the Middle Ages the spectacle was a court favorite, and kings and lesser royalty participated in the bull ring. Sometime in the eighteenth century the sport passed out of the amateur class and into the hands of professional bullfighters. It was introduced into Mexico by the soldiers of Cortés early in the sixteenth century. It has been popular throughout Mexico ever since.

It is our secret and studied opinion that more Americans like and enjoy Mexican bullfights than is generally believed. They are more "conditioned" to this sport than they realize. Boxing and wrestling matches as performed in the United States are part of this background, but mainly it is a characteristic much more basic and fundamental. All our so-called civilized SPCA propaganda to the contrary, a large proportion of Americans are inherently savage in their basic instincts. Watch any group of small boys for very long and you will see what we mean; and it is our contention that they change very little from this basic pattern during the process of growing up. What, then, is the reason for their outward show of moral fastidiousness? Obviously it is the direct result of our ascetic education and puritanical environment.

That this education is little more than a thin veneer covering the real American character of some is obvious to anyone who has watched the audience at a Madison Square Garden boxing match—or many Americans in the audience of a Mexican bull ring. Certainly, those Americans who have taken the trouble to learn the meaning of a few of the essential features of a bullfight appear to enjoy it as much as the average Mexican fan. We do not guarantee that a more thorough knowledge of the *corrida* will cause you to enjoy a bullfight, but in all fairness to the Mexicans one should have some logical basis for judgment before the expression of any opinions.

First of all, perhaps we should explain that a bullfight is not a fight. Once upon a time a long time ago—in Spain in the Middle Ages—a *corrida de toros* was indeed a true fight, performed on horseback and on foot. But through the years a great many changes have taken place. Today the English word "bullfight" is not only insufficient to indicate what happens, but actually misinterprets the whole idea.

A bullfight is a combination of courage, skill, and elegance. Every bullfighter must show these three things. When he holds his red cape and makes the bull charge at him, he directs the charge of the beast with the movements of the cape. The cape *points* for the bull the direction that the man wants the bull to follow. If the bull is of good stock, the fighter may be sure that he will follow the cape. When the bull has started his rush, the bullfighter must plant his feet firmly on the ground. He must maintain this stance while he directs the bull with the cape, moving his body and his arms only in a pattern established by precedent. He must have poise and elegance; he must adopt positions that are pleasant to the eye; and at the same time, he must let the horns of the bull come as close as possible.

The combination of all these movements and gestures makes a *lance* or a *pase.* Consequently, a good *lance* must be performed on one spot, with an elegant and controlled pose. Above all, the bullfighter must let the bull come as close as possible, the closer and more dangerous the better. It is to see these *lances* and *pases* performed that the people go to a bullfight. The killing of the bull is only an incident of the performance, which also should be accomplished according to definite rules and patterns. Even the most vociferous denouncers are thrilled when they see this colorful spectacle: a slender man dressed in a tight-fitting costume of gold and silk, elegantly poised, moving a brilliant cape in the sun, while a powerful beast rushes by in a mad charge, its horns passing a few inches from the man's body.

If you would like to be a real *aficionado* (fan), then get a copy of

Going to a Bullfight? by James D. Carter and Carlos González, published in Mexico and obtainable at any bookstore in Mexico City. It tells you how to understand and enjoy every phase of the bullfight.

CABARETS

You can enjoy all the night life you want in Mexico City. New *clubs de noche* (night clubs) blossom at the drop of a peso, and each new season finds the city's elite, lesser elite, and plain lesser society swarming into the new spots and still having enough left over to keep most of the old ones in business. We will not presume to make any suggestions beyond "Watch your pocketbook." Slightly inebriated tourists who have difficulty understanding menus in Spanish are too often the victims of unscrupulous waiters. Prices, generally, are a little less than one would pay for similar service and entertainment in the United States.

COCKFIGHTS

You probably won't see a cockfight in Mexico. They are outlawed in Mexico City, and clandestine fights in the outlying villages are seen only by chance encounter with some native who will take you.

FOOTBALL

Futbol, as they say in Mexico, is actually the Mexican adaptation of Rugby. This and baseball are played throughout the year. See the daily newspapers or *Esta Semana* for announcements of games.

HORSE RACES

Mexico City's fashionable new Hipódromo de las Américas (ee-POH-droh-moh) is as American as anything you will find in Mexico. That is easily understood when you learn that its operation is about a fifty-fifty deal between well-known United States track operators and Mexican financiers. The grandstand seats seventeen thousand with standing room for twice that many. The season is in winter, from October to May. Whether or not you speak Spanish you will encounter no more difficulty getting rid of your money here than you would at Jamaica or Santa Anita. The pari-mutuel system of relieving you of it operates the same as in the United States. Special busses run between the Hipódromo and the Zócalo during racing days.

HORSE SHOWS

The most picturesque horse shows are the frequent *charro* contests. The costume of the *charro*, or Mexican cowboy, is a Mexican elaboration of a costume that originated in Salamanca, Spain. It is very picturesque and usually highly adorned with silver. The sombrero alone frequently costs many hundreds of pesos. There are several *charro* riding associations, and one may see the riders in their fancy costumes any morning on the bridle paths around Chapultepec. The contests are exhibitions of riding, roping, and jumping. *Charro* contests are held at frequent and irregular intervals throughout the year. They are worth seeing if your visit happens to coincide with one of their dates.

LOTTERY

Mexico's National Lottery (the full name includes "for the Public Welfare") is as ingrained and institutionalized as fiestas and bullfights, and as necessary, in the minds of Juan and Juanita, as tortillas and *frijoles*. It is under the strict supervision of the Junta de Beneficencia Pública (Board of Public Welfare), and its history is commendable. In a land long famous for graft and political *mordida,* the lottery has never been accused of dishonesty in the drawing of lucky numbers or in the distribution of profits to the various hospitals and welfare institutions that it supports. Strait-laced Americans who are shocked at the popularity of the lottery in Mexico should remember that probably the same amount of money is regularly being gambled in their own home state—without taxation or any public-welfare benefits. The Mexican lottery distributes about 7,000,000 pesos ($1,250,000) annually to orphanages, hospitals, and other charitable institutions. It takes the place of the Community Chests of United States cities. Imagine a country where there is no annual "drive." Or a situation where your contribution has a fair chance of returning a small fortune and a long chance of returning a sizable one.

Just don't try bringing or mailing lottery tickets to the United States.

MARIACHIS

The wandering guitar-playing troubadors of Mexico are usually called *mariachis.* You'll see them in the middle-class cabarets, sometimes in restaurants, frequently on the streets and in the market places. The name originated in Jalisco, where at one time these strolling folk orchestras were composed of stringed instruments only —guitar, *guitarrón* (large guitar), and violin. In recent years, as the name has spread to other regions, and as the bands have added cornets and even saxophones, the *mariachis* have lost much of their picturesque and folkloric flavor, if not their flamboyance. Still, around fiesta gatherings one will see enough of them to satisfy that desire for "atmosphere." They are easily found in Guadalajara, usually around the markets, where they wait for customers. The Plaza Garibaldi in Mexico City is another good place to find them.

MUSEUMS

National Museum of Archaeology and Anthropology. During the colonial days when Mexico was still New Spain all buildings on a large scale were done either by the viceregal government or by the Catholic Church. One of the first buildings of importance to be erected in the colonial seventeenth and eighteenth centuries was the Real y Pontificia Universidad de México. It was in this university that the museum had its unofficial, meager beginnings. Antonio Bucareli in 1743 ordered the archives of the viceroy to be installed in that university, and thus the very first beginnings of a museum were at last under way. But as a cramped dependency of that institution it could hardly expand and progress. The museum received a good shove at the hands of one of New Spain's greatest viceroys, Conde de Revillagigedo, when he ordered all archaeological pieces to be placed in that museum.

It wasn't, however, until the time of the Austrian archduke, Emperor Maximilian, sent by France to rule Mexico, that the museum was definitely installed in its present location. That huge building, once the Casa de Moneda (or mint) of New Spain, formally became, in 1866, the Museo Público de Historia Natural, Arqueología, e Historia, being inaugurated in the presence of Maximilian and his renowned wife, Carlota.

In 1944 the huge museum, filled beyond capacity, became a museum of archaeology and anthropology exclusively. The museum of history then moved to historic Chapultepec Castle.

The present Museo Nacional de Arqueología y Antropología, on Calle de Moneda one block from Mexico City's Zócalo (or main square), now has all of the old Casa de Moneda for the exhibition of the famed products of Mexico's great civilizations.

National Museum of History. This is a new museum, or at least its location is new. Its contents are mostly the treasures of the Conquest and the colonial period. It occupies a part of the famous old Chapultepec Castle, which in itself is a museum piece worth visiting. Visiting hours are from nine to two.

Other, smaller museums of interest to specialists are the Natural History Museum on Calle Chopo at No. 10; Institute of Geology on Plaza de Santa María la Ribera; Commercial and Industrial Museum in the Secretariat of Agriculture Building; and the Hygiene Museum, occupying an old church on Avenida Juárez, opposite the Juárez Monument.

San Carlos Academy of Art. Here is Mexico's best collection of old masters, Mexican as well as European.

The Fine Arts Galleries and the Popular Arts Museum occupy salons in the Palacio de Bellas Artes. The former comprises a nineteenth-century collection and some frescoes by Rivera, Orozco, and Siqueiros. The latter is mostly a collection of representative handicrafts and folk arts, much of which you will find for sale in the shops and bazaars along Avenida Madero.

PELOTA

Pelota or *jai alai* (high ah-LIE) is played at the *frontón* located near the tall arched Monument to the Revolution. This is a fast and spectacular ball game, played by two teams of two men to the side, something like tennis doubles except that both teams are on the same end of the court. The ball is caught in a *cesta*, a long curving basket secured to the right hand and forearm, and thrown against a high wall at the opposite end of the court. Players are usually high-salaried professionals, most of them Basques from Spain. You wouldn't be able to understand the game from any description we could write, so our advice is to seek out a friendly Mexican who can explain it in detail as the game progresses. Have him explain, also, the strange betting procedure.

THEATERS

The principal theaters (*teatros*) of the country are in Mexico City, though every village of any size has its *cine* (movie). Some of the *cines* of the capital are as elaborate and impressive as Hollywood's best. American, Mexican, and Argentine films are shown, productions from the latter two countries being in Spanish and the American films usually in English with Spanish titles. One American company (M-G-M) dubs all its features, shorts, and newsreels in Spanish for release in Mexico and Latin America. So if you would like to hear your favorite movie star mouthing Spanish, try one of this company's pictures while in Mexico. Mexico City newspapers carry large advertisements (generally in Spanish and English) of current and coming features, and the excellent free publication *Esta Semana en México* (This Week in Mexico) has a weekly program.

Cine shows are seldom "continuous" as in the United States. Usually two shows are given daily, *funciones de moda* beginning about six P.M. and the night performance at nine P.M. With the increase in movie audiences in recent years, some of the larger city *cines* now have afternoon shows also. Admissions are 10 to 25 per cent below those charged in the United States for similar shows.

If you understand Spanish, then by all means try to attend one of the performances of one of the many *teatros*. There is a new movement afoot to encourage interest in the drama in Mexico, and some of the recent productions have been outstanding. Perhaps the best entertainment in this field, however, is to be found in the variety theaters when the program includes a wide range of dance and musical numbers. Although staging, lighting, and general effects are usually inferior to American little-theater standards, some of the productions are worth seeing if only for a basis of comparison.

Excellent opera and symphony concerts are given at the Palacio de Bellas Artes during the winter months.

MOUNTAIN CLIMBING

With a clear, dry climate and some of the world's highest peaks, Mexico offers many attractions for mountain climbers. The highest peak is Mount Orizaba (18,320 feet), which, next to Mount McKinley in Alaska, ranks as the highest peak in the North American continent. The nearest town is Orizaba, a delightful health and vacation resort, where a local association supplies information and assists climbers in obtaining guides.

The starting point for the climb is the village of San Andrés Chalchicomola, a few miles from Orizaba. On the way to the summit several caves furnish desirable spots for camping. In scaling the mountain climbers pass from tropical vegetation to the temperate region, where oaks and pines cover the slopes. Beyond this extends the snow cap. There are wonderful views at many points. A good model of Mount Orizaba is exhibited in the Museum of Natural History in New York City.

Next in height to Orizaba is Popocatépetl, 17,520 feet, the starting point for which is Amecameca, two hours by rail or auto from Mexico City. Experienced guides can be hired there, but the climbing outfit must be brought from Mexico City.

The start is usually made after an early breakfast, with a halt in the foothills for lunch. From there the ascent continues, on horse- or muleback, to Tlacamacas, at 12,782 feet, where there is a good view. The night is passed in a hut there. The next morning at seven the ascent is resumed, and at about nine o'clock horses are left at La Cruz, 14,104 feet, from which point the climb is continued on foot. If little snow is encountered a good climber should reach the summit by one o'clock. In clear weather the view is indescribably grand, taking in the entire Valley of Mexico, the domes and spires of the capital, and several towns, including Puebla, together with thousands of square miles of highlands and lowlands.

The crater, about 2,700 feet across, has a depth of over 550 feet. It is encrusted with sulphur, and occasionally there is sulphurous smoke. According to history it was from this crater that Cortés obtained sulphur to make gunpowder during his siege of the Aztec capital, Tenochtitlán.

Ixtaccíhuatl ("Sleeping Woman," from the resemblance of the snow cap to a recumbent woman), the adjacent mountain, is 17,330 feet high. Although the ascent presents few difficulties, this mountain has never been so popular with climbers as the higher Popocatépetl. The ascent is usually made from Amecameca, and the surrounding sierras have much interest for the mountaineer, naturalist, and geologist. In the lower foothills are groves of evergreen trees and a large variety of wild flowers, while the plains stretching away from the base are a patchwork of farms and gardens.

Watch the weekly issues of *Esta Semana* for announcements of the mountain-climbing clubs and special excursions.

FISHING

Mexican waters are internationally known to sportsmen as among the world's finest fishing grounds. Most celebrated is the deep-sea fishing in the tropical waters off both Mexican coasts; but stream fishing and to a lesser degree lake fishing also deserve mention.

The attitude of the Mexican government is friendly toward those who come to Mexico to fish solely for the love of the sport. As long as the visiting fisherman complies with the simple requisites and generous laws of Mexico governing the taking of fish, he will not be molested in any way.

Fishing Regulations. Apart from the observance of the federal regulations governing seasons, the only requirement for the foreign visitor is a fishing license, which may be obtained at the border, in Mexico City and other major cities, or from local fish and game wardens. The cost is small. The taking as well as the protection of fish and game in Mexico is under the exclusive control of the federal government, hence there are no state or municipal licenses or regulations to contend with. A fishing license is good in any state or states or territory of the Mexican republic, and permits any or all kinds of sport fishing, whether deep-sea, stream, or lake. In the interests of conservation, limited areas are occasionally closed to fishing, but generally for a relatively short time; the few cases in which this has been done need cause no concern, however, as the limits of these prohibited zones are well known and always may be determined by local inquiry.

Following is a schedule of license fees, which permit fishing for sport only. Fees are expressed in pesos, Mexican currency.

One Month:

For foreign nonresidents of Mexico $4
For citizens and foreign residents of Mexico 1

Three Months:

For foreign nonresidents of Mexico $10
For citizens and foreign residents of Mexico 3

One Year:

For foreign nonresidents of Mexico $20
For citizens and foreign residents of Mexico 10

Foreign yachts that intend to fish for sport in the coastal waters of Mexico must pay a fee of $25 for a thirty-day fishing permit; for small craft the fee is $4. Qualified members of scientific societies or museums and faculty members or research students of universities or other scientific institutions who wish to take specimen fish for scientific study or use may obtain a special permit in lieu of a license; such a permit is issued without cost by the Federal Fisheries Bureau in Mexico City, upon application accompanied by proper credentials.

Fishing Tackle and Equipment. The customs laws of Mexico permit the sportsman visitor to bring into the country, free of duty or special permit, any reasonable quantity of tackle when intended for personal use. In the case of bringing into Mexico any elaborate kinds or quantity of tackle having considerable value, it would be wise to list such equipment with the American customs at the border before crossing over to Mexico, so as to avoid any question upon returning as to where such equipment was purchased. The sportsman also should advise the Mexican immigration authorities at the border that he intends to fish for sport in Mexico, so that the proper notation can be made on his tourist card.

Whether for stream, lake, or deep-sea fishing, it is advisable that visitors bring their own tackle to Mexico. Although tackle can almost always be rented from boat owners, in the case of deep-sea fishing such tackle is liable to be of inferior quality and not likely to please the experienced fisherman. For stream or lake fishing tackle must be brought, as there are no facilities in Mexico for renting equipment of this kind. In Mexico City there are sporting-goods stores that carry small stocks of fishing tackle for deep-sea as well as stream fishing, but the assortments are limited and may not always include certain necessary or desired items. Furthermore, as most of this tackle is imported from the United States, prices are correspondingly higher because of duties and other import costs.

Boat Rentals. Many types of power launches and other boats suitable for deep-sea fishing are available at Guaymas, Mazatlán, Manzanillo, Acapulco, Veracruz, Tampico, and Coatzacoalcos, and to a more limited extent at fishing ports of lesser importance. Rental charges usually vary directly according to the size of the launch and the number of persons in the party (assuming that the launch is wanted for the exclusive use of the party); in any case, the costs are very moderate, beginning at around $2.50 per hour. There are no established tariffs for this class of service, hence a little good-natured bargaining is usually indicated. The launch owners customarily provide all tackle and bait. The majority are themselves expert fishermen, and know intimately the best fishing grounds in their respective localities as well as the habits and wiles of each class of fish; their judgment in piscatorial matters usually merits the confidence of the angler. Many of these boat owners speak English or understand it sufficiently for all the necessities of the sportsman; thus they can serve in the dual capacity of launch pilot and fishing guide. Professional fishing guides are usually available for those who want their services. Such guides are very useful when the boat owners do not speak English or when they are not themselves skilled fishermen, or when a fairly large party goes together in one boat.

Hunting and Fishing Clubs. Although it is not necessary for deep-sea fishing, the visitor who expects to fish the streams or lakes of Mexico may find it convenient to affiliate himself with one of the many fishing and hunting clubs that enjoy the official recognition and support of the Federal Fisheries Bureau. A temporary or courtesy membership usually can be arranged, and will prove particularly useful in making arrangements for local fishing trips, obtaining guides, securing special information, etc. All of the following clubs are officially registered with the Federal Fisheries Bureau and include among their members some of the most prominent sport fishermen in Mexico:

Centro Nacional de Caza y Pesca
Deportiva .... Piedras Negras, Coah.
Club Deportivo Don Martín .... Don Martín, Coah.
Club Regiomontano Deportivo .... Monterrey, N.L.
Club de Caza y Pesca Acuna .... Villa Acuna, Coah.
San Diego Sport Fishing Assn. .... San Diego, Calif.
Club Totoaba .... Tijuana, Baja Calif.
Club Martín .... Mexico, D.F.

Seasons. Fishing is a year-round sport in Mexico. There are definite seasons, of course, when some fish are more abundant than others, but there is never a time when deep-sea fishing is poor. The various seasons when different kinds of fish are running will be mentioned later under the places described.

Glossary of Fish Names. Except among foreigners, Spanish names are generally used in designating fish in Mexico. For this reason the angler will do well to study the following glossary, which gives the Spanish names and English equivalents of the most abundant varieties. Occasionally one finds a special regional or local name, often of Indian origin, applied to a common fish species, but with a few exceptions these names have not seemed important enough to warrant inclusion in the glossary. The Spanish word *trucha*, which means "trout," is often applied erroneously to other varieties of fresh-water or lake fish, principally small bass.

Albacore	Albacore
Arenque	Herring
Atún	Tuna
Bacalao	Codfish
Barrelete	Skipjack
Bagre	Catfish
Baya	Sea bass
Baya	Spotted rock bass (Guaymas)
Bonito	Bonito
Cabrillo	Rock bass
Carpa	Carp
Cherna	Jewfish
Curbina	Silver sea trout
Curbina	Gulf sea trout
Dorado	Dolphin
Gallo	Roosterfish
Guachinango	Red snapper
Jurel	Yellow-tailed shark
Leguado	Halibut
Lisa	Mullet
Lisa	Smallmouthed black bass (Lake Chapala)
Lobina	Smallmouthed black bass
Lobo Marino	Sea lion
Mantarraya	Giant manta ray
Mero	Jewfish
Palomita	Moonfish
Pargo colorado	Red grouper
Pargo mulato	Black grouper

Pez puerco	Marlin
Pez espada	Triggerfish
Pez vela	Sailfish
Piltontle	Smallmouthed black bass (north Mexico)
Pampano	Pompano
Robalo	Smallmouthed black bass
Roncador	Striped bass
Sabalo	Tarpon
Sierra	Spanish mackerel
Tiburón	Shark
Toro	Bullfish
Tortuga	Turtle
Totoaba	White sea bass
Trucha	Trout
Trucha	Smallmouthed black bass (misnamed) (Lake Pátzcuaro)

DEEP-SEA FISHING ON THE GULF COAST

Veracruz. This interesting tropical seaport, the oldest in continental America, may be reached from Mexico City by an all-paved highway via Puebla and Jalapa. It is also accessible by train and plane from the capital and by boat from New York and New Orleans. There are fishing craft of all kinds available, and at comparatively reasonable rates. Most of the owners of these boats are professional fishermen, hence also excellent guides. The visitor should encounter no language difficulties in Veracruz, since a great deal of English is spoken there.

The best fishing grounds are found outside Veracruz harbor, especially around the shoals and banks of Isla Verde, Antón Lizardo, Anegada de Afuera, and La Gallega, and around other islands in the vicinity. The *jurel*, or yellow-tailed shark, are abundant in these waters and attain immense size. Tarpon are plentiful during their season, from May to the end of summer, but are more difficult to catch as they are commonly found only in the open water rather than inshore, as at Tampico. Red snapper, pompano, common shark, mackerel, bonito, palomita, and sailfish are also plentiful.

As in all waters of the Mexican Gulf coast, fishing during the winter season is occasionally interrupted by severe storms, called *nortes,* which make it impossible for any small craft to leave port. These storms come only at infrequent intervals, however, and between times the ocean waters are quite calm.

Tampico. From Ciudad Mante on the Pan American Highway a paved branch highway leads direct to the important seaport and oil center of Tampico. Good hotels and an ample supply of fishing launches and other facilities answer most of the needs of the deep-sea fisherman. Tampico also may be reached by train from Mexico City, Monterrey, and Laredo, Texas; by plane from Brownsville, Texas, and Mexico City; and by boat from New Orleans.

The fishing here is similar to that at Veracruz. Tarpon, which are abundant, offer thrilling sport and are easier to catch than at Veracruz, in that they are found inshore at the mouth of the wide Pánuco River. Red snapper, pompano, shark, red grouper, sea bass, and yellowtail are among the most plentiful of other varieties. Sailfish, croaker, palomita, and jewfish are found in considerable numbers.

Between Tampico and the Texas border, but closer to the latter, is the large Madre Lagoon, which parallels the coast for a hundred miles and has several openings into the Gulf. A large variety of fish abounds in its sheltered waters, offering excellent sport. This area may be reached by seagoing launch from Tampico, or from the mouth of the Rio Grande.

Beginning a short distance south of Tampico and continuing for almost fifty miles along the coast is Lake Tamiahua, another large salt-water lagoon, noted for sea-bass fishing and easily reached from Tampico.

Coatzacoalcos (Puerto Mexico). This small seaport at the eastern extremity of the Isthmus of Tehuantepec is noted for its excellent deep-sea fishing. Its only disadvantage is that it cannot be reached by car, as no highway yet extends into this region. The port is accessible by train from Veracruz or Mexico City and by plane from either of these points to Minatitlán, near the town. The broad Río Coatzacoalcos, one of the most beautiful tropical rivers in Mexico, flows into the Gulf at this point. Hotels are of the simple country type, but sufficient for the sportsman's needs. Despite the handicaps, a fishing trip to this region usually compensates in sport for the slight inconvenience in reaching the place.

Fishing launches may be rented cheaply at Coatzacoalcos. However, little English is spoken here, hence a working knowledge of Spanish will prove useful. Upstream from the wide mouth of the Coatzacoalcos River the tidal waters abound in a great variety of fish, including tarpon, snook, and both red and black snapper. Even greater sport is found offshore, where the range of species is very similar to that of Veracruz.

Peninsula of Yucatán. Along the north coast of the Yucatán peninsula the fishing is poor. The east coast of the peninsula provides good fishing, but it is practically isolated from the rest of Mexico. This is a fishing ground only for the sportsman who has his own yacht or who can afford to hire a coastal schooner for a trip of several days. There are practically no towns or safe seaports in this virgin region.

Between Puerto Mexico and the Yucatán peninsula are the small ports of Álvaro Obregón (Frontera) and Ciudad del Carmen—two excellent fishing regions but accessible only with difficulty except by plane from Veracruz.

DEEP-SEA FISHING ON THE WEST COAST

Guaymas. This famous fishing ground is easily reached from Nogales, Arizona, by a paved road. Guaymas is also on the west-coast line of the Southern Pacific Railway, which operates the splendid Playa de Cortés Hotel at Bacochibampo Bay, near the town. Here one will find facilities to satisfy the most luxurious tastes, including fine power launches operated by the hotel for the benefit of its fishermen guests. For those who must seek a more economical fare, there are a few simple, comfortable hotels in the village. Fishing boats and facilities are generally plentiful.

Fishing at Guaymas is good throughout the year. During the winter season (October to May) the most abundant fish are the *totoaba* (white sea bass), rock bass and spotted rock bass, silver sea trout, bullfish, jewfish, pompano, red snapper, Spanish mackerel, and yellowtail. The summer season (May to September) finds the waters alive with tuna, swordfish, shark, sailfish, mackerel, roosterfish, dolphin, giant ray, and many other species. Marlin is another favorite found here in abundance.

Best fishing spots out of Guaymas: Bay of Guaymas, Cabo Horno,

Isla de San Pedro Martir, Bacochibampo Bay, San Carlos (to the north of Guaymas), and Lobos Island (to the south).

Topolobampo. A small seaport town south of Guaymas, reached by a branch-line railroad that connects with the Southern Pacific. Hotels are very simple and facilities are limited, but the fishing is excellent. A few small launches are available for hire at very low cost. Varieties of fish as well as the seasons in which they are found are practically the same as at Guaymas.

Mazatlán. This picturesque seaport and popular coast resort city may be reached only by the Southern Pacific Railway, or by plane from Mexico City or Los Angeles. There are good hotels in the town and every facility for the sport fisherman, including a number of fishing launches for hire. Besides being a good fishing ground, Mazatlán is a delightful place to spend a few days' vacation. Swimming is excellent in the beautiful bay.

Most plentiful varieties of fish in the region around the Bay of Mazatlán are the rock bass and black sea bass, roosterfish, mackerel, bullfish, sea trout, swordfish, grouper, sailfish, jewfish, yellowtail, dolphin, and the giant manta ray. Seasons are similar to those at Guaymas. The huge manta ray is best hunted with the harpoon; many launches are available that are adapted to this exciting sport.

Manzanillo. A very old tropical sea town between Mazatlán and Acapulco and an important port of call for deep-water ships. Many civic improvements have been made in the town in recent years. Manzanillo may be reached only by a branch-line railroad from Guadalajara, or by plane from Mexico City. Hotels are second-class but adequate in the necessities.

Practically the same general species of fish are found in the waters off Manzanillo as are common at Mazatlán, although in lesser quantity. There are a number of fishing launches available at inexpensive rates.

Zihuatanejo. This is a small, isolated seacoast town between Manzanillo and Acapulco, which can be reached only by boat from either of these two points. Accommodations are primitive but the fishing is among the finest to be found anywhere. These waters seem to be alive with everything that swims; particularly plentiful are the marlin, sailfish, barracuda, roosterfish, and swordfish. Unfortunately this remarkable fishing ground can be worked only if one has available a boat sufficiently seaworthy for a coastwise trip in the open ocean. Arrangements for a suitable launch sometimes can be made at Acapulco.

Acapulco. Surrounded by towering mountains and laced by golden beaches, Acapulco has a compelling beauty that makes it a popular resort for fishermen and vacationists. The town is the terminus of an all-paved highway from Mexico City, and on a daily air service from the capital. It has an abundance of excellent hotels; its beaches offer the finest swimming; it is probably the grandest place in Mexico to relax and loaf happily. The beautiful landlocked harbor is a popular port of call for yachts and sportsmen fisherfolk from all over the world. Facilities of every kind and boats of all types are offered the angler, and at price ranges to meet any budget.

Marlin and sailfish are found in large numbers in the waters off Acapulco Bay. The barracuda, dolphin, shark, yellowtail, pompano, tuna, bonito, roosterfish, mackerel, red snapper, palomita, and amberjack are among other plentiful species. The giant rays, which are larger here than in the waters farther north, as well as huge sea turtles, are hunted with the harpoon.

Other West-Coast Fishing Grounds. The immense stretch of shore line comprising the entire west coast of the peninsula of Baja (Lower) California is one continuously fine fishing ground, but it has the serious disadvantage that it can be reached only by boat, necessitating a long trip on open water. If and when good roads are built into this sparsely inhabited territory, it will seriously compete for the fishing popularity that other west-coast ports now enjoy.

Near the northwest corner of Lower California is the town of Ensenada, easily reached by all-weather highway from San Diego, California. The town has good hotel accommodations, and the adjacent waters offer good fishing. Even better sport is found off the Coronado Islands, close to the American boundary; these may be reached direct from San Diego, where the Mexican government maintains an office authorized to issue the necessary fishing license and permits.

Puerto Ángel, a tiny seaport considerably south of Acapulco, is also celebrated for its fishing grounds, but its isolation is so complete that it can be reached easily only by boat.

Salina Cruz, at the western extremity of the Isthmus of Tehuantepec, is accessible from Mexico City by the Isthmus Railroad, but this is a long, arduous trip that is not justified unless one plans to spend some time in the picturesque isthmus region. Hotels are poor and fishing facilities such as boats are limited; nevertheless, if one is visiting the isthmus region, a fling at deep-sea fishing at Salina Cruz should not be passed up.

STREAM FISHING

The best stream fishing in Mexico is for the most part found in the streams that flow to the Gulf of Mexico. The rivers and creeks on the Atlantic side of the continental divide are larger and more numerous, because of a heavier rainfall. During the rainy season, from June through September, stream fishing is likely to be uncertain and haphazard because of the immense volumes of water in the form of freshets that follow every heavy rainfall. Peaceful creeks suddenly become raging torrents, at times only for a few hours and at other times for a matter of days. It is, of course, practically impossible to fish during these freshet periods, but between times some sport can be realized. At other seasons of the year, however, stream fishing in Mexico provides fine sport.

Trout, black bass, and catfish are the most abundant species in Mexican streams. Trout are more plentiful in the upland country, whereas bass and catfish are found more commonly in the lower reaches of the rivers.

Rivers of Tamaulipas. The Pan American Highway traverses the state of Tamaulipas, in the northern part of Mexico. Both rivers and small streams are plentiful. Many of them are stocked with black bass and all have catfish of unusual size as well as sunfish. Of these various streams, the river Tamesi is probably the best possibility. Headquarters can be established at any of the highway towns in this region.

Rivers of San Luís Potosí. This state, south of Tamaulipas, is also crossed by the Pan American Highway. In some of the rivers that cross the highway, catfish weighing up to fifty pounds have been taken. Sunfish and black bass are found in most of these tropical and subtropical rivers. The Pánuco and Moctezuma Rivers are the most important ones in the region, and in many places offer good fishing.

Rivers of Veracruz. This long narrow state parallels the Gulf coast from Tampico to the Isthmus of Tehuantepec, and is crossed by a great number of rivers that have their sources in the towering

Sierra Madre del Oriente range to the west. The Cazones and Teco-lutla Rivers, together with their major tributaries, offer good bass fishing, but are difficult of access. Farther south, the river Nautla (known as the river Bobos in its upper reaches) is well supplied with bass; the important tributaries known as the Quilate and San Pedro Rivers are also good streams to fish. This river system may be reached by driving to Perote (Veracruz highway), thence over an all-weather road to Teziutlan; from there to Martínez de la Torro the trip had best be made by commercial auto stage. This town is in the center of this river region, from which point one may explore the main river or its tributaries on foot or horseback. Accommodations are simple but the fishing is good. Farther south, the various rivers run through districts that are more heavily populated, and fishing there cannot be recommended. In the Orizaba region, however, the rivers have been stocked with rainbow trout and offer good sport. The Tenejapa and Blanco Rivers are probably the best in the region.

Hacienda de Santa Engracia. This famous old hacienda has been converted into a delightful dude ranch. It lies a few miles off the Pan American Highway near Ciudad Victoria, in Tamaulipas. Streams in the vicinity are stocked with black bass, catfish, and sunfish.

Hacienda de Hueyapan. Another old hacienda, at San Miguel Regla in Hidalgo state, has been converted into a private fish and game preserve. It is but a few hours' drive from Mexico City. Fishing is good, especially for rainbow trout.

Hacienda de Texcaltenco. A private fish preserve near Lerma, just off the Toluca highway. Accommodations are good, fees are reasonable, and exciting sport is assured. Rainbow trout is the specialty of this preserve.

Other Streams. Many streams that formerly yielded good catches have not yet been restocked because of inaccessibility. In others, the local population manages to keep them pretty well fished out. The streams listed previously offer what we believe to be the best general possibilities at the present time, although there are of course many other streams in the republic, especially in sparsely populated or isolated regions, where one may fish. The average visiting sportsman, however, will rarely have the time necessary to make a long trip into the hinterland of Mexico.

LAKE FISHING

Lake fishing in Mexico is becoming an increasingly better sport, owing to the work of the federal government in restocking these inland waters. Much of this commendable work is being offset by the local natives, who fish with nets, to the destruction of the smaller fish. Black bass is the principal species found in the Mexican lakes, although rainbow trout is found in the lakes of high altitude.

Lake Pátzcuaro. This picturesque lake, beloved of tourists and Mexicans alike, is situated in the state of Michoacán. It may be reached over a scenic paved highway from Mexico City. The local Indians conduct a large business of fishing on this lake, but its waters are seldom worked by the sportsman angler. The daily catches of black bass and whitefish from this lake feed a large population in the surrounding country. There are good hotels in Pátzcuaro. Launches are available on the lake at a nominal charge.

Lake Chapala. The same highway from Mexico City to Pátzcuaro continues on to Lake Chapala before reaching Guadalajara. This lake, the largest in Mexico, contains black bass, trout, catfish, and carp. The fishing industry on the lake is even larger than on Pátzcuaro, as it supplies the market for the large city of Guadalajara, some twenty miles distant. There are resort hotels at the town of Chapala, at the lake's edge. Launches and other lake craft are always available for rental. Apart from fishing, Lake Chapala is a delightful place to spend a few days' vacation. Swimming is very popular in its pleasantly warm waters.

Other Lakes. There are only two other lakes of importance in Mexico, judged from the fisherman's point of view. These are Lake Cuitzeo and Lake Zirahuen, both in the state of Michoacán in the Pátzcuaro region. Lake Cuitzeo may be reached by a dirt road from Morelia; bass is the principal species found here. Lake Zirahuen, much smaller than Cuitzeo, is a few miles from Pátzcuaro, with which it is connected by a dirt road difficult during the rainy season. Black-bass fishing is fair. It is a beautiful little lake, however, and a delightful place to visit.

HUNTING

No description of Mexico would be complete if it did not mention the big industrial plants and ultramodern skyscrapers that stand cheek by jowl with the more picturesque evidences of Spanish colonial history and ancient civilizations. The visitor who desires a proper balance in his conception of the country should spend some time studying Mexico's modernization and industrial progress. However, there is still another side to this protean country. One might call this other side still another civilization, for there are primeval forests and remote deserts wherein dwell a variety of animals and birds little changed in quantity or design from those known to the prehistoric hunters who roamed the continent even before the Toltecs and the Aztecs. Further, American sportsmen who read this with surprise will be happy to learn that there is big-game hunting in Mexico within comparatively easy access, and that some of its adventure potentials are fully equal to anything encountered on an African safari.

There are several obvious reasons for this continuance of the Mexican fauna's *status quo*. Adverse climate and inhospitable lands have discouraged human encroachment on vast areas; the difficulties involved in obtaining wild animals for food caused the indigenous races to be herbivorous or at least partially vegetarian; and maladjustments in the modern economic situation in Mexico have not permitted any wide use of such expensive food-getting instruments as firearms. So the animal population of Mexico has probably grown and prospered through the centuries rather than dwindled as it has in the United States.

Mexican Hunting Regulations. Compared to other countries, the game limits and the open seasons in Mexico are generous and the license fees modest. All the hunter needs to enter Mexico is a tourist card (see page 16) obtainable at the nearest Mexican consulate or at the place of entry. Sportsmen should specify on their applications for this card that they wish to hunt. The regulations for taking firearms into Mexico for hunting purposes are not strict, provided the visitor complies with a few simple requisites. He must obtain a firearm permit from the Mexican consul, and the documents necessary to get it are: (1) a letter of recommendation from a bank, chamber of commerce, police department, or other recognized institution, stating that the applicant is a respectable, law-abiding citizen; and (2) two passport-size photographs of the applicant. This permit entitles the holder to take four guns, each of a different caliber, into Mexico. However, only one gun (either a shotgun or a rifle) is admitted duty-free; the others must be bonded (about $4 per gun), and the bond is refundable when the guns are taken back out of the country. No guns of the same caliber as used by the Mexican military forces are allowed entry (at present these are the Mausser 7 mm. rifle and the Colt .45 automatic). Those who wish to bring in guns not made in the United States should register them with the United States customs office before taking them out of the country to avoid payment of duty when they are returned to the United States. Ammunition up to one hundred cartridges or five hundred grams of powder for each gun is allowed entry duty-free.

All hunters must carry a hunting license; in fact, in so far as hunting is concerned, visitors should consider themselves Mexican citizens, for the license laws make no distinction between Mexicans and foreigners. Hunting licenses may be obtained from the Oficina de Caza (Office of the Game Warden) at the border port of entry; at the office of the Secretaría de Agricultura y Fomento (Agriculture and Public Works) in any state capital; or at the federal office of the Secretaría de Agricultura y Fomento, Dirección General Forestal y de Caza, Avenida Edison 145, in Mexico City. In addition, there are forestry and game wardens in various parts of Mexico (usually near forested areas) from whom one may obtain hunting licenses. In making his application the sportsman must present his tourist card and furnish a bond. The bond may be secured from any reliable Mexican bonding company or from a responsible business firm. The easiest, perhaps, is to join one of the many officially licensed hunting clubs, membership in which includes the furnishing of a bond. The cost of a hunting license to hunt anywhere in Mexico for six months is eighty pesos, or about $16.50. A license for one state, which may not exceed thirty days, costs fifty pesos.

Hunting and Fishing Clubs. The following clubs are licensed by the Hunting and Fishing Departments of the Mexican government and authorized to provide the above services according to the hunting and fishing laws:

Club de Cazadores Rancho El Carrizo, Ensenada, Baja California.
Club de Cazadores La Grulla, S.A., Baja California.
Club Nacional de Caza y Pesca Playa de Cortés, Apartado 22, Guaymas, Sonora.

Club Deportivo de Caza y Pesca Santa Engracia, Hacienda Santa Engracia, Hidalgo, Tamaulipas.

Club Deportivo de Cazadores de Baja California, Avenida B, No. 144, Apartado 121, Tijuana, Baja California.

Club de Cazadores de Mazatlán, Calle Juárez 613–615, Mazatlán, Sinaloa.

Asociación Internacional Deportiva de México, 205 South Broadway, 216 Civic Center Bldg., Los Angeles, California.

Club Deportivo Tiradores del Norte, Apartado 192, Ciudad Juárez, Chihuahua.

Club de Cazadores Mexicanos, Edificio Salido, Oficina 4, Nogales, Sonora.

Club Deportivo de Caza y Pesca Rosarito, Edificio Barbachano, Apartado 6, Tijuana, Baja California.

Centro Nacional de Caza y Pesca Deportiva, Piedras Negras, Coahuila.

Club Cinegetico y de Tiro Alcones, San Luís Potosí, San Luís Potosí.

Asociación Deportiva Mexicana de Caza y Pesca La Tropical, A.C., Avenida 5 de Mayo 23, México, D.F.

Asociación Deportiva Mexicana de Caza y Pesca Marlin, Avenida 5 de Mayo 23, México, D.F.

Club Cinegetico Morelia, Esquina Dr. Silva y Avenida Serdan, Morelia, Michoacán.

Club de Caza y Pesca Casa Blanca, Apartado 2, Monterrey, Nuevo León.

Club Deportivo de Caza y Pesca Costa Occidental de México, Tucson, Arizona.

Where, What, and When to Hunt. The Mexican Tourist Association, a government agency, has issued an illustrated brochure entitled *Hunting in Mexico,* which gives a complete list of all game birds and animals and the seasons covering them. It also lists the game supposedly available in the various states or hunting regions. The state of Chihuahua, for instance, sounds like a Noah's ark with this list: gray bear, black bear, mountain sheep, wild turkey, cougar, jaguar, Mexican panther, wolf, coyote, wild duck, wild goose, light and dark heron, boar, black-tailed deer, and white-tailed deer. But ask any Chibaba from Chihuahua and he will say, "*Si, señor,* they are all common game animals in this state."

CHAPTER XI

FIESTAS AND HOLIDAYS

BECAUSE the climate is generally delightful throughout most of the regions usually visited by tourists, one should say that any time of the year is the ideal time to visit Mexico. There is another factor, however, that influences the travel plans of the experienced. At least, it is important in the minds of those who want full value for their travel dollar. That factor is the annual fiesta.

Since there are as many saints as there are days in the year, there is a fiesta or holiday every day of the year someplace in Mexico. Each Mexican village annually celebrates its patron saint's day with festivities and reverent religious ceremonies, and frequently there are a colorful market, folk dances, bullfights, and fireworks. Indians for miles around bring to the market the serapes, pottery, baskets, fruits, and grain that they have been working to produce for a whole year. Churches and streets are decorated with streamers of colored tissue paper; primitive musicians play even more primitive musical instruments; and what the fireworks may lack in brilliance they manage to make up for in noise.

In addition to these celebrations, which are religious in origin though generally pagan in expression, there are many important civic or national holidays that are the occasions for simultaneous fiestas throughout the republic.

During the fiesta no one thinks of rest or sleep. The native dances may begin at three o'clock in the morning and continue until sundown of the following day. At nightfall the entire population gathers in the central plaza to watch the fireworks, which are the high point of the celebration.

Mexican fireworks are really something to watch. The central piece, called the *castillo,* is a reed structure often reaching to a height of thirty feet. It consists of a series of complicated fireworks that, setting each other off in sequence, builds up to an impressive drama of light and color. The *globo,* also typical of these celebrations, is a huge balloon made of myriads of tiny pieces of bright-colored paper. From innumerable threads affixed to its sides dangle cylindrical lanterns. When the *globo* is released into the air it rises in the dark night and flames into a mass of fire, soaring above the heads of the onlookers; then suddenly it falls to earth in a shower of dripping sparks. The entire spectacle lasts only five minutes, but weeks of patient work go into its preparation. The fireworks mark the climax and the end of the fiesta.

The best time to visit any community, therefore, is during the most important of its annual fiestas. However, although we give below a complete calendar of official holidays and outstanding festivals, one should ascertain after arrival in Mexico whether or not any change or slight postponement has taken place in the fiesta plans. If the fiesta is a religious celebration, the saint's day may fall on a week day and be celebrated the following Sunday because the men are busy in the fields. Or it may be postponed until the harvest is gathered, for in the hearts of many Indians the festival is still one of direct thanksgiving to an agricultural deity. Or Don José's mother may have gone to the holy shrine of Chalma to give thanks for her daughter's miraculous recovery from a major illness, and Don José may have accompanied her, traveling on his knees over the stony paths as an expression of his great piety. But it so happens that Don José is in charge of the fireworks, because he can build cleverer *castillos* than anyone else, and the townspeople, having become accustomed to the fine *castillos* of Don José, would not enjoy an inferior display of fireworks. A fiesta, of course, would be unthinkable without fireworks. Consequently, it must be put off until Don José's return. When will he return? *Quién sabe?*

There may be a dozen different reasons for changing the date of a fiesta, but when you see your first one you will decide it was worth all previous disappointments.

PRINCIPAL CIVIC HOLIDAYS

January 1. New Year's Day.

February 5. Constitution Day, anniversary of the establishment of the constitutions of 1857 and 1917, now in effect.

March 21. Anniversary of the birth of Benito Juárez and Day of the Indian Child.

Benito Juárez was president of the republic from 1858 to 1872. He was a statesman, patriot, and author of liberal reforms, and led his people in resistance to the French invasion (1861–67), which culminated in the capture and execution of Archduke Maximilian of Austria and in the withdrawal of the invaders.

The Day of the Indian Child is also celebrated on this date. Special exhibits are held of the paintings, handicrafts, and other arts of the Indian children.

April 14. Pan American Day—anniversary of the founding of the Pan American Union.

May 1. Labor Day.

May 5. National Day, commemorating the Mexican victory over the French at Puebla in 1862.

The French, under General Laurenez, marching ten thousand strong on Mexico City from Veracruz, were met at Puebla, May 5, 1862, by four thousand Mexicans under General Zaragoza and soundly defeated on this memorable date. The city was attacked again, however, by a strongly reinforced army, and finally capitulated to the French a year later.

September 15–16. Independence, commemorating Hidalgo's Declaration of Independence, the Mexican equivalent of our Fourth of July. The most impressive fiesta takes place in Mexico City at midnight of the fifteenth, when it is customary for the president of Mexico to stand on the central balcony of the National Palace and repeat Hidalgo's call to freedom:

"*Viva México!* Long live independence!"

The answer echoes back from thousands of Mexicans who fill every corner of the huge square in front of the National Palace.

"Long live independence! *Viva México!*"

Bells of the cathedral ring out over the square, and a military band crashes into the notes of the Mexican national anthem. Factory whistles scream and church bells all over the city ring above the crowds welcoming Mexico's greatest national holiday, the independence celebration of the sixteenth of September.

Thus Mexico hails its George Washington, a village priest in the state of Guanajuato who in 1810 shouted the first *grito* and called his congregation to follow him in revolt against the harsh colonial rule of Spain. Although the rebellion started by Miguel Hidalgo was crushed and the priest was captured and shot by the Spaniards, his uprising marked the beginning of Mexico's struggle for freedom. The climax to Hidalgo's heroic efforts did not come until some years later, when the Mexican Republic was founded.

Usually there is a reception for the foreign ambassadors and representatives following the ceremony, with toasts to the future prosperity and continued freedom of Mexico.

The annual Independence military parade takes place about noon on the sixteenth. Sidewalks are crowded with spectators, as picked troops from every part of the republic pass through the downtown streets.

October 12. Discovery of America or Columbus Day, called Día de la Raza (Day of the Race) in Mexico.

The twelfth of October is a historical date to which all peoples of the Western Hemisphere, from Alaska to the Straits of Magellan, have a common claim, although so far it has been celebrated with special zeal and devotion only in Latin America. Most of the Spanish-speaking republics call it El Día de la Raza, as they stress their common origin, language, and culture. In the United States it is generally observed as Columbus Day, except in Alabama, where it is called Fraternal Day; North Dakota, which prefers Discovery Day; and Wisconsin, where it is known as Landing Day.

November 20. Revolution Day, commemorating the beginning of the 1910 revolution.

In 1877 General Porfirio Díaz became president and ultimately dictator. He ruled Mexico for over thirty years. Although the country made much progress during that time, foreign interests gained wide control, while education was neglected and labor oppressed. In 1910 the rule of Díaz ended as the result of a revolution headed by Francisco Madero. For ten years thereafter Mexico witnessed great political upheavals. Peaceful conditions were restored in 1920, since which time, under eight presidents—Obregón, Calles, Portes Gil, Ortíz Rubio, Rodríguez, Cárdenas, Camacho, and Alemán—Mexico has witnessed a new era of progress and prosperity.

PRINCIPAL RELIGIOUS FIESTAS

Since Roman Catholicism is the dominant religion of the country, the chief feast days of the Church are generally observed. As a rule, government departments are closed on these days, but stores sometimes remain open. The most important religious celebrations take place in December and January. During these months there is a continuous round of religious and folk festivals in Mexico. These begin early in December, with Indian dances and miracle plays carrying the heritage of medieval Spain and of the great Indian civilization that preceded the Conquest. Most noteworthy are those celebrated the second and sixth of December in the Indian churches of San Francisco and of Santa María Tonantzintla, near Puebla; the Monterrey ceremonies centering on the Purísima Church and plaza on December eighth; and, also on the eighth, the Pátzcuaro festival honoring Our Lady of Health.

All Mexico pays homage to the miracle-making Virgin of Guadalupe on December 12 (see below), and the *Posadas* begin on the sixteenth. Almost every family holds one before Christmas Eve. In the patios the guests, holding candles and plagued by the firecrackers set off by the children, follow an image of the Virgin and Joseph. Re-enacting the search for shelter, they stop at the door of each room and plead in Latin chant for entry. In the last room they are admitted, and there they sing their thanks.

After this charming ceremony is completed, the merrymaking begins with the breaking of the *piñata*. This is a huge earthenware jar covered with streamers or with a papier-mâché facsimile of a grotesque figure. The jar is filled with candy and chewing gum. The *piñata* is suspended from a doorway, and each guest in turn is blindfolded and handed a stick. He must try to break the *piñata,* while the other guests call out confusing directions and the *piñata* is jerked out of his reach by a rope. At last someone strikes the lucky blow, and the children scramble for the shower of goodies that fall from the jar.

Mexicans spend much time and artistic ingenuity in arranging the miniature mangers that, instead of Christmas trees, are the center of Christmas Eve ceremonies in both churches and homes. However, the Christmas tree has finally invaded the republic, and today the northern visitor can celebrate his kind of Christmas in Mexico as well as the traditional one of the country. *Pastorales,* or Nativity plays, are held everywhere, very much as they were in medieval Europe.

January 1–7. Fiesta of Chalma. This remote mountain village has a famous miracle-working Spanish crucifix in a magnificent sanctuary. For centuries the pilgrims, tramping through mountain and forest, have worn the dirt trails as hard as stone. If you should camp in the forest preserve of Zempoala, near Cuernavaca, during this time, you would see throughout the night an endless line of bobbing torches winding over the old mountain trail. The pilgrims travel day and night. The Chalma festival is one of the most colorful and unspoiled in Mexico.

January 6. Day of the Three Wise Men, primarily a children's holiday. The children dress in costume or in their best, and everyone buys for them the cleverly formed candies and cakes that are for sale in the plazas.

January 15. The ancient plume dance draws visitors to Zimatlán, near Oaxaca. Tenango del Valle, not far from the capital, also has an interesting fiesta on this date.

January 17. Everyone visits the town nearest his own named San Antonio. This is the day of St. Anthony, when domestic animals and pets, decked out with ribbons and streamers, are taken to the church to be blessed.

January 27–28. The Dance of the Conquest is a feature of the fiesta at Cuilapan, in Oaxaca.

February 2. In Mexico February is the traditional month for the planting of gardens and crops. It is a month of mild rains and warm, sunlit afternoons, and therefore the belief that any seeds planted on Candlemass Day will flourish into fine plants is usually substantiated. The custom of planting in February has come down through the years from Mexico's pagan history. Now, however, Candlemass Day is a much celebrated and revered fiesta. The festival is most interesting and colorful in the little town of San Juan de Los Lagos, not far from León, Guanajuato. There is a miraculous image of St. John in this town that is believed to protect the pilgrims against death by drowning. The devout journey from all parts of Mexico to this shrine, and just before Candlemass Day one may see them, laden with their bedding and cooking utensils, trudging along the country roads that lead to San Juan de Los Lagos. At night they make camp under a tree or in a village street; some have their sick with them and others their animals, and all anticipate blessings and miracles.

This day is also celebrated with dances and fireworks in the village of El Pueblito, a village known as the site of interesting archaeological ruins. El Pueblito is near Querétaro and may be reached by car from that city.

From February first through the seventh there are fiestas and dances at Tzintzuntzan, a primitive colonial town on the shores of Lake Pátzcuaro. This village was once the center of the powerful and artistic Tarascan empire, and after the Spanish Conquest it was for some years the seat of the Catholic archbishopric. In the square before the old church and convent, built in the best plateresque style, one may still see the olive trees planted by the Spanish priests early in the sixteenth century. During the week that terminates on Ash Wednesday, native Passion plays, with much naïve charm, are presented.

The town itself is interesting as the center of the ancient feather work brought to such a high degree of beauty by the Tarascans. Tzintzuntzan, the name of the town, means Place of the Hummingbirds, and it was hummingbird feathers that were used most in the delicate feather tapestries.

February 9. Fiesta of San Juan Teotihuacán. This city is famous as the site of Mexico's most imposing Toltec archaeological ruins. The Pyramids of the Sun and the Moon, the Temple of the Plumed Serpent, and the Fortress are well worth a visit at any time of the year, but they are especially imposing at this season, when the sunlight is bright and intense, and one may see clearly the surrounding mountains. The native dances and bazaars of today make one meditate on what scenes of fiesta must have been some seven centuries ago, before the subjugation of the Indians and the conversion of their pagan rituals.

Carnival. Carnival in Mexico, usually a week in late February (preceding the abstinences that begin with Ash Wednesday), is marked by gay festivities wherein cares, restraints, and everyday routine are forgotten and the great king Good Humor rules the land. Poets and peasants, philosophers and politicians, businessmen and bureaucrats join hands to have a rip-roaring good time into which, with typical Mexican hospitality, visitors are invited to join. The merrymaking is especially animated at the colorful port towns of Mazatlán, Manzanillo, Acapulco, and Veracruz. Mexico City, as the nation's capital, is the center of elaborate and lively celebrations. In every town, large and small, there are native dances, balls, fireworks, special ceremonies, and rodeos.

One of the most interesting of the rural carnival celebrations takes place at Huejotzingo, a picturesque little village just an hour's drive from Mexico City on the Puebla highway. Here several hundred inhabitants enact a three-day drama with the entire village as a setting. The theme of this outdoor play, which dates back at least two centuries, is the elopement of a village maiden with the famous bandit Agustín Lorenzo. The latter is portrayed as a rather charming fellow, somewhat on the Robin Hood type. The maiden, generally acted by a stalwart Indian in chintz shirts and a bright felt hat, is rather less appealing. She performs, however, some rather startling acrobatic feats, descending from a second-story balcony of the city hall to a fiery steed on which she rides off with the daring Agustín.

On the third day, after considerable blood and thunder and a series of stirring events including the actual burning of the honeymoon hut, all ends well. The girl's parents are reconciled to her marriage with the daring young bandit, and the tempestuous romance terminates on a happy note.

Meanwhile there have been exciting encounters between the French and Spanish soldiers and the Indian warriors, portrayed by hundreds of local participants. The Indians, resplendent in many-colored plumed headdresses, their faces painted in intricate white and gold designs, perform a series of native dances. The soldiers, mounted on horseback, stage mock combats with very real rifles. As the play unfolds the natives and visitors trail the all-star cast of several hundred local artists through the streets and plazas of the town.

The drama lasts for three days, with time out for sleeping, eating, drinking (delicious Huejotzingo *manzanilla*, a locally brewed beverage that is between champagne and cider), and talking. Visitors are invariably thrilled by the spectacle, though they generally find the twelve-hour, three-day performance rather wearing and compromise by driving out for the morning or afternoon. Fortunately, the time of arrival doesn't make much difference. The actors, who never seem to tire, keep a continuous show going, and at Huejotzingo the spectacle, not the plot, is the thing.

Holy Week is an inspiring and deeply religious period observed with fiestas and Passion plays. One of the most interesting takes place in Tzintzuntzan, the ancient Tarascan capital on the shores of Lake Pátzcuaro. Here, on Holy Thursday, pious Indians enact the Last Supper, and on the following day perform the drama of Calvary. During Easter week vendors in all the markets of Mexico are busy selling fireworks for the celebration of the ending of Lent on Holy Saturday. Most popular of the fireworks are the large papier-mâché images of Judas.

March 19. St. Joseph's Day, widely celebrated throughout Mexico.

August 15. The Assumption of the Blessed Virgin, a religious feast celebrated with processions throughout the republic.

November 1 and 2. All Saints' Day and All Souls' Day.

"It's almost as much fun to die as to live in Mexico," says the Mexican Tourist Association in describing the celebration of All Souls' Day. During the last days of October, gay placards in all the bakeries announce a fine supply of Dead Men's Bread. The round loaves surmounted by well-baked dough skulls are relished by the living. Children beg their mothers for one of the tinsel-decorated sugar skulls that peer enticingly from shopwindows and market stands. Dapper skeletons with plumed hats beckon with a friendly gesture. Toy skeletons leap cheerfully out of cozy coffins at the pull of a cleverly arranged string. And as a fascinated youngster winds the handle of a little box, a toy funeral passes in and out of a cardboard cathedral. November first and second are dedicated to the dead, but the Mexican spirit turns the occasion into a festive holiday.

Improvised altars decorated with black and white paper cutouts are arranged in Indian homes. Food is specially prepared for the dead of the family, who, according to the Indian tradition, return on this night to eat with their loved ones. The graveyards are visited by picnic parties who decorate the tombs and wooden crosses with pungent bright yellow calendulas. This is the flower that the Indians always use to cheer up the dead. The ceremony and Tarascan singing at midnight on the island of Janitzio, in Lake Pátzcuaro, provide an impressive and unearthly spectacle. The narrow graveyard is turned into a sparkling fairyland where myriads of gleaming candles cast a weird light on mounds garlanded with fruits and flowers. The Indians have a primitive attitude toward death, and the fact that they do not fear it is reflected in their gay celebration of this day.

December 12. Guadalupe Day.

The day of Our Lady of Guadalupe finds Mexico in gala attire. Children dressed in colorful national costumes swarm the streets. Long lines of devout pilgrims wend their way toward the churches dedicated to this saint. During the festival they camp for miles round, while the plaza outside the church resembles a great country fair.

After the church services the celebration goes into full swing with dancing, feasting, and fireworks. In the open square before the church, *matachín* dancers and musicians pirouette in quaint costumes hung with mirrors, bright ribbons, and fringe.

In the little suburb of Guadalupe itself, twenty minutes from downtown Mexico City, tourists may see the streets bustling with people: thousands of pilgrims converging on the shrine, thronging the narrow walks, flooding the large courtyard of the cathedral, all patiently awaiting their turn to enter and leave an offering. The rich and the poor, the healthy and the infirm, crowd within the impressive, richly decorated church. Nothing in all Mexico is more exciting to the pious Indians than this great religious celebration, in which, following their own primitive forms and customs, they pay homage to the Virgin of Guadalupe.

According to legend, the Virgin of Guadalupe first appeared to Juan Diego, an innocent Indian peasant, in December of 1531. Her sainthood was proclaimed by papal bull in 1754, 223 years later.

The church and shrine of Guadalupe is a "must" on all tourist itineraries.

December 25. Christmas Day (see *Posadas,* above).

FIESTA CALENDAR

January 1. Dolores Hidalgo, state of Guanajuato, Mexico's cradle of independence, where Father Hidalgo rang the bells that started the struggle for freedom from Spain. It is about twenty-two miles north of the town of San Miguel Allende (where there are hotels). As a rule there are dances of *Los Comanches, El Torito, Los Compadres,* etc., though these are not held every year. Reached via railway, Ferrocarriles Nacionales, and busses from Guanajuato, San Miguel Allende, San Felipe, and San Luís de la Paz.

Tlaxcoapan, state of Hidalgo, reached by Laredo highway; turn off at Actopan on road to Tula. The latter town is one of the most interesting archaeological sites. Between Tula and the thermal baths of Ajacuba is Tlaxcoapan, where dances of *Los Segadores, Vaqueros, Conquistadores,* and *Contradanzas* may be seen. Also reached via railway; the Ferrocarriles Nacionales. There are no hotels in the village.

January 1–7. Chalma, state of Mexico. Take the paved road toward Toluca to Kilometer 60, turn south, and continue to the town of Tenancingo, where it is advisable to stay overnight (or return to Toluca). From this point continue on horseback or afoot. Upon entering the town everyone is supposed to dance to the Sanctuary of the Miraculous Lord of Chalma, in whose honor the fiesta is held. For centuries pilgrims have tramped through mountain and forest to this shrine. Religious ceremonies, native dances, fireworks, and fair. Principal day is the sixth. Other interesting visiting days are August 28, September 29, and December 25.

January 5–6. Throughout the republic, on the eve of the sixth, the children in Mexico leave a shoe in the window (instead of hanging their stockings) because they say this is the night on which the three holy kings pass by and leave toys and presents. It commemorates the pilgrimage of Melchior, Gaspar, and Balthazar, who visited the child Jesus and brought him presents. It is customary on the sixth to invite close friends to dinner and have a *reyes* ring cake, which contains a surprise. The person who happens to cut the piece of cake that holds the doll or surprise immediately becomes a *compadre* (godfather) of those who give the party, and is bound to give another party on the second of February.

January 6–7. Almoloya del Río, state of Mexico. Take Toluca road as far as Kilometer 45; turn off on dirt road for ten miles. Noted for the pretty napery embroidered in primitive designs by the natives. There are several typical dances and the usual street fair.

January 8. Ahila, state of Puebla. This village is very near Pahuatlán. May be reached by train or road from Mexico City to Tulancingo, Hidalgo, thence by rail to Honey Station; continue on horseback or car to Ahila. Generally there is a fair with native dances and the daring, dangerous game of *El Volador,* seldom seen anywhere else. Check with the National Tourist Association.

January 17. Throughout Mexico. Celebration of St. Anthony of Padua and blessing of the animals.

January 18. Taxco, state of Guerrero. A very beautiful fiesta is held in honor of Santa Prisca, patroness of the artistic church built by José de la Borda. Dances called Moors, *Tecomanes, Blanca,* and Shepherds may be seen.

January 20. San Luís Potosí, state of San Luís Potosí. In the suburb of San Sebastián there is a fiesta typical of the region with typical dances and fireworks.

León, state of Guanajuato. Accessible by railroad from Mexico City or El Paso; also by highway from Guanajuato, San Luís Potosí, or Guadalajara. Principal manufacturing and leather-goods center. The town celebrates with popular fair, bullfights, etc., the anniversary of its foundation.

January 20–25. Tehuantepec, state of Oaxaca. Celebration in San Sebastián and Laborío (sections of the town); typical dances.

January 25–February 2. Talpa de Allende, state of Jalisco. This village is off the beaten path but can be reached by bus or plane from Guadalajara. A fiesta is held in honor of a much venerated Virgin. Talpa is famous for its strange curios made of chewing gum. See also March 19, below.

Arenal, state of Jalisco. A village near Guadalajara. Can be reached by automobile, bus, or the Southern Pacific train. A colorful fair that includes bullfights, cockfights, and the original *jarabe* and *La Conquista* dances.

January 29. Pahuatlán, state of Puebla. Off the beaten path; reach it from Huauchinango, a town on the highway from Mexico City to Tuxpan, or by bus from Honey Station on the railway. This region is very interesting, and dances such as *Santiagueros, Tocotines,* and *Quetzales* may be seen. If this fiesta is postponed, visit the village during Holy Week.

January 31–February 8. Tlacotalpan, state of Veracruz. To reach this village, go first to Veracruz by train or highway, then to the town of Alvarado. The journey from there to Tlacotalpan is made by motorboat on the Papaloapan River, famous as one of the most scenic in the republic. On February 1 there is a procession of grotesque figures parading through the streets at night and a rodeo in which the *charros* from near-by towns participate. February 2 is dedicated to the religious ceremony in honor of the Virgin of Candelaria, patroness of the town, to which many devotees from distant parts come. This Virgin possesses a noteworthy collection of jewels.

There are also native dances, especially the *huapangos,* typical of this region. Although the festivities really begin on the thirty-first of January and end on the eighth of February, the first and second of February are usually the principal days. Hotels are primitive.

February 2. San Juan de Los Lagos, state of Jalisco, 325 miles from Mexico City. Reached by train to Ciudad Juárez or bus from Guadalajara. The feast is in honor of the patroness of the town and pilgrims come from all over the republic. Typical articles from several central states are sold in the adjoining fair: ceramics from Jalisco, flowers made from chewing gum, hand-drawn work from Aguascalientes, serapes, *rebozos,* liquors, sweet-potato candy, *alfajores,* and others. Many dances may be seen, but the most interesting one is the "Moors and Christians." Also held on August 15 and December 8.

February 5. Throughout Mexico. Anniversary of the establishment of the constitutions of 1857 and 1917, now in effect.

February 15. Tzintzuntzan, state of Michoacán. In pre-Conquest days this village was the capital of the Tarascan empire. Noted for its pottery. Located near Pátzcuaro, where there are several good hotels. On this day there are usually several dances, among them one called *Los Viejitos* (Old Men).

February 25. Telcalpulco, state of Guerrero. About two miles from Taxco. Fiesta at Chavarrietas Chapel, lively and traditional. Native dances of *Tecomates, Gallitos, Tecuanes,* and *Santiagos* with fireworks and *Toritos.*

March 5–6. Amecameca, state of Mexico. A pretty village at the foot of Ixtaccíhuatl and Popocatépetl volcanoes, thirty-five miles southeast of Mexico City, on the paved Cuautla highway. The fiesta is celebrated at a church on top of a hill, in honor of an image of Christ that is greatly venerated. Natives come from far and near to pay homage to this image. As usual there are numerous native dances. See information sources in Mexico City, as this fiesta is frequently changed to coincide with Holy Week or the earlier carnival.

March 11–19 (principal day is the nineteenth). Talpa de Allende, state of Jalisco. This village is about an hour's flight from Guadalajara, on the air line from Guadalajara to Puerto Vallarta, Jalisco; also reached by bus from Guadalajara. A Virgin venerated by natives far and near is honored by an interesting pilgrimage during these days. Talpa is noted for its ingenious way of working chewing gum, which is colored and modeled into an immense variety of shapes such as flowers and animal figures. This is one of the native arts less known, perhaps because this village is difficult to get to, except by plane. Fiestas also on February 2 and September 19.

March 12. Taxco, state of Guerrero. At the chapel called Chavarrieta, near the San Bernardino Convent, there is a religious ceremony celebrated with a fiesta and dances such as the *Tecomates, Gallitos,* and others. Not regularly active.

March 21. Throughout Mexico. Anniversary of the birth of President Benito Juárez and Day of the Indian Child.

March 29. Taxco, state of Guerrero. At the little church of Santa Veracruz there is a religious festival in which dances of the *Pastores, Las Tres Potencias* (The Three Potentials; i.e., Body and Soul, Devil and Angel, and the Virgin), and other typical events take place. Not regularly active.

April 25–May 5. Aguascalientes, state of Aguascalientes. This is the annual spring festival, celebrated since the early seventeenth century. The fiesta originated as a religious commemoration of the founding of San Marcos in 1604. The festivities are very animated and include bullfights, regional dances, *mariachi* orchestras, typical songs, parades, contests, fireworks, expositions of art, athletic events, bazaars, and serenades. Reached by railroad, plane, or car.

April 30. Tepatitlan, state of Jalisco. Reached from Guadalajara, on the highway to San Luís Potosí. Typical dances, serenades, fireworks, bullfights, etc.

May 1. Throughout Mexico. Labor Day. Parades, dances, etc.

May 3. Mexico City. Celebration of the Santa Cruz, the feast day of bricklayers. A traditional ceremony in which a cross, decorated with bright paper ornaments and flowers, is erected at the highest point of all constructions.

Tehuantepec, state of Oaxaca. Celebration in the Santa Cruz (section of the town). Dances, typical costumes. Fiestas also on May 31, June 21–29, July 25 (in San Blas region), August 15 (Santa María), September 8 (Laborío), September 30 (San Jerónimo), October 15, and November 2.

Amatlán de los Reyes, state of Veracruz. Located one mile from Córdoba. Festival in honor of the Holy Cross (*Santa Cruz*), celebrated with native dances, among them "Moors and Christians," *zapateados,* and *jaranas.*

Jiménez, state of Coahuila. Reached via Piedras Negras to Villa Acuña highway, very close to Texas border. Dances with costumes from Conquest epoch.

May 5. Throughout Mexico. National celebration commemorating the Mexican victory over the French at Puebla in 1862.

Fortín de las Flores, state of Veracruz. Celebration called Fiesta da la Flor (of the Flower). Dances, fireworks.

May 19–20. Tasquillo, state of Hidalgo. Situated on the Pan American Highway at Kilometer 178 (about 110 miles from Mexico City). Popular fair celebrated with dances, etc. Not regularly active.

May 20. San Bernardino, state of Puebla. Four miles from Puebla on the road to Atlixco. Small festival in honor of the patron saint of the town.

May 22. Chihuahua, state of Chihuahua. Popular fair (Fiesta of Santa Rita) where one may see some of the natives dressed in their Tarahumara costumes.

June 4. Zaachila, state of Oaxaca. Near the city of Oaxaca. Pagan-religious festivity in honor of the Holy Trinity, during which the famous native Dance of the Feathers may be seen. This village was once capital of the great Zapotec nation.

June 5–13. Río Verde, state of San Luís Potosí. Renowned fair celebrated every year in honor of St. Anthony. There are religious ceremonies and popular dances, cockfights, horse races, etc. The Fiesta of Santa Catarina is held here on November 25. Other fairs June 13 and 24.

Teotitlan del Valle, state of Oaxaca. Near the city of Oaxaca. Dance of the Feathers and market day. Also September 29.

June 8. Metepec, state of Mexico. Highway to Toluca; at Kilometer 60 take side road to Metepec. A "crazy" fiesta takes place where men dress as women; there are also a colorful parade with decorated yokes of oxen and some native dances. Not regularly active.

June 9. Chalma, state of Mexico. Interesting pilgrimage. People come from all parts of Mexico to venerate the famous image of the Lord of Chalma. Dances of interest.

June 24–29. Tehuantepec, state of Oaxaca. Celebration in Guichivere and Vishana (sections of the town). Dances, typical costumes.

June 29. San Pedro Tlaquepaque, state of Jalisco. This village is famous for its pottery and is a few minutes from Guadalajara by trolley car, bus, or automobile. There is a fair in which there are cockfights and other attractions. Not regularly active.

June 29–30. Tianguistengo, state of Mexico. Take Toluca highway to Kilometer 45; follow side road to this village, where famous natural colored serapes with beautiful designs are made. In the San Pedro suburb of this village there are dances such as *Lobos* (wolves), "Apaches," and "Moors." Not regularly active, though almost any day is a good day to visit.

San Pedro Actopan, D.F. Fair and celebration in honor of St. Peter, patron saint of the place. Music, fireworks, native dances.

July. Oaxaca, state of Oaxaca. On the two following Mondays after July 16, there is a folkloric celebration at the Cerro del Fortín. Dance of *La Pluma.* Other fiestas are held on December 23 (called Noche de Rábanos) and December 24. The annual regional fair is held on December 8.

Villa Álvaro Obregón, D.F. (San Ángel). Suburb of Mexico City. Fair, fireworks, dances; celebration during the whole month of July in honor of The Virgin of El Carmen.

July 4. Acámbaro, state of Guanajuato. A fiesta with fireworks and typical dances; fiesta locally called Fiesta de la Virgen del Refugio.

July 7. Tlacotepec, state of Puebla. Take highway toward Tehuacán to Kilometer 215 (135 miles from Mexico City). The village has a church on top of a hill, where a fiesta takes place that is especially interesting because of the many Indians who gather there in native costumes from the states of Oaxaca, Puebla, and Veracruz. Human hair and personal articles are left as offerings by the natives. Tehuacán is close by and would be the place to stop.

July 8. Teotitlan del Valle, state of Oaxaca. Near the city of Oaxaca. The Dance of the Feathers is one of the attractions. Not regularly active.

July 8–16. Motul, state of Yucatán. Not far from Mérida. The dance of *Jarana Yucateca* is one of the main attractions of the fiesta and fair.

July 13. Ejutla, state of Jalisco. Southwest of Guadalajara, on the road to Barra de Navidad. Dances, fireworks, and other typical games and exhibitions.

July 24. Candela, state of Coahuila. Reached by railroad between Laredo and Monterrey. As a rule one may see the dance typical of northern Mexico called *Los Matachines*. Natives dance interminably to the monotonous sound of drums and *chirimías*.

July 25. Cuilapam, state of Oaxaca. About an hour's drive from the city of Oaxaca. Main interest of the fiesta is the Dance of the Feathers, originally of this region.

San Luís Potosí, state of San Luís Potosí. In the suburb of Santiago del Río is celebrated a festival in which people wear ornaments of flowers in many designs.

Santiago Tianguistengo, state of Mexico. On the road to Toluca. Religious fiesta in honor of the patron saint of the town with dances, market, and other attractions.

July 26. Santa Ana Tlacotenco, D.F. Religious ceremonies in honor of Our Lady of Santa Ana. Fair, dances, fireworks.

August 6. Saltillo, state of Coahuila. Best reached by train from Mexico City, or by highway from Monterrey. Feast in honor of the image of the Christ of the Chapel; a big event, for which natives begin arriving several days in advance. Celebrated by fireworks, dances, extensive market, and other attractions. An important center for the weaving of serapes, those typical of this city being the multicolored striped ones, usually with a diamond-shaped center.

August 8. Paracho, state of Michoacán. On the highway from Mexico City to Guadalajara. Girls parade in typical costumes and form part of a procession headed by a bull gaudily ornamented with all the ingredients needed to prepare the typical dish *shuripo*, in which its own flesh is also used.

August 10–17. Zacatlan de Las Manzanas, state of Jalisco. Apple fair. This town is noted for its excellent apples.

August 10–20. Amozoc, state of Puebla. This village is a short distance from Puebla on the highway to Veracruz. It is noted for its silver-inlaid steel objects, such as buckles, bits, spurs, irons, etc. There is a fair with cockfights, bullfights, and popular dances. August 15 is the principal day.

August 12. Santa Clara del Cobre, state of Michoacán. This village is beyond Pátzcuaro and can be reached by train or automobile. It is noted for its copper objects as well as gold and silver filigree.

August 15. Capácuaro, state of Michoacán. On the highway from Mexico City to Guadalajara. The best place to stay in order to see this fiesta is Uruapan, eleven miles beyond. There is a pagan-religious festival with typical dances.

August 24. San Bartolo Naucalpan, state of Mexico. Eight and a half miles northwest of Mexico City. Festival with fair, games, and, usually, native dances.

August 28. Tlalpam, D.F. Suburb thirty minutes from downtown Mexico City. Traditional fair; Aztec dances.

September 1–8. Los Remedios, state of Mexico. Fourteen and one-half miles northwest of Mexico City on paved road. Festivity in honor of the Virgen de los Remedios, deeply venerated throughout the region. There is a legend dating from the sixteenth century regarding the apparition of this Virgin in the locality. People come from all parts of the republic to this pagan-religious festival, which lasts several days. A typical fair.

September 8. Cholula, state of Puebla. To the east of Mexico City, eighty miles on the Puebla highway. Religious feast in honor of the Virgen de los Remedios, celebrated by typical dances of the region, fair, and other popular amusements. The festivities center around the Church of Los Remedios. While in Cholula, visit the pyramid dedicated to Quetzalcoatl, god of the ancient inhabitants; and the San Francisco Church with its Royal Chapel having forty-seven domes supported by sixty-four columns.

September 10. Ramos Arizpe, state of Coahuila. San Nicolás Fair, dance of the *Matachines,* cockfights and bullfights, fireworks, etc.

September 14. Uruapan, state of Michoacán. Fiesta in honor of the patron saint, who was greatly venerated in the town of Parangaricutiro, now covered with the lava of Parícutin volcano. The inhabitants of the town moved with their crucifix to a village called Los Conejos, close to Uruapan, where this interesting fiesta takes place. According to the story, it is a custom to dance with faith in front of this crucifix to make up for the irreverent dancing performed by the Indians when it was first brought here four hundred years ago.

Querétaro, state of Querétaro. Interesting festival at Convento de la Cruz, where Maximilian of Austria spent his last hours as emperor of Mexico. In an inner patio of this convent there is a unique bush: The thorns are peculiarly shaped like the cross. As a rule there are native dances. Visit the churches of San Agustín, Santa Clara, Santa Rosa, etc. At a short distance is the famous Hill of Las Campanas, on which a chapel was erected at the spot where Maximilian and his companions were shot.

San Juan de las Colchas, state of Michoacán. Festival in honor of an image of Christ on the Cross. Dances, fireworks, etc.

September 15–16. Throughout the republic. Commemoration of Mexican independence. On the fifteenth, at eleven P.M., a ceremony called El Grito takes place in all state capitals. At that hour the governor addresses the people from a balcony on the Government Palace. Music, fireworks, and other amusements. On the sixteenth, a parade composed of regular troops and military organizations is reviewed by the president in Mexico City. All stores and business places are closed during the day.

September 21. Ahuiran, state of Michoacán. This village is near the town of Paracho, crossed by the paved highway that leads to Uruapan. The fiesta is typical of the region. Paracho is noted for its carved wooden objects. Near by is the famous volcano Parícutin.

September 29. San Miguel Allende, state of Guanajuato. Regional dances, cockfights, fair, etc. Reached by railway and highway.

Cocula, state of Jalisco. Sixty miles from Guadalajara on highway to Barra de Navidad; typical town of Jalisco. Noted for its *mariachis* (native singers) and the dance of *La Conquista*. Other fiestas on May 22, June 24, and July 4.

Chalma, state of Mexico. Pilgrims generally walk to Chalma, but probably the best way is to stay overnight at Tenancingo, where there are regular hotels, and make arrangements to go by car and horseback. The place is famous for its many dances.

San Miguel Regla, state of Hidalgo. Festival in honor of the patron saint of the town. Fair, races, cockfighting, dances.

September 29–30. San Miguel Tlaixpan, state of Mexico. This village is beyond Texcoco and is accessible by car or bus.

Chiconcuac, state of Mexico. This village is close to Texcoco; a primitive native fiesta, sometimes with dances. In this village are made the serapes with the blue background.

September 30. Coatepec, state of Veracruz. Half an hour from Jalapa. Fiesta in honor of San Jerónimo, patron saint of the town. Religious ceremonies and dances of the *Tocotines* and others.

October. Atzcapotzalco, D.F. Suburb twenty minutes' ride from downtown Mexico City. Festival in honor of the Virgen del Rosario. Celebration during the whole month; fair, dances, fireworks, horse races; pagan-religious in origin. It used to be held in honor of King Maxtla.

October 4. Autlan, state of Jalisco. Festival with *Pastorelas,* Dance of the Conquest, games, and other amusements.

Zapopan, state of Jalisco. Interesting religious festival, dances from different parts of the country. The Dance of the Conquest is worth seeing because of the rich attire of the dancers. An easy trip from Guadalajara, half an hour's drive by taxi or bus. If you are a good hiker it is interesting to walk with the crowd.

October 7–15. Alvarado, state of Veracruz. Festival in honor of Our Lady of the Rosary. Parades, masquerades, and exhibitions.

October 10–12. Tlacolula, state of Oaxaca. The fiesta at Tlacolula takes place on the tenth, and on the twelfth it is celebrated at Santa María del Tule. Both towns are on the road from Oaxaca City to Mitla. Regional dances.

October 12. Throughout Mexico. Día de la Raza, Discovery of America (Columbus Day).

October 15–23. Ciudad Guzmán, state of Jalisco. Celebrations and festivals during the whole month, but more particularly during the days mentioned. Religious services in honor of St. Joseph, patron saint of the town. Processions, floats, dances of *La Conquista, Los Sonajeros, Los Paistes, Los Pastores,* etc.

October 29–November 2. Zacualtipan, state of Hidalgo. Take Laredo highway to Pachuca, famous mining center, then follow interesting road through ravine. Great variety of cactus abounds around village of Zacualtipan, "Place of the Huasteca." Other fiesta May 1–6.

November 1 and 2. Throughout Mexico. All Saints' Day and All Souls' Day. Religious ceremonies. See above, page 259.

Janítzio, state of Michoacán. An impressive ceremony takes place on this island in Lake Pátzcuaro during the night of the first and daybreak of the second of November. During these hours the natives render honor to their dead with a candlelight procession in the local cemetery.

November 10–12. San Martín Texmelucan, state of Puebla. A festival where several native dances may be seen. The fair is of importance and well attended. The town is at Kilometer 91 on the Mexico-Puebla highway, and twenty-three kilometers from Tlaxcala. Serapes and excellent woolens are manufactured here.

November 17–25. Río Verde, state of San Luís Potosí. This town is reached by train or highway from San Luís Potosí. A fiesta is celebrated in honor of the patron saint of this region.

November 20. Throughout Mexico. The whole country celebrates on this day the anniversary of the 1910 revolution with parades, dances, and popular games.

November 22. Zapotitlan, state of Jalisco. South of Guadalajara. This village has a warm climate and the fiesta is original. Musicians honor St. Cecilia, their patron saint.

November 25. San Marcos, state of Guerrero. Take Mexico-Acapulco highway and deviation at Las Cruces. Fair and fruit exhibits, *cancioneros,* and dances of the *Tlacololeros, Tlamiques, Diablos,* "The Eleven Pairs of France," "Moors," "Cockerels," etc.

November 30–December 15. Atotonilco, state of Jalisco. East of Guadalajara; can be reached by train or highway, through La Barca, about twenty-six miles away. There are typical cockfights, bullfights, and a colorful fiesta. The main attraction is the variety of fruit; the place is famous for its orange groves.

November 30. Texcoco, state of Mexico. Thirty-two miles from Mexico City. Native festival. On this trip one may visit Chapingo Agricultural School, where some of Rivera's best paintings may be seen; also the Cuautlinchan monolith and the archaeological ruins at Huexotla. At the Texcoco market one of the typical foods is barbecue. There are generally dances, the *Sembradores,* the *Vaqueros,* the *Serranitos,* etc.

December 5–9. San Francisco del Rincón, state of Guanajuato. Festival commemorating the foundation of the city. Serenades, cockfights, bullfights, horse races, fireworks, dances, etc.

December 8. San Juan de Los Lagos, state of Jalisco. Reached through Guadalajara. Popular festival where some interesting dances may be seen, such as "Moors and Christians." Fair with the usual amusements.

Pátzcuaro, state of Michoacán. Reached by paved highway or by train. Traditional festival in honor of Our Lady of the Immaculate Conception. Interesting native dances typical of this state, among which are *Los Viejitos* (The Old Men), *Sembradores* (Planters), *Los Negritos* (Negroes), and others. The usual fair. Pátzcuaro is notable for its delicate whitefish.

Tenancingo, state of Mexico. Located about sixty-five miles from

Mexico City, on the road to Ixtapan de la Sal, a branch of the Guadalajara highway before it reaches Toluca. There are many beautiful surroundings such as Santa Ana, El Desierto, Los Balcones, etc. Fine *rebozos* are woven here, and nice fruit liquors are manufactured. Fair with the usual amusements, and in general the typical dances.

December 9–18. Oaxaca, state of Oaxaca. During each one of these days, every section of Oaxaca takes its turn celebrating the feast in honor of the Virgin of La Soledad. An interesting feature is the parade of girls carrying on their heads beautiful flowers formed into different shapes such as lyres, swans, etc.

December 10–12. Otumba, state of Mexico. Just a little beyond the Teotihuacán Pyramids. Fair with dances of *Los Apaches and Santiagueros.*

December 12. Santiago Tianguistengo, state of Mexico, Religious fiesta in honor of the patron saint of the town. Dances, market, and other attractions.

Villa de Guadalupe, D.F. Suburb four miles from the center of Mexico City. Trolley, bus, or taxi. One of the greatest festivities in the country, in honor of Our Lady of Guadalupe, patroness of the Americas. According to history she appeared to an Indian, Juan Diego, asking him to get the archbishop to build a sanctuary on the spot in her honor. Devotees from all parts of the republic come in pilgrimage, and typical dances are performed by large groups of dancers.

Zinapécuaro, state of Michoacán. Town between Morella and Tacambaro, reached by gravel road from Morelia. Its name Zinani means "curative place" (near by are the radioactive springs called Atzimba and Taimeo). Many typical dances. Handicrafts can be obtained such as palm objects, chairs, serapes, etc. Visit its orchards, especially one called Bocaneo. This fiesta is sometimes held November 1 and 2. Check with tourist offices in Mexico City.

December 12–15. Autlan, state of Jalisco. Pagan-religious festival with fair, fireworks, and native dances, particularly that of "The Conquest."

December 12–24. Celaya, state of Guanajuato. Fair, dances, and other amusements.

December 13. Jonacatepec, state of Morelos. Interesting celebration of the fiesta of *La Vaquerita* with popular fair, native dances, and other amusements.

December 16–24. Querétaro, state of Querétaro. The festival of the *Posadas* is celebrated in Querétaro more sumptuously and animatedly than in any other city in the republic. The Posadas begin the sixteenth, when floats representing the peregrinations of Mary and Joseph in search of lodging call at different places in the city every evening for nine days. Other floats parade on the twenty-fourth, representing Biblical scenes characterized as "The Paradise," "The Law Tables," "Jephthah's Vow," "Belshazzar's Banquet," "Solomon's Judgment," "The Hut," etc. This is a good time to visit the town, which is most interesting for its colonial buildings and picturesque surroundings.

December 23. Oaxaca, state of Oaxaca. There is an old custom during this fiesta of making different shapes and figures out of radishes and other vegetables.

December 24. Oaxaca, state of Oaxaca. On this day the people of Oaxaca like plates of *buñuelos* (a sort of flour wafer with molasses); after eating they break the dish. The *buñuelos* are served in private homes or in the market.

Quiroga, state of Michoacán. Religious fiesta with singing and dancing, usually songs alluding to the birth of Christ.

December 24–26. Santa Isabel Ixtapa, state of Mexico. Festival in honor of the patroness of Ixtapa. Fair and dances of the *Santiaguitos* and *Vaqueritos*.

First Friday of Lent. Chalma, state of Mexico. Upon entering the town everyone is expected to dance to the sanctuary of the miraculous lord of Chalma, in whose honor the fiesta is held. Pilgrims come from all parts of Mexico.

Holy Thursday and Good Friday. Ixtapalapa, D.F. Nine miles from downtown Mexico City. Pagan-religious festivities to commemorate Holy Thursday and Good Friday. A representation of the Passion of Christ is staged.

Holy Friday. Ixtapalapa, D.F. Passion play.

Good Friday. Santa Anita, D.F. Suburb southeast of Mexico City. Fiesta most renowned in Mexico in honor of the Virgin of Los Dolores (Sorrows). Bullfights, rodeos, contest of best typical costumes, races, dancing, and fair.

Holy Saturday. Throughout Mexico. Judas Day. Feast throughout the republic. Signifies the death of Judas, and figures are burned with fireworks representing Judas. Frequently some represent living persons.

Carnival. Mérida, state of Yucatán. The carnival festivals in Mérida are famous.

Veracruz, state of Veracruz. Carnival festivals, dances, parades, etc.; the same at Jalapa, Córdoba, Fortín de las Flores, and Orizaba.

Mazatlán, state of Sinaloa. Traditional carnival celebration.

Huejotzingo, state of Puebla. Carnival is celebrated for two consecutive days. The ancient story of a fiery bandit, Agustín Lorenzo, is enacted.

Xochimilco, D.F. Fair during carnival time. Dances of the *Santiagos, Pastores,* and *Vaqueros.*

Carnival and Ash Wednesday. Amecameca, state of Mexico. Thirty-five miles southeast of Mexico City on the Cuautla highway. Fiesta celebrated at the church on top of a hill in honor of an image of Christ that is greatly venerated. Pilgrims come from all over the republic.

Corpus Christi Day (one Thursday in June). Throughout Mexico. Celebrated especially at the cathedral in Mexico City, with a procession in which many children dressed in typical costumes take part.

CHAPTER XII

RESIDING IN MEXICO

I N EVERY hundred tourists who visit Mexico there are at least ten who say they would like to live in Mexico for a year or two or more. Of these we do not know what percentage actually do remain in Mexico or return at a future date armed with the necessities for setting up housekeeping and a long residence in the country. But as the years and taxes and spiraling living costs and severe winters roll inexorably on, the so-called American colony in Mexico grows larger and larger.

The following information, therefore, is included for those who may be planning to reside in Mexico, either for business or for pleasure. It is taken from the most recent reports on Americans living in Mexico published by the United States Department of Commerce, Washington.

The first question asked by those contemplating a long residence in Mexico is: "What about health?"

HEALTH CONDITIONS

Mexico's larger cities have modern water and sewage systems, and these facilities are being improved in centers like Mexico City, where the population has increased rapidly during recent years. There is also a fairly extensive program of development throughout Mexico of water and sewage systems to supply smaller places. In 1943 an agreement was entered into by Mexico and the United States, involving the financial and technical assistance of the United States, for the construction of important sanitation projects in border towns and along the Pan American Highway.

The usual contagious diseases common to every large city are likewise to be found in Mexican cities, and these should be guarded against just as in the United States. Although typhus fever exists, it is confined to the congested areas inhabited by the very poor. Since there are occasional outbreaks of smallpox throughout the country, it is necessary to be vaccinated before going to reside in Mexico.

Perhaps the most important health problem in Mexico at present is the prevention of water-borne diseases such as typhoid and dysentery. Typhoid fever is more prevalent than in many of the large cities in the United States, particularly at the beginning of the rainy season, and typhoid inoculations are imperative. Dysentery, including amoebic, is endemic, but may be avoided with fair success by drinking only boiled or bottled water and by eating only such fruits and vegetables as are cooked or peeled. Sporadic cases of undulant fever are attributed to milk; it is therefore advisable to use boiled, canned, or powdered milk. Pulmonary infections are fairly common, and in the low tropical areas there is some malaria.

In addition to the basic sanitation work of establishing the modern water and sewage systems mentioned above, intensive work is being carried out by the government to improve health conditions through antilarval work (especially at ports), distribution of quinine in malaria regions, organization of tuberculosis hospitals and free dispensaries, infant hygiene centers, educational health programs, and improved diet and housing conditions.

Although the newcomer to Mexico City, and other places where the altitude is high, may find the climate stimulating, precautions should be taken against overwork, strenuous exercise, or intemperance, which may bring on nervous and organic disorders, particularly in those who suffer with heart, lung, and kidney trouble and high blood pressure. However, moderate living and occasional visits to near-by sections at low altitudes, such as Veracruz or Acapulco, enable those of sound constitution to remain in good health.

Some of the cities in lower altitudes, such as Guadalajara, Monterrey, Cuernavaca, and Puebla, have almost ideal climates, with no great variations in seasons and temperatures, bracing air, plenty of sunshine, and year-round production of fruits and vegetables.

LIVING COSTS

Although the cost of living in Mexico has been rising steadily since about 1934, this rise has been greatly accentuated since the end of 1942. While wages have increased to some extent, the increase in the average workingman's salary between 1939 and 1944, according to a recent report of the Minister of Labor, was only 46 per cent, whereas the increase in the cost of living during the same period was 155 per cent. Efforts of the government to control the rising cost of living through the establishment of ceiling prices, importation of primary foodstuffs, and control of distribution and sale of essential products have been only partially successful, and prices of both domestic and foreign goods are high and are expected to remain so for some time. The scarcity of goods and speculative activities have been primarily responsible for inflation, but lack of transport facilities and inadequate distribution have also contributed their share.

Government control of rents has been fairly effective, although only those tenants who occupied their quarters prior to July 1942, when rents were frozen by executive decree, have been fortunate enough to continue paying reasonable rentals.

HOUSING

Housing facilities in Mexico include the so-called "leading hotels," the smaller and less expensive hotels, apartments, houses, furnished rooms, and a few tourist courts. The *Directory of Hotels in the Republic of Mexico,* published by the Mexican Hotel Association, lists 180 hotels in the country, of which 33 are in Mexico City and the Federal District, 42 in Acapulco, 17 in Monterrey, 7 in Guadalajara, 5 each in Saltillo and Taxco, 4 each in Ciudad Victoria and Tehuacán, 3 each in Chihuahua, Guanajuato, and Morelia, and the remaining 54 in other cities and towns throughout the republic.

In Mexico City most of the hotels operate on the European plan —that is, the rate is for the room without meals—and charges per day range from 10 to 30 pesos for a single room and from 17 to 50 pesos for a double room. Hotels in Mexican cities and towns outside the capital are on either the American or European plan, at the option of the guest. In these cities American guests usually eat most of their meals at the hotels, inasmuch as the restaurants that cater to the public do not in every case come up to the standards of restaurants in the United States. In cities outside of the capital rates for similar accommodations run somewhat lower than in Mexico City, or from 8 to 13 pesos per day for single room and 15 to 25 pesos for double room (European plan), and 18 to 50 per day for single room and 36 to 80 for double room (American plan). Rates in the popular tourist resorts, such as Veracruz and Acapulco, are higher than in other cities.

It is advisable for Americans to make hotel reservations in Mexico City several weeks in advance.

In addition, there are many smaller hotels that offer less expensive but suitable accommodations, and furnished rooms are available in private residences. Mexico City is adequately served by boardinghouses that offer satisfactory accommodations, and many Americans eager to learn Spanish patronize these establishments. Generally speaking, Americans in Mexico find the hotels satisfactory only as temporary living quarters, and when they remain for any length of time they obtain other types of accommodations.

Owing to the shortage of living quarters in Mexico City, it is advisable for Americans who plan to rent a house or apartment to communicate with rental agencies in advance. Names of rental agencies may be obtained from the American Republics Division, Department of Commerce, Washington 25, D.C.

The following prices are currently paid for living quarters of the type usually required by Americans visiting or residing in Mexico: Unfurnished apartments, four rooms or more, range from 250 to 550 pesos ($51.50 to $113.30) per month; furnished apartments, four rooms or more, range from 350 to 1,500 pesos ($72 to $309) per month; unfurnished houses with three or more bedrooms, 450 to 1,000 pesos ($92.70 to $206) per month; and furnished houses with three or more bedrooms, 600 to 1,500 pesos ($123.60 to $309) per month. These prices are representative of rentals paid by present tenants. Competition is very strong at the lower prices quoted above, and prospective renters may have to pay as much as 50 per cent more than these prices, or wait a number of weeks to find what they want. As in the case of hotel rates, house and apartment rentals in cities other than the capital are somewhat lower.

A fairly satisfactory apartment usually consists of a living room, dining room, two bedrooms, bath, kitchen, and servant's room, and a house usually has a living room, dining room, hall, kitchen, two or possibly three bedrooms, a bath, servant's quarters, garage, and small garden. Some allowance is customarily made for outlays on minor maintenance or remodeling work. The water supply is generally paid for by the landlord. Light fixtures are ordinarily purchased and installed by the tenant.

HOUSEHOLD EXPENSES

Food. Food is generally plentiful in Mexico City and throughout the country, but, like all other products, has risen rapidly in price since the latter part of 1942. The food index, which averaged 179 during 1942 (1934 = 100), rose to 354 in December of 1945. The latter figure represents an increase of 123 per cent over the index of 1941 and approximately 254 per cent over that of 1934, while estimates at the end of 1947 were higher still than 1945. Local prices in small towns and rural areas are sometimes reported to be as much as 50 per cent below those prevailing in Mexico City.

The cost of food in Mexico varies with the season and the geographical area, and insufficient transportation facilities coupled with poor distribution methods are frequently the cause of local shortages and high costs. Imported articles are usually considerably higher than domestic goods because of transportation costs and duties. Formerly canned foodstuffs were almost entirely imported, but in recent years Mexico has been building up its canning industry, and as a result, increasing amounts of very good domestic canned fruits, fish, and vegetables are available. Evaporated, condensed, and powdered milk and dehydrated fruits and vegetables are also being produced in the country in limited amounts.

Fresh vegetables and fruits are plentiful and more varied than in most parts of the United States. Vegetables usually on sale in sufficient amounts at all times are squash, eggplant, cabbage, carrots, peas, beans, tomatoes, peppers, cucumbers, radishes, potatoes (white and sweet), onions, and corn. In addition to oranges, pineapples, bananas, limes, peaches, pears, plums, grapes, melons, and strawberries, there is a wide variety of native tropical fruits, such as avocados, papayas, guayabas, and sapotes, which find favor in the diet of both foreigners and Mexicans. Fresh vegetables and fruits are bought on the market daily; few persons purchase supplies for more than a day or two at a time.

Meat is plentiful, but in general it is of poor quality and not graded. Tender cuts are especially expensive. The chief meat products available in the local markets are beef, mutton, pork, lamb, goat, turkey, and chicken. Because of the lack of refrigeration in most cities, meat is offered for sale immediately after slaughter.

In Mexico City, as in other places in Mexico, care should be taken to boil raw milk. It is the opinion of many doctors that the milk supplied in Mexico City lacks some of the nutritive qualities found in milk produced in the United States, and for this reason there is a considerable consumption of canned milk, which is available in all grocery stores.

The marketing in Mexico is generally done by servants, although the larger grocery stores in Mexico City offer delivery service on telephone orders. Arrangements can also be made for the delivery of ice if needed. Grocery stores open daily from eight A.M. to two P.M. and from four P.M to eight P.M.

Utilities. Mexico has a telegraph and cable service, which is under the Ministry of Communications and Public Works and has connections for transmitting international messages by wire and radio to all parts of this hemisphere and Europe. The Western Union, a branch of the company in the United States, has its principal office in Mexico City with branch offices at Salina Cruz, Veracruz, Tampico, and Puerto Mexico.

Local, long-distance, and international telephone service is available throughout Mexico.

The central area of Mexico, which includes the capital, is fairly well supplied with electric current for household use, industry, and agriculture. The larger cities outside this area, however, are not so well supplied. The government has plans for increasing electric-power facilities generally throughout the country and expects to spend during the next few years between 200,000,000 and 300,000,-000 pesos on the construction of electric-power plants that will increase production capacity by about 200,000 kilowatts, and benefit zones having a population of 4,500,000, or approximately 20 per cent of the present population of Mexico.

In the central area of Mexico the electric-current characteristics are alternating 50 cycles, 120 volts, for domestic purposes. Higher voltages may be arranged for where required for industry. In the rest of the country, current is generally supplied at 50 or 60 cycles, 110/220 volts.

The cost of electric current in Mexico is fairly moderate, and an average family, consisting of two adults and two children and living in a medium-sized house in Mexico City or its suburbs, would spend from twenty to twenty-five pesos monthly for electricity. This would include lighting and the use of such household electric appliances as refrigerator, washing machine, iron, toaster, and radio.

Except for a few towns adjacent to the United States, gas is not piped to homes anywhere in Mexico at present, although the Mexican government-owned oil company, Petroleos Mexicanos, is reported to be investigating the possibilities of piping gas for both industrial and domestic uses from Mexican oil fields to such important centers as Mexico City and Monterrey. The latter city has for a number of years used gas piped from Texas for industrial purposes.

Petroleos Mexicanos manufactures a butane gas that it supplies to subscribers for home cooking and heating water at about $4 for cylinders containing about one hundred pounds. There are also a number of private companies that import gas from the United States in cylinders, at a cost slightly higher than that quoted above. Most houses and apartments of the type ordinarily rented by Americans are equipped with gas ranges. It is estimated that an average American family in Mexico City would spend from thirty to forty pesos a month for gas for cooking and heating water.

The heating of homes in Mexico is generally not necessary, and very few dwellings have central heating. Even in the higher altitudes, climatic conditions are pleasant most of the year, but some heating, although not absolutely indispensable, is welcome during the months of November through February. Gas and electric heaters are usually sufficient, and these are available in the larger cities. Recently the government has been requiring the use in private residences of oil heaters and stoves to replace the wood and charcoal burners in general use for many years.

The larger cities in Mexico have municipal water systems; however, most of these systems were installed years ago, and with the rapid growth in urban population in recent years many of them have become inadequate. In Mexico City, improvements in the public water system are under construction by the federal and municipal governments. This should do much to alleviate the present situation. It is estimated that upon completion of the Lerma project, the city will have adequate water reserves for supplying 2,500,000 inhabitants with about 423 quarts of water daily per inhabitant.

Municipal water systems are supplemented by wells. In smaller places and in rural districts most of the population is at present dependent on streams, open wells, and trapped rain water. Of course, there are throughout Mexico many developed farms and estates that have their own water-supply systems. The Mexican government has as one of its major projects the development of water and sanitation systems for urban as well as rural districts, and some progress has already been made along this line. However, in view of the fact that electric power is essential to carrying out many of these projects, water systems for suburban and rural districts are not expected to be adequate for some years.

It is always advisable for foreigners who visit small towns or rural districts to boil the drinking water, or better still, to use bottled water, which is available in most places. Visitors who make short trips to Mexico may find it advantageous to use bottled water altogether during their stay.

Servants. The number of servants in an American household in Mexico is determined by the size of the household. Servants' wages are generally lower than in the United States. However, when servants live in the household, the cost is usually more than their wages. It is generally necessary to employ more servants in the average household in Mexico than in a household of the same size in the United States. A nursemaid is desirable if there are children in the family. If the dwelling includes a garden, it is customary to hire a gardener by the day. Laundry is customarily done at home, and this requires a laundress to work by the day. If a car is maintained, a chauffeur is usually employed.

Persons who work by the day are entitled to one or two meals furnished by employers; other servants live in the household. Most houses are constructed with living quarters for servants in the rear of the house or above the garage.

Under Mexican labor laws medical care must be provided for domestic servants in case of illness. If dismissed without just cause, the servant is entitled to three months' salary plus compensation equivalent to twenty days' pay for each year of service. The employer also is required to defray burial expenses in case of the death of the servant.

Servants' wages vary with the experience and efficiency of the individual employed. The following are typical wages (quoted in pesos) paid by Americans to servants in Mexico City:

Cook..........................	$ 80 to $125
General maid..................	60 to 90
Nursemaid....................	60 to 100
Chauffeur....................	250 to 400
Laundress (daily wages)........	6 to 8
Gardener (daily wages).........	6 to 10

Furnishings. Furniture and house furnishings are comparatively more expensive in Mexico than in the United States. Furniture, either ready-made or custom-made, is available in all of the principal cities. In Mexico City, Guadalajara, Puebla, and Monterrey, upholstered furniture and heavy rugs are customarily used. In the lower altitudes and in coastal cities, such as Tampico, Veracruz, Acapulco, and Mazatlán, wicker furniture is most satisfactory, and floor coverings, if used, are generally of grass or reed.

Americans who plan to establish a home for any length of time in Mexico would find it advantageous to take their own household accessories and electrical appliances, since these are more expensive and less easily obtainable in Mexico than in the United States. Most electrical appliances except clocks will operate satisfactorily on current used in Mexico City. The majority of these items, at present available in the local market, are imported from the United States. Domestic production of household electrical appliances is limited and often of poorer quality than similar American products.

CLOTHING

The type of clothing needed in Mexico is dictated by the altitude of the city in which residence is established. The following may serve as a guide to Americans planning to reside in Mexico:

Altitude of place of residence	Type of clothing used in central part of United States during
More than 6,000 feet.........	Late fall and early winter
4,000 to 6,000 feet...........	Late summer and fall
2,000 to 4,000 feet...........	Late spring
Less than 2,000 feet..........	Summer
Coastal cities..............	Warmest part of summer

In the higher altitudes, which include Mexico City, Puebla, and Guadalajara, woolen suits of medium weight are usually worn by men, and light-weight woolen suits and dresses are worn by women. The evenings are quite cool and a light topcoat is necessary. The rainy season extends from June to October, and during this season a raincoat is needed. Cocktail parties and receptions call for afternoon dresses, and formal occasions call for formal evening dress.

The cities in coastal areas and tropical regions of Mexico experience intense heat during the day, and in these places the lightest and most comfortable summer clothing is worn.

Shopping centers in Mexico City, Guadalajara, and Monterrey carry adequate stocks of clothing, both domestic and imported.

The larger cities of Mexico have adequate dry-cleaning establishments. In Mexico City the cost of dry-cleaning a man's suit or a woman's dress is six pesos. Cleaning of silk and evening dresses varies in price, depending on the dress.

Suits and dresses may be made to order, as there are many competent tailors and seamstresses in Mexico, and prices for this type of work are about the same as in the United States.

Mexico City has several department stores similar to those in the United States, with the usual departments for furniture, household appliances, and men's, women's, and children's wear. Large department stores of the type found in American cities do not exist outside the capital, although the larger cities have many medium-sized shops that specialize in dry goods, house furnishings, hardware articles, or electrical appliances, as the case may be. There are no five-and-ten-cent stores in Mexico, such as operate in the United States. Throughout the cities and towns of Mexico there are open-air markets where native-made merchandise can be obtained at reasonable prices. In most cities the afternoon siesta or rest period is no longer observed, and shopping hours are from nine A.M. until five P.M., except on Saturdays, when department stores are open until seven P.M. Grocery stores observe different hours, as previously noted.

MEDICAL FACILITIES AND SUPPLIES

Competent physicians and surgeons are available in most Mexican cities, many of them having done postgraduate work in the United States and Europe. Also a large number of foreign doctors, including American, who have had excellent medical education and wide experience, practice in Mexico City, Monterrey, Guadalajara, and some other cities. Fees vary considerably, but in general are as follows: for office calls in Mexico City, from ten to fifteen pesos; home calls, fifteen to twenty-five pesos. There are specialists in almost all fields of medical science whose fees range from forty to one hundred pesos per visit to the office.

The Mexican government, through the Health Department and Institute of Social Security, maintains a number of general hospitals and clinics. However, members of the foreign colonies in Mexico usually utilize the services of private hospitals. The British-American Cowdray Hospital is located in Mexico City and is modernly equipped. The chief of staff and a number of the surgeons are American or British. The average cost per day for a room is from 25 to 40 pesos ($5.10 to $8.24). The cost of an appendectomy is about 500 pesos ($103), exclusive of the cost of anaesthetics, X rays, laboratory analyses, and medicines. As in the United States, some doctors combine their facilities in professional buildings and maintain clinics or small hospitals.

First-class dental work is obtainable in the larger cities, and, like doctors, many of the dentists in Mexico have obtained their education abroad. Dental fees are generally lower than in the United States, and vary in accordance with the amount of work and time involved. Prices for first-class work are as follows: alloy filling, 20 pesos ($4.75); gold filling, 75 pesos ($15.46); cleaning, 35 pesos ($4.72); simple extraction, 10 pesos ($2.06).

Most of the medical and pharmaceutical products commonly used in the United States are available in Mexico City and the larger centers, and medical prescriptions are accurately filled at reasonable prices. The prices of all drug and patent-medicine preparations are strictly controlled by the Department of Health and all packages bear the price of the article on a small sticker attached thereto. Vitamin pills and calcium are considered necessary to supplement diet; both domestically manufactured and imported varieties are available.

EDUCATION

Because the courses of study offered by Mexican public schools are substantially different in the length and period of the school term, as well as in the curricula, from those in the United States, they are usually inadequate for the needs of American children residing in Mexico. The two semesters run from July until December and from February through June, respectively, with the long vacation in the winter. Changes of classes and transfers are generally made in June.

Children of foreign residents may attend Mexican public schools, but most of them prefer to attend private schools that are designed to prepare students for further study in American colleges and universities. The most important of these private schools in Mexico City is the American School, a nonprofit institution established by the American colony, in which instruction is given in both English and Spanish. The faculty is composed principally of American teachers. The school consists of a kindergarten, grade school, and high school, and is recognized by leading colleges in the United States. Its graduates are also prepared to meet the entrance requirements of the National University of Mexico. Fees vary from thirty to sixty pesos per month.

Other American and English schools include the Maddox Academy, Helena Herlihy Hall, Williams School, Fitz-Gibbon School, the Garside School, and the Gordon College. For those American residents who want more intensive schooling in Spanish for their children, there are a number of Spanish-language private schools, such as the Colegio Anglo-Español, Colegio Cervantes, and the Academia Hispano-Mexicana. The word *colegio* designates an educational institution and not a college as the term is used in the United States. There are also a number of very good private French schools. For visitors who require tutoring in Spanish, special courses are offered by the National University at twenty-five pesos for enrollment and ten pesos for each course per semester. Private tutors may be engaged at the rate of five pesos per hour.

Detailed information concerning educational facilities in the various cities in Mexico may be obtained from the Inter-American Schools Service of the American Council on Education, located at 744 Jackson Place, N.W., Washington, D.C.

LOCAL TRANSPORTATION AND COMMUNICATION

Busses and streetcars are found in all of the chief urban centers of Mexico, although only the larger cities have modern electric streetcar systems. Taxi service is available in all cities. The possession of an automobile in Mexico is a great convenience because of the inadequacy, according to United States standards, of public transportation facilities. All of the American automobile makes are represented in Mexico by authorized dealers and service stations. The purchase price of a car in Mexico is higher than in the United States because of freight, import duty, and insurance costs. The cost of maintenance is about the same. Although the majority of houses in Mexico are built with garages, an outside or public garage may be rented for about thirty pesos a month.

Bus lines in the capital extend to all parts of the city, radiating from the Zócalo or heart of the city. The bus fare on all lines is ten centavos (two cents), and on lines extending to the suburbs it is twenty centavos. Busses and streetcars are greatly overcrowded as a result of the recent great increase in the capital's population. There has likewise been considerable deterioration in streetcar equipment in recent years. It is advisable to avoid using streetcars during rush hours whenever possible.

By mid-1948, Mexico City's five thousand taxicabs will be equipped with taxi meters, according to a Federal District Traffic Department regulation published late in 1947. The department contracted with a local firm to install the meters and the firm set up an assembly plant in the city. Some special parts are being manufactured locally, and standard parts were imported from the United States. To modernize the taxi system further, the department also ordered all cab owners to paint their vehicles gray and blue before January 1, 1948.

However, for those taxis that have not yet installed meters the old established rates by the trip and by the hour should still be in effect in Mexico City. These fares are as follows: for a minimum trip, 1.25 pesos ($0.25); by the half hour, 2.50 pesos ($0.50); by the hour, 3.50 pesos ($0.70). On Sundays and holidays fares are as follows: for a minimum trip, 1.50 pesos ($0.30); by the half hour, 3 pesos ($0.60); by the hour, 4 pesos ($0.80). It is customary for passengers to arrange with the driver in advance for the cost of the trip.

The domestic postage rate for ordinary letters is 12 centavos ($0.024) for less than 20 grams (1 gram equals 0.03527 ounce), plus an additional .01 centavo ($0.002) stamp tax. Ordinary mail to the

United States costs 13 centavos for less than 20 grams, and air mail is 25 centavos ($0.05) for the first 5 grams and 25 centavos for each additional 5 grams or fraction thereof.

Three of the principal morning newspapers of Mexico City, which carry one page in English, are *El Universal, Excelsior,* and *Novedades.* Bookstores and the larger hotels sell current American magazines and popular fiction in English.

RECREATION

There are a number of social and sports clubs in the principal cities of Mexico that Americans resident in the country may join. For more information about sports and recreation, see Chapter X, "Mexican Recreations," page 225.

TAXATION

The principal Mexican federal taxes affecting business firms and individuals are the income tax and the stamp tax; in addition, if any undertaking is situated in the Federal District (i.e., Mexico City and its environs), it will be subject to certain local taxes, usually referred to as a capital or business tax, and a tax on proceeds of capital. In general, taxes are reasonable.

The present income-tax law of Mexico became effective January 1, 1942, but owing to the fact that this law is amended from time to time, it is advisable for Americans who are engaged in business in Mexico or planning to establish a business there to have legal counsel in all matters pertaining to taxation.

MISCELLANEOUS EXPENSES

When living costs in Mexico for an American household are computed, certain expenditures occur as a consequence of the climate, local customs, and other factors that are proportionately larger than similar expenses in the United States. For example, insect pests are numerous and the liberal use of insecticides is necessary. Tipping is much more frequent in Mexico than in the United States, and watchmen, either public or private, are more often employed. It is not unusual for a sizable annual outlay to accrue from breakage and waste. While these individual expenditures are not great, their accumulation throughout the year represents a significant amount and should be allowed for in estimating a family budget.

MISCELLANEOUS DATA

CHURCHES

Roman Catholicism is the predominant religion in Mexico, and Mexico City is the seat of the archbishopric. In the capital there is a Protestant Union church of nondenominational character, with services in English; an Episcopal church, with services in English; a Lutheran church, with services in Spanish. In addition, there is one Christian Science church, with English and Spanish services, a Methodist church, and Jewish synagogues. There is also a Young Men's Christian Association and a Young Men's Hebrew Association. In the three or four leading cities outside the capital where there are American or British groups, there is usually a Protestant church where services are conducted in English.

BANKING FACILITIES

There is a branch of the National City Bank of New York in Mexico City located at Isabel la Católica Number 54. All of the Mexican banks, such as the Banco de Mexico (Central Bank of Mexico), Banco Nacional de Mexico (National Bank of Mexico, a private institution), the Banco de Comercio, the Banco Mexicano, the Banco Internacional, the Banco Continental, and others, operate with correspondent banks in all of the principal cities in the United States. The Bank of Mexico has branches in Guadalajara, Mazatlán, Mérida, Monterrey, and Torreón. The National Bank of Mexico has forty-six branches located in the larger cities and towns throughout the republic.

DIPLOMATIC REPRESENTATION

The United States is represented in Mexico by an embassy in Mexico City and twenty-two consular offices located in all of the important cities.

ENTRANCE REQUIREMENTS FOR FOREIGNERS

Visitors to Mexico will not be vaccinated against smallpox at the port of entry, provided they show their tourist cards or other documents. It is advisable, however, to be in possession of a vaccination certificate to show the American authorities on return to the United States.

Tourists. Requirements for United States and Canadian citizens entering Mexico as tourists are given in Chapter II, page 16.

Commercial Travelers. Commercial travelers or representatives, in order to enter Mexico, must obtain a special permit, which may be procured through a Mexican consul in the United States. The issuance of such permits generally involves a delay of from four to six weeks, since approval from Mexico must be obtained by the consul. The commercial traveler or representative is required to post a bond of five hundred pesos at the port of entry to guarantee his departure from Mexico within the period specified on his *visitante* card. The maximum period of issue is six months. To assure return of his bond in case he leaves by a border point other than that by which he entered, the commercial traveler is required to have his card stamped on the date of his departure at the nearest office of the Mexican Immigration Department; promptly on his return to the United States he should apply at the Mexican consulate through which he obtained his *visitante* status for a return of the amount of his bond, and should present his stamped card in evidence of compliance with legal requirements. Should he leave via his port of entry, he should apply at the customs office for the return of his bond.

Commercial travelers entering Mexico by automobile may take their automobiles into Mexico for a period of six months, free of import duty, upon posting a satisfactory bond at the customhouse of entry.

The commercial traveler must verbally inform the Mexican customs at the point of entry that he wishes to take his automobile into Mexico under the temporary admission provisions of the Mexican customs law. The commercial traveler will be required to fill out Form 141 (supplied by the Mexican customs authorities) giving such information as identification and serial numbers of the car. The commercial traveler is then required to post a bond equal to the amount of the import duty assessed on the particular type of car that he is importing, plus 10 per cent. This bond will be refunded to the commercial traveler upon the exportation of the car within the six-month period. Should the commercial traveler desire to export the car through a different customhouse than the one through which it was imported, it will be necessary for him to write to the customhouse of entry and explain his intentions, so that they may forward the papers to the proposed customhouse of exit. Commercial travelers should carry their bill of sale covering the automobile and a driver's permit or other document authorizing them to operate the vehicle in the United States.

Immigrants. Foreigners desiring to enter Mexico for the purpose of engaging in agriculture, industrial development, or foreign trade must have permission of the Mexican Minister of Foreign Relations before entering upon any business in the country. Cash bonds may be required. Interested persons should write direct to the ministry, describing in detail the work in which they propose to engage.

Professionals. Professional persons will be permitted to enter the country to practice only if the Minister of the Interior authorizes their entry because their services are essential and when some official agency requests their admission.

Technicians. Technical personnel will be permitted to enter Mexico to practice only when similarly qualified individuals are not available within the country.

Colonists. Colonists will be admitted to the country only with the approval of the Minister of Agriculture and in accordance with the Federal Colonization Law, provided this does not conflict with immigration requirements to which they are subject.

Others. Men of letters and artists will be permitted to enter the country and carry on remunerative activities, provided their applications for admission are made by some institution or enterprise that intends to use their services. *Scientists* and *artists, newspaper correspondents, sportsmen,* and persons desiring to study conditions in Mexico will be admitted as *visitors,* provided they fulfill the requirements established in each individual case by the Minister of the Interior.

ARTICLES ADMITTED DUTY-FREE

According to the Mexican customs law, persons entering the country to live under one of the above classifications have the right to import their baggage and household effects free of the payment of import duties. This includes used furniture, clothing, articles for the personal use of those entering, and articles, equipment, instruments, or personal tools of the trade of the individual.

OFFICE OPERATING COSTS

Rent and utilities, office equipment, business taxes, wages and salaries customarily paid, labor legislation, social security, and similar factors involved in establishing a business in Mexico should be investigated in some detail. The latest information about such conditions should be secured from the United States Department of Commerce, Washington, D.C., or from the following sources of information.

INFORMATION INDEX

Few Mexicans you meet will admit they do not know when you ask them for information. They feel it is a matter of courtesy to give you some kind of answer, whether or not the information includes any element of accuracy. This is a very friendly trait, once you get to know the Mexicans, but not much appreciated by the average American traveler. However, there are a few sources of information we can vouch for, and if you need more facts in more detail call on the following:

IN THE UNITED STATES

Mexican Embassy, 2829 Sixteenth Street, N.W., Washington, D. C.

Consulate General of Mexico, 70 Pine Street, New York, N.Y.

Mexican Chamber of Commerce of the United States, Inc., 60 Wall Street, New York, N.Y.

Mexican Tourist Information Bureau, Rockefeller Center, 630 Fifth Avenue, New York, N.Y.

Mexican consulates in Albuquerque, Boston, Brownsville, Buffalo, Chicago, Cleveland, Dallas, Denver, Detroit, Douglas (Arizona), El Paso, Galveston, Houston, Kansas City, Laredo, Los Angeles, Louisville, Miami, Milwaukee, New Orleans, Nogales, Norfolk, Philadelphia, Phoenix, Pittsburgh, Portland (Oregon), San Antonio, San Diego, San Francisco, Seattle, St. Louis, Tampa, and Tucson. See your telephone directory if you live in one of these places.

Pan American Sanitary Bureau, 17th St. and Constitution Ave., N.W., Washington 6, D.C.

Pan American Union, 17th St. and Constitution Ave., N.W., Washington 6, D.C.

American Automobile Association, Washington, D.C. Most state or regional auto clubs are affiliated with the AAA. If you are a member of one of these, then see your local auto club office. Motorists to Mexico will find many advantages in membership in a club affiliated with the AAA.

Bureau of Foreign and Domestic Commerce, Washington 25, D.C.

IN MEXICO

Asociación Mexicana de Turismo (Mexican Tourist Association), Juárez 76 (across from the Regis Hotel), Mexico, D.F., Mexico.

American Chamber of Commerce of Mexico, San Juan de Letrán 24, Mexico, D.F., Mexico.

Departamento de Turismo, Secretaría de Gobernación, Bucareli 99, Mexico, D.F., Mexico.

Asociación Mexicana Automovilística (AMA), Paseo de la Reforma 46, Mexico, D.F., Mexico.

Asociación Nacional Automovilística (ANA), Balderas 39, Mexico, D.F., Mexico.

Pemex Travel Club, Avenida Juárez 212, Mexico, D.F., Mexico.

American Consulate, Insurgentes 105, Mexico, D.F., Mexico.

INDEX

Note: Page numbers in italics refer to the convenient general information contained in Chapter VIII, Encyclopedia of Places, beginning on page *167*.